The Kaiser's Last General

The Kaiser's Last General

*The East Africa Campaign
and the Hunt for
Paul von Lettow-Vorbeck,
1914–1918*

R.G. Gladding

McFarland & Company, Inc., Publishers
Jefferson, North Carolina

LIBRARY OF CONGRESS CATALOGUING-IN-PUBLICATION DATA

Names: Gladding, R. G. (Rob G.), author.
Title: The Kaiser's last general : the East Africa campaign and the hunt for Paul von Lettow-Vorbeck, 1914–1918 / R.G. Gladding.
Other titles: East Africa campaign and the hunt for Paul von Lettow-Vorbeck, 1914–1918
Description: Jefferson, North Carolina : McFarland & Company, Inc., Publishers, 2021 | Includes bibliographical references and index.
Identifiers: LCCN 2021061182 | ISBN 9781476685991 (paperback : acid free paper) ∞
ISBN 9781476644752 (ebook)
Subjects: LCSH: Lettow-Vorbeck, Paul Emil von, 1870–1964. | World War, 1914–1918—Campaigns—German East Africa. | World War, 1914–1918—Aerial operations, German. | Germany. Heer. Schutztruppen. | Germany—Armed Forces—Colonial forces. | BISAC: HISTORY / Military / World War I
Classification: LCC D576.G3 G53 2021 | DDC 940.416—dc23/eng/20220103
LC record available at https://lccn.loc.gov/2021061182

BRITISH LIBRARY CATALOGUING DATA ARE AVAILABLE

ISBN (print) 978-1-4766-8599-1
ISBN (ebook) 978-1-4766-4475-2

© 2022 R.G. Gladding. All rights reserved

No part of this book may be reproduced or transmitted in any form or by any means, electronic or mechanical, including photocopying or recording, or by any information storage and retrieval system, without permission in writing from the publisher.

Front cover: World War I poster art of General Paul von Lettow-Vorbeck on horseback, 1918 (Library of Congress); (background) map of the Schutztruppe movements in German East Africa, 1916–1918 (Berlin State Library)

Printed in the United States of America

McFarland & Company, Inc., Publishers
Box 611, Jefferson, North Carolina 28640
www.mcfarlandpub.com

For Mo

Contents

Preface   1

Introduction   3

ONE. East Africa, 1914   7

TWO. Disaster at Tanga   20

THREE. Operations in the Rufiji Delta   32

FOUR. The Action at Jasin and Early Operations in the West and Northwest   38

FIVE. The Destruction of the *Königsberg*   48

SIX. The Bukoba Raid and the Action at Saisi   56

SEVEN. The Naval Africa Expedition   64

EIGHT. Operations on the Northern and Northwestern Frontier   71

NINE. The Battle of Kilimanjaro   85

TEN. Portugal Enters the War and the Allied Offensive Begins   96

ELEVEN. Into German East   113

TWELVE. The Long Pursuit   137

THIRTEEN. Mahiwa, Lukuledi Mission and Withdrawal to the Rovuma   158

FOURTEEN. Portuguese East Africa   175

FIFTEEN. The Last German General   190

APPENDIX I. *British Order of Battle, January 1916*   197

APPENDIX II. *British Order of Battle, March 1916*   198

APPENDIX III. *Versailles Treaty—Articles Regarding German Overseas Territories*   200

Chapter Notes   205

Bibliography   209

Index   211

Preface

COMING FROM A MILITARY FAMILY I have always been interested in military history; however, it was only after I joined the armed forces that I became interested in the East African Campaign of World War I. After coming off duty one night in the late '60s, I read an article in a magazine I had purchased in the NAAFI regarding the hunt for the cruiser *Königsberg*. It was unlike anything I had read about the First World War, and I wanted to know more. I then obtained a copy of *The Victoria Cross: The Empire's Roll of Valour*, where I read the citations for the VCs awarded in Africa but which contained only the bare bones of the actions for which they were awarded. Since then, I have become passionate about the subject, which I have been researching—on and off—for some 30 years.

What fascinated me about this campaign and how it developed was the fact that the belligerents were mainly African colonial troops from German East Africa, the Belgian Congo and the British West, Central and East Africa, along with South African volunteer formations—including the Cape Corps, which was recruited from South Africans of mixed race—and Indian troops. Only three British Imperial Regiments took part in the campaign. (One of those was from the West Indies, while a second was a war service battalion.) I was also frustrated by the fact that most modern publications on the subject were biased in one way or another and, being so, slanted the story according to the author's biases. The Allies, generally, were made out to be either incompetent racists or amateurs without a clue—which diminished what the German commander accomplished. The more I researched personal accounts and contemporary documents, I realized that this was not the case. In a number of instances in the early days of the war there were strongly held views about the superiority of one race over another. For example, the white South African troops believed they were superior in every way to the black soldiers. This belief was quickly dispelled. Equally the African soldiers initially despised the Indian troops, who they thought were no better than shopkeepers and traders because of their experience with the Indian population in East Africa prior to the war. Again, this belief was quickly dispelled. These fighting men soon learned that they had to trust and rely on their fellow soldiers regardless of their ethnicity or religious beliefs; all that mattered in the end was how good, steadfast and trustworthy were those units they fought beside.

I realized early on that few people knew about the war in East Africa—or for that matter the campaigns across Africa in general—and those who do are left dealing with the subject of Imperialism and the Scramble for Africa rather than the story of the campaign and the fighting men, who very quickly came to respect their fellow soldiers and the enemy. I decided then to write an account of the campaign which told the story of the fighting men. When writing about a particular action or operation, I have refrained from criticism based on hindsight and current operational procedures and based any criticism on contemporary practice and instruction as laid down in the Field Service Regulations of the time. This then is the story of that campaign, the story of the soldiers of the then Great European Empires who fought their war in Africa.

Oberstleutnant Paul von Lettow-Vorbeck, Officer Commanding the Ostafrikaschutztruppe (Bundesarchive, Bild 183-R05765).

Introduction

AT THE OUTBREAK OF WORLD WAR I, the commander of the Protection Force—*Ostafrikaschutztruppe*—in Germany's East African colony, Lieutenant-Colonel Paul Emil von Lettow-Vorbeck, with a force of only 2,732 officers and men, was determined to force the British to dispatch troops needed in Europe to East Africa. He was commissioned into the army as a lieutenant in 1890, and his first assignment had been to the German General Staff. In 1900, now a 1st Lieutenant, he was sent to China to take up duties with the German Legation Guard in Peking (Beijing), where he served throughout the Boxer Rebellion of 1900–1901 and the siege of the legations. He returned to Germany in 1901 and was again assigned to the General Staff. Promoted to captain in 1904, he was ordered to German South West Africa to take up duties as adjutant to Lieutenant-General Lothar von Trotha, the military commander. He served throughout the Namaqua and Herero insurrection, firstly as Lieutenant-General von Trotha's adjutant and then as a company commander, but having been wounded in the chest and left eye, he was evacuated to British South Africa for treatment and was still in Cape Town recovering when General von Trotha began the infamous Herero genocide. Promoted to major in 1907 and returning to Germany, he was appointed to the Staff of the XI Corps at Kassel in Hesse. He held this appointment until March 1909, when he took command of the marines of the *II Seebataillon* at Wilhelmshaven in Lower Saxony. He was promoted to lieutenant-colonel in October 1913 and was assigned to the command of the *Kamerun Schutztruppe* in West Africa. But before he left to take up this assignment, his orders were changed, and he was instructed to proceed to German East Africa as commander of the *Ostafrikaschutztruppe*. He arrived in Dar es Salaam in January 1914, even though the effective date of his taking command of the Protection Force was April 13, 1914.

Von Lettow-Vorbeck, convinced that a general war in Europe between Germany and the Entente Powers—France, Russia and

Britain—was imminent, as soon as he landed in the colony, set out on a tour of inspection and a reconnaissance. It did not take him long to realize that the only way he could compel the British, should war come, to divert troops and material to East Africa was to initially raid their territory and then fight only when the odds were in his favor. He used the invaluable knowledge and experience he had gained as a captain in German South West Africa—that in savage and inhospitable lands it is not always the big, modern armies that win campaigns, even if they eventually win the war, and that small, well-trained and -led troops conversant with the environment and bushcraft skills are perfectly able to contain, frustrate and sometimes defeat the biggest and most modern armies. He knew he could not defeat the British and her Allies in a set-piece battle but that once he had enticed them to commit to fight in East Africa, he would need to rely on fighting withdrawals into his own colony. Von Lettow-Vorbeck deduced, correctly, that by constantly withdrawing into his own colony, he ensured he had the advantage of interior lines of communication, whereas the Allies would be disadvantaged by being forced to advance into hostile territory with vulnerable exterior lines. As he foresaw, when the Allies invaded the colony, the further they advanced, the longer and more vulnerable their lines of communication became, making it harder and harder to ensure a constant flow of essential supplies and war material as they became overstretched.

Despite opposition from the Colonial Governor, von Lettow-Vorbeck was not prepared to fight for territory. This strategy forced the British, Belgians and Portuguese to commit in excess of 160,000 troops—drawn from Britain, Portugal, India, the Congo, East, West and South Africa—to operations in East Africa during the course of the war. Eventually the campaign deteriorated from an operation to take the German colony into a hunt for the elusive German commander and his small army, which never exceeded more than 15,000 officers and men, as they undertook a virtual guerrilla campaign. Von Lettow-Vorbeck was also quite willing to abandon German territory and invade Portuguese East Africa (now Mozambique) to pursue his self-imposed war aims. Throughout the campaign von Lettow-Vorbeck led the Allies in a merry dance of "catch me if you can" and punished them severely for any and every mistake. Unlike the war in Europe, the British and German commanders were, throughout the war, in the thick of the action, sharing the hardships endured by their men.

As the campaign was fought in countryside that varied from open savannah to dense forest, bushland thick with thornbushes and desert, command and control of the armies became a formidable task which tested to the limit the skills of the commanders. Besides the arduous

Introduction

country and climate, the soldiers also faced the dangers of the wildlife—lions, elephants, rhinoceroses and crocodiles. On top of this the troops had to contend with mosquitoes, tsetse flies, jiggers and ticks as well as numerous tropical diseases such as malaria, bilharzia from the waters of the rivers and lakes, yellow fever, blackwater fever and sleeping sickness.

Promoted to major-general by the Kaiser in 1917 for his resistance, Paul von Lettow-Vorbeck commanded the only undefeated German force to surrender to the Allies, well after the end of hostilities in Europe. This history follows the campaign from its inception to the surrender of the German forces in Northern Rhodesia (modern Zambia) and to the fate of von Lettow-Vorbeck following the end of hostilities. What follows is not a political history or a biography, nor does it deal with the rights or wrongs of colonialism; it is the story of the soldiers and civilians of all colors, creeds and nationalities who fought and endured the rigors of the First World War in East Africa and how a campaign of conquest became a hunt for a single general and his small, highly efficient and loyal command.

ONE

East Africa, 1914

ON JUNE 28, 1914, news of the assassination of the heir to the Austro-Hungarian Empire, Archduke Franz Ferdinand, and his wife in Sarajevo was flashed around the world. Following weeks of tension and fighting in the Balkans, Germany invaded Belgium, and Britain, France and Russia found themselves at war with the German and Austro-Hungarian Empires. Following the outbreak of war in August 1914, the Governor of German East Africa—present day Tanzania, Burundi and Rwanda[1]— Dr. Heinrich Albert Schnee, having conferred with his superior, Minister Dr. Solf, at the *Kolonialamt* in Berlin, ordered that no hostile actions were to be undertaken against his colony's neighbors, while in British East Africa, the governor, Sir Henry Belfield, declared that his colony had no interest in the war. The governors of these vast territories had met on a number of occasions prior to the outbreak of hostilities in Europe to discuss what they would do in the event of war. And both agreed to try and adhere to Article II of the 1885 Congo Act, which called for all overseas possessions of the colonial powers to remain neutral in the event of a general war in Europe.

The recently appointed commander of the German colonial forces, the *Ostafrikaschutztruppe*, Lieutenant-Colonel Paul Emil von Lettow-Vorbeck, on the other hand, was determined to open hostilities as soon as possible: "I considered it to be our military object to detain enemy, that is English forces if it could by any means be accomplished. This, however, was impossible if we remained neutral."[2] He hoped that this would force the British to divert men and material required in Europe to East Africa and that the longer he resisted the more troops would have to be sent. He assessed that the most sensitive point in British territory was the Uganda Railway, and it was against this target he planned to move when the time came. Von Lettow-Vorbeck had available to him, in August 1914, 14 regular *Feldkompanies*, or Field Companies, which were native units with white officers and NCOs, numbering 260 German officers and NCOs and 2,472 native askaris troops. These independent

Field Companies were deployed at strategic locations throughout German East Africa for internal security. Von Lettow-Vorbeck had initially planned to concentrate them in the Kilimanjaro area, from where he could threaten British territory, but because of objections by the Governor that such a move would be seen as provocative by the British, this concentration took place in the Pugu heights 12 miles (19 kilometers) to the west of Dar es Salaam.

Having already supplemented the *Schutztruppe*'s strength by the addition of four Field Companies—numbered 15th to 18th—by the incorporation of police askaris and former askaris recalled to service at the beginning of hostilities, Von Lettow-Vorbeck had quickly realized he had the means and material to double his army at hand. And having established his Headquarters at Pugu, he had been busy preparing to implement the increase of the *Schutztruppe*'s strength from 18 Field Companies to 52 by recruiting a further 34 companies. He eventually raised an additional 27 Field Companies numbered 19th to 30th and a number of temporary companies with lettered prefixes (i.e., "A" Company). When hostilities began, the German colonists that volunteered for service were formed into two *Schutzenkompanies* or Rifle Companies. And these Rifle Companies he reorganized along the lines of his Field Companies by filling their ranks with askaris, which allowed him to increase them from the original two to ten numbered 1st to 10th. By the end of 1915, his force numbered 2,998 Europeans and 11,300 askaris.

Unfortunately for the *Schutztruppe*, Commander Governor Schnee—who was also the Commander-in-Chief of the *Schutztruppe*—opposed his plans and ambitions and took every opportunity to try and thwart them by countermanding orders and refusing to cooperate with his military commander, much to von Lettow-Vorbeck's chagrin. At one stage he threatened to relieve von Lettow-Vorbeck of his command and place him under arrest if he did not follow his orders as Commander-in-Chief. This intolerable situation would dog von Lettow-Vorbeck throughout the campaign. "According to an ordinance, which certainly did not contemplate the case of foreign war, the supreme military power in the Colony was in the hands of the Governor, and communication with home having ceased, it was anyhow physically impossible to get this altered. So I was obliged to make the best of this, from a military point of view, very serious difficulty and to reckon with the possibility that, if the Governor's instructions were faithfully executed, Dar-es-Salaam and Tanga for instance, the termini of our railways and the obvious bases for hostile operations from the coast towards the interior, would fall into the enemy's hands without a struggle."[3]

Opposing him, the British had three battalions of the King's

One. East Africa, 1914

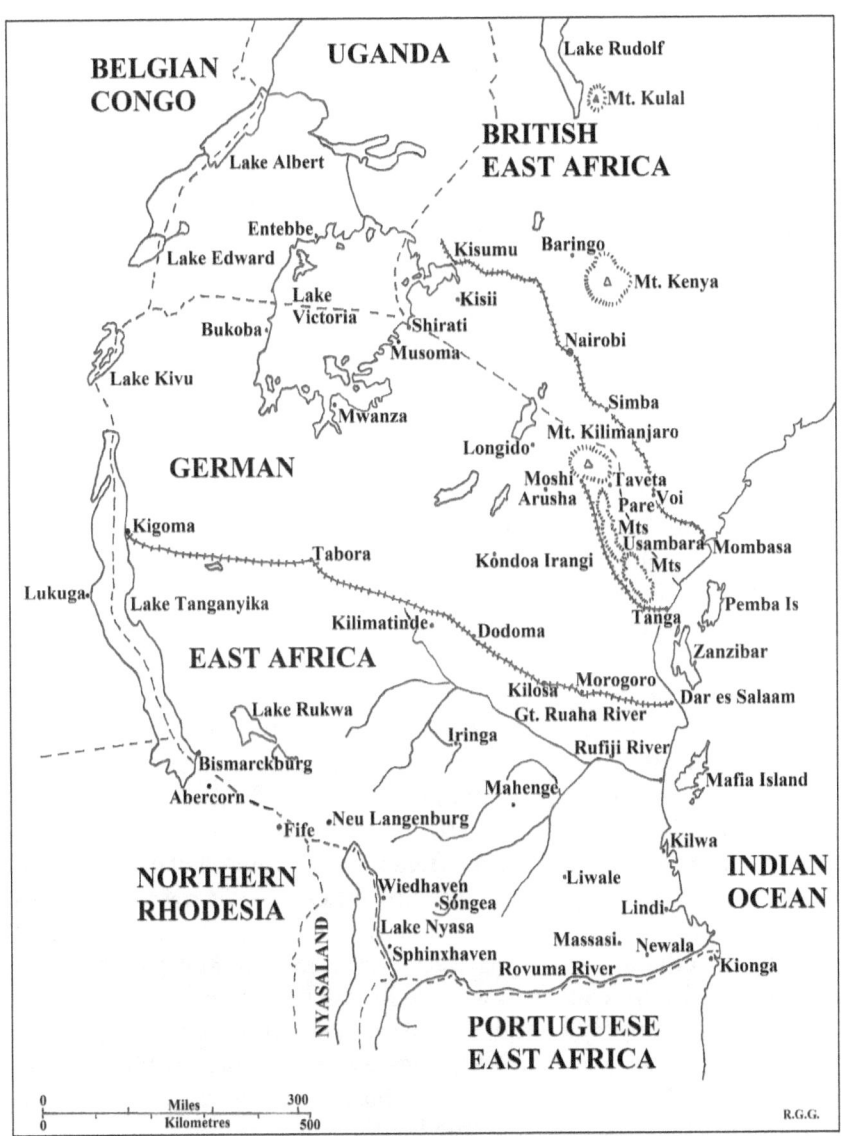

The East African Theatre 1914 (map by the author).

African Rifles (KAR). The 1st KAR were in Nyasaland (now Malawi) less four companies; the 3rd KAR of five Rifle and a camel Company had three companies deployed in half companies throughout British East (now Kenya) with their HQ in Nairobi, while two companies, along with the four detached companies of 1st KAR, were undertaking punitive operations in Jubaland on the frontier between British East and Italian Somaliland and a company in garrison on the island of Zanzibar. The third of the British battalions, the 4th KAR, with its HQ at Bombo in Uganda, had seven companies: two were stationed near the northwestern shore of Lake Victoria, three along the Uganda-Kenya frontier, one northwest of Mount Kenya at Baringo, and one at Kisumu in Kenya, on the northeastern shore of Lake Victoria with a half company of 3rd KAR.[4]

The opportunity for von Lettow-Vorbeck to begin hostile operations was provided within two days of the outbreak of war. The catalyst was the modern German light cruiser, SMS *Königsberg*. The *Königsberg*, Commander Max Looff, had arrived in Dar es Salaam, the capital of German East Africa, in June 1914, to take up duties in the colony and to take part in the colonial exhibition that was due to begin that August. Looff, however, had received advanced warning of a general war in Europe from German Naval High Command. Accordingly, at 4:30 p.m. on the afternoon of July 31, *Königsberg* steamed slowly out of Dar es Salaam, her ship's company at "action stations," and the ship darkened. As she cleared the harbor and passed Makatumbe Lighthouse, she increased speed to ten knots. Her destination was the Gulf of Aden where she was to commence operations as a commerce raider as soon as hostilities began.

To remove this potential threat to the British trade routes from India and the East, in the event of war, the Royal Navy's Cape Squadron, Vice-Admiral Herbert King-Hall, DSO, RN with the 2nd and 3rd Class cruisers *Hyacinth*, *Pegasus* and *Astraea*, had been standing off the coast since *Königsberg's* arrival in East African waters. King-Hall had orders to hunt her down and destroy her once hostilities began. Now ten miles (16 kilometers) off the East African coast, with the night sky darkening and heading into the squalls of the southwest monsoon, *Königsberg's* lookouts reported ships closing. It was the British Cape Squadron.

Admiral King-Hall had his cruisers take up station within 3,000 yards (2,743 meters) of the *Königsberg*—*Astraea* on her port beam, *Pegasus* ahead and *Hyacinth* astern. With this unexpected development and knowing that he had to escape the British, Commander Looff ordered his engineer officer to build up steam as quickly and unobtrusively as possible so as not to alert the British cruisers as to his intentions. He wanted sufficient steam available to be able to quickly increase his speed to maximum revolutions at a moment's notice, so he could break free and evade the British squadron before they could react. All he needed, once this had been achieved, was the right opportunity.

Forty-five minutes later, as the warships proceeded at 12 knots towards the eastern edge of Zanzibar Island, Looff was informed by his engineer officer that a sufficient head of steam was available for the cruiser to go to full speed. Shortly after, a squall from the southwest enveloped the ships, reducing visibility to a few hundred yards; Looff immediately ordered the cruiser to turn hard to starboard and for her speed to be increased to 22 knots. *Königsberg*, having turned 180 degrees, swept past the *Hyacinth*, which was desperately attempting to increase her speed. Shortly after passing *Hyacinth*, Looff turned 90 degrees to port and steamed south towards Mafia Island, and then reducing speed to conserve coal, she turned east to disappear into the Gulf of Aden. To Admiral King-Hall's chagrin the *Königsberg* had successfully given the Cape Squadron the slip.

Korvettenkapitän Max Looff, Commanding Officer of the light cruiser SMS *Königsberg* (Wikimedia Commons).

Two days after the declaration of war, *Königsberg* attacked and captured the SS *City of Winchester*[5] off Aden, and along with two German merchant ships—*Goldenfels* and *Zeiten*—which she had intercepted earlier, steamed for Makallah Bay on the Hadhramaut coast of South Arabia, where *Königsberg* was due to rendezvous with the collier SS *Somali*.

On August 6, the supply ship *König* attempted to leave Dar es Salaam to rendezvous with the *Königsberg* but was forced to return to harbor when warning shots from *Pegasus* straddled her. The next day *Pegasus* and *Astraea* steamed into the main roads and opened fire on the radio tower situated on the headland. Governor Schnee, fearing a British invasion, raised a white flag over Government House and handed over control of the capital to the chief of police. He then fled in his special train to Morogoro, stopping at Pugu long enough to advise his military commander of what had occurred. Von Lettow-Vorbeck recorded, "He seemed quite surprised by the English hostilities."⁶

These actions gave von Lettow-Vorbeck all the excuse he needed to consider the restraints of the Congo Act breached. He immediately took the initiative, ordering the senior officer at Neu Moshi on the southern slopes of Mount Kilimanjaro, Captain Tom von Prince, to begin offensive operations. "In the north of the Colony, the 1st Company at Arusha had been reinforced by the 13th Company, coming by rapid marches from Kondoa, and by another company formed at Moshi from Police Askari. Further, a large part of the Europeans of the northern districts had combined to form a detachment under Captain von Prince. Most of those troops were in the neighbourhood of Moshi. Taveta, which lies to the eastward, in English territory, was held by the enemy, who thereby secured a valuable sally-port against our European settlements in the north; it was, therefore, an urgent matter for us to capture this important point without delay."⁷ Von Prince sent a demand to the commander of the British frontier post at Taveta to evacuate the settlement. This demand was ignored, and on August 15, the 1st Field Company, along with mounted German volunteers, under the command of Colonel (Rtd) Heinrich *Freiherr* von Bock, crossed the frontier and seized the post before advancing northeast to the railway.

Lieutenant-Colonel LES Ward (Oxs & Bucks Light Infantry) deployed a company of 3rd KAR to meet the incursion, which was repelled after a short skirmish, the Germans retreating to Taveta. The immediate response to this incursion—the first of a number of poorly planned and executed raids—got the reaction von Lettow-Vorbeck wanted. Sir Henry Belfield sent an urgent plea for reinforcements, to counter his perceived threat of invasion, to the Colonial Office. The Colo-

Captain Tom von Prince (*Deutsch-Ostafrikanische Zeitung*).

nial Office passed this request to the Committee of Imperial Defence, who instructed the Indian government to dispatch two expeditionary forces to the region: one to reinforce British East Africa, the second, and larger of the two, to take the Germans' principal port and capital, Dar es Salaam.

At Makallah Bay, meanwhile, Commander Looff learned that the Cape Squadron had attacked Dar es Salaam, destroying the port facilities and wireless station. As a result of this news, *Königsberg*, accompanied by the three merchantmen, sailed to the Kuria Muria Islands. Here the *City of Winchester* was stripped of all food, water and other supplies and her crew put aboard the *Zeiten* to be repatriated to Portuguese East Africa. As for the coal the *City of Winchester* was carrying, this was considered too inferior in quality, and the ship was scuttled without it being removed. *Königsberg* then set sail to try and find the *Somali*, which had missed her prearranged rendezvous at Makallah Bay.

The first of the Indian Expeditionary Forces, Force "C," under the command of Brigadier-General JM Stewart, CB, was of brigade strength and consisted of the 29th Punjabis, Bengal Infantry, two Imperial Service Battalions[8] formed from half battalions of the state forces of Bhurtpore, Jind, Kapurthala and Rampur, the 27th Mountain (Artillery) Battery, 1st Battery, Calcutta Volunteer Artillery, and a machine-gun battery. The 29th Punjabis arrived in British East on September 1 and were immediately sent up country to the area around Kilimanjaro and the Tsavo River. They were soon in contact with the Germans, when on September 6, elements of the 29th Punjabis and 3rd KAR made contact with an enemy force west of Tsavo. A brisk skirmish followed, and the Germans withdrew.

Two days later the 5th Field Company crossed the southwestern frontier into British Nyasaland. Evading a flying column of 1st KAR sent to intercept them, they attacked Karonga on the northwest shore of Lake Nyasa (now Lake Malawi) at dawn on September 9. The settlement's garrison of a British officer and 50 men of 1st KAR and eight armed civilians successfully held the town for three hours before being relieved by the flying column. The KAR charged the Germans with fixed bayonets, and after, a vicious hand-to-hand fight forced them to withdraw across the frontier to Songwe, having abandoned two field guns and two machine guns.

Earlier, on September 5, a German force of four Germans, 50 police askaris, 60 armed porters and 250 Ruga-Ruga (native irregulars) and a 3.7-cm field gun, under the command of Medical Lieutenant Dr. Westhofen, crossed the frontier of Northern Rhodesia (now Zambia) and was marching on Abercorn (now Mbala). Abercorn was garrisoned by

40 men of "D" Company, Northern Rhodesia Police (Military Branch), under the command of Lieutenant JJ McCarthy. On learning of the approach of the German force, McCarthy had the town jail turned into an armed post and successfully repulsed the attack.

Meanwhile, a mobile column of three officers and 80 men of the Northern Rhodesia Police (Military Branch), commanded by Major HM Stennett, which had been moving up to the border from Livingstone, had arrived at Kasama on the 5th. Here he received notification of the German incursion and a request for assistance from the magistrate at Abercorn. He immediately marched out of Kasama with his column, arriving at Abercorn at 3 a.m. on the 9th, having covered the 100 miles (160 kilometers) from Kasama in 66 hours.

Three hours later Westhofen's field gun began shelling the town, opening a second attack which lasted throughout the day. All attempts to take the town were repulsed. The next morning the German column began withdrawing. Lieutenant McCarthy followed up with his command. His machine gun and ammunition were carried by the prisoners in the jail, who had volunteered to act as carriers in return for a remission of their sentences at the end of the war. McCarthy pressed the withdrawing Westhofen and, following a short skirmish at the Lumi River, forced him to withdraw across the frontier.

Shortly afterwards Belgian colonial troops, the *Troupes de Katanga* of the *Force Publique*,[9] began offensive operations between Lake Tanganyika and Lake Victoria Nyanza with moderate success. The Belgian colonial authorities had tried to adhere to Article II of the 1885 Congo Act, even though Belgium itself had been invaded and occupied by the Germans. However, on Lake Tanganyika, von Lettow-Vorbeck had ordered Lieutenant-Commander Gustav Zimmer—former captain of the survey ship SMS *Möwe* which had been scuttled in Dar es Salaam harbor on August 9 and been sent with his ship's company to man the lake flotilla—to form an askari marine detachment 400-strong to support his three gunboats: the *Hedwig von Wissmann, Graf von Götson* and *Kingani*. On August 22 the gunboat *Hedwig von Wissman* entered Belgian waters, attacked and sank a number of canoes and badly damaged the Belgian government steamer *Alexandre del Commune* before landing a shore party to cut all telephone and telegraph lines in the lake area. *Alexandre del Commune* was completely destroyed on October 9, 1914, when German marine askaris landed at Mtoa, where she had been beached, blew a hole in her bottom and finally shelled her.

On learning of these attacks the Belgian authorities ordered the Vice-Governor of Katanga—General of Division Charles Tombeur[10]—to defend Belgian territory and assist where possible the British

Askaris of the Northern Rhodesia Police (Military Branch) entrenching the Mount Saisi post, Northern Rhodesia (*Illustrated London News and Sketch*).

Operations in East Africa. This request for assistance came soon after from the British. And on September 22, an advance company, preceding a column commanded by Major Frederik Olsen which consisted of the *Ie* and *IIIme Bataillons de Marche, Troupes de Katanga*, arrived in Abercorn. When the main column began arriving on the 25th, they were deployed between Abercorn and Fife (now Mwenzo). Here they successfully repelled a number of German raids in conjunction with the Northern Rhodesia Police.

As a number of these raids were carried out by brutal Ruga-Ruga gangs against border villages, where they pillaged and raped, a fortified post was established on a rocky knoll known as Mount Saisi, 30 miles (48 kilometers) east of Abercorn, which lay between the Saisi and Mambala rivers and overlooked the crossings used by the Ruga-Ruga. The farmhouse of Jericho Farm, which was built on the knoll, was fortified and entrenched, and from here the garrison—228 officers and men of the Northern Rhodesia Police with two machine guns and a 7-pdr mountain gun of the British South Africa Police, 206 officers and men of the *Ie Bataillon de Marche, Troupes de Katanga* with one machine gun and a 4-pdr Nordenfelt gun—under Colonel FA Hodson, commandant of the Northern Rhodesia Police—patrolled along and across the border.

In the north, meanwhile, Captain Theodor Tafel—one of von Lettow-Vorbeck's staff officers—had crossed the frontier with 1st

Lieutenant Udo von Chappuis's 10th Field Company and was advancing on the Magadi railway junction southwest of Nairobi. News of the incursion was reported by Masai scouts on September 25, and a 30-strong troop of "C" Squadron, East African Mounted Rifles—a locally raised volunteer unit commanded by Captain Chapman—rode to intercept them. They eventually located a small group of enemy preparing a meal in the thick bush and immediately dismounted and engaged them. Unknown to Chapman, however, Tafel and the main body of the enemy, numbering around 250 men, was close by, and they immediately counterattacked the troop, who retired in contact to their horses, then withdrew with the loss of four men wounded and eight missing. Following this skirmish, Tafel aborted his mission and withdrew towards Longido, having lost 11 killed and 22 wounded. The Mounted Rifles returned the next day and found that their eight missing men had been killed.

In mid-September von Lettow-Vorbeck began preparations for an advance on Mombasa, which was not only the best seaport on the East African coast and of strategic importance to the British; it was also within easy striking distance of the frontier. The British had been expecting such an attack since hostilities began and had recalled the companies of 1st and 3rd KAR from their operations in Jubaland. Until they and the remainder of Indian Expeditionary Force "C" arrived, which was expected at any time, the defense of Mombasa was entirely in the hands of the locally raised volunteers of the East Africa Regiment and East African Mounted Rifles.

The German attack, meanwhile, had been postponed until September 29 so that the *Königsberg* could assist the *Schutztruppe* in the capture of Mombasa Island. *Königsberg* was to land a party to seize Mombasa while the *Schutztruppe* took the Salisbury Bridge which joined it to the mainland. The bridge was to be destroyed by the *Schutztruppe*, who were to take it before the arrival of the *Königsberg* and then cover the cruiser's landing parties as they came ashore to take the town.

The German column that subsequently crossed the frontier and advanced along the coast from Vanga was 600 strong with six machine guns, comprising the recently embodied 15th, 16th and 17th Field Companies. When news of the enemy advance reached the British authorities, a scratch force of motorcycle volunteers, a detachment of 3rd KAR, brought down from Jubaland by sea, and a company of the Arab Rifles—recruited from Adeni and Hadhramaut Arabs working on the British East African coast—under the command of Captain AJB Wavell (Special Reserve and Welsh Regt) was rushed south to intercept them. They made contact at Margerini, 12 miles (19 kilometers) north of the frontier, on the 25th.

From first contact Wavell's force became engaged in a fighting withdrawal in the face of the strong German column. On the 27th Captain WG Stonor's (Middlesex Regt) "C" company of 1st KAR from Jubaland, which had undertaken a forced march of over 300 miles (482 kilometers), reached Wavell, who had suffered heavy losses in the two days fighting his little force had endured. Between them they were able to halt and contain the Germans at Gazi, 25 miles (40 kilometers) south of Mombasa.

The main body of Indian Expeditionary Force "C" had begun landing at Mombasa by this time, and a relief column—consisting of elements of the 29th Punjabis, the Jind Infantry, the Reserve Company, 1st KAR and Indian Volunteer Maxim Company—was assembled under the command of Major GMP Hawthorne (Liverpool Regt and KAR). It was immediately sent south by Brigadier-General Stewart, reaching Wavell and Stonor on October 2. Wavell and Stonor now came under Hawthorne's command, which, with the addition of these units, now numbered 850 rifles.

The *Schutztruppe* launched a dawn attack against Hawthorne's position at Gazi on the 7th, driving in his outposts and forcing them back towards the village. With mounting pressure on his perimeter, he ordered Stonor's company to counterattack, which they successfully did, halting the enemy assault. But the Germans maintained their pressure on the British perimeter, and it became necessary for Stonor's company to mount a second counterattack, during which all the company officers became casualties. Colour-Sergeant Sumani, the most senior man left standing, immediately took command. He rallied the faltering company, leading them again into the attack. Shortly after Sumani was reinforced by one and a half companies of the Jind Infantry and the German attack was broken, Captain Paul Baumstark, the German commander, ordered his troops to break contact and withdrew south across the frontier, abandoning large quantities of stores and ammunition. Colour-Sergeant Sumani was awarded the African Distinguished Conduct Medal for his gallantry and leadership.

Königsberg too had failed in her part of the operation; Looff had learned that HMS *Pegasus* was in Zanzibar harbor undergoing a refit. *Pegasus* had been forced to dock in Zanzibar as her machinery required extensive work and her boilers desperately needed cleaning, having become furred by the continuous use of poor-quality coal. At 5 a.m. on the 20th, *Königsberg*, steaming out of the dawn mist, entered Zanzibar harbor, catching *Pegasus* anchored and in the middle of her refit.

The German cruiser opened fire immediately, and though *Pegasus* returned fire, she was hopelessly outgunned. Having been hit 300 times in ten minutes, she was ablaze along her entire length. *Königsberg* ceased fire, turned away, and steaming out of the harbor, vanished. *Pegasus* sank at 1 p.m., having lost 31 of her ship's company killed in the action and 49 wounded.

On being advised of the loss of the *Pegasus* the Admiralty dispatched the 1st Class cruiser HMS *Chatham*, Captain Sidney Drury-Lowe, RN, from its station in the Red Sea to East Africa, along with the cruisers, *Dartmouth* and *Weymouth*, to hunt down and destroy the *Königsberg*. Drury-Lowe, as Senior Naval Officer, commanded the squadron, which on arrival in East African waters began its hunt.

Unbeknown to Drury-Lowe, the *Königsberg* was herself badly in need of a refit. But as no port was available or safe for him to use Looff, who had been advised of the arrival of the British cruiser squadron, decided to take his ship, accompanied by his collier SS *Somali*, up the Rufiji River opposite Mafia Island. *Königsberg* anchored six miles (nine and a half kilometers) upriver, near Salale. Her decks were camouflaged with nets and foliage to blend her into the surrounding bush. Her torpedo tubes were then removed and set up at the mouth of the Rufiji to engage any enemy vessels that came too near.

Meanwhile, Drury-Lowe's squadron hunted tirelessly for her and despite obtaining three significant indicators as to her whereabouts, failed to evaluate correctly the intelligence they had captured. The first came when *Dartmouth* took a German tug trying to reach the Rufiji, which was ordered to return to port; the second when *Chatham*, making a routine inspection of Lindi harbor in the Lukuledi River estuary, discovered the German merchantman *Präsident* anchored there. A boarding party was sent aboard the *Präsident*, which was flying a Red Cross flag, and quickly established that she was not a hospital ship. The boarding party dismantled her engines and seized her papers and charts, one of which was an up-to-date chart of the Rufiji Delta—recently compiled following a survey by the *Möwe* by her captain, Lieutenant-Commander Zimmer—much more accurate and detailed than the Admiralty charts. They also interrogated the crew, who revealed that the *Präsident* had recently carried a consignment of coal from Lindi to a location up the Rufiji where it was unloaded. Even now the British failed to correctly evaluate what they had learned.

The final piece of intelligence came two days later while the squadron was cruising off Komo Island, opposite the entrance to the Rufiji. A lookout spotted a figure in khaki running from the beach into a clump of palms. A party was sent ashore to apprehend the man, who turned out to be a German reserve officer manning a signal station on the island. Among the papers taken from him was a diary which mentioned the *Königsberg* and a place called Salale, which was not marked on the

Admiralty charts. None of *Chatham's* officers thought to consult the chart taken from the *Präsident,* which had Salale clearly marked on it.

On October 21, after responding to much disinformation from German agents, *Chatham* stood off Dar es Salaam. Her lookouts could see a number of masts in the obscured inner harbor but not the actual vessels. Drury-Lowe and his officers convinced themselves that one of the masts they could see belonged to the cruiser, and as the German authorities failed to respond to his demand that a boat be sent out to his ship to confirm or deny the presence of the *Königsberg,* he opened fire on all the ships in the harbor.

But by the 30th, Drury-Lowe had found the elusive German. He had begun to suspect that the *Königsberg* was sheltering in the Rufiji Delta and had landed parties to question local natives, who confirmed the presence of a warship in the Rufiji. That afternoon he stood off the delta and landed a party at the head of the Kiomboni arm of the river. A rating climbed a palm tree from where he was able to see the mastheads of both the *Königsberg* and *Somali*—right where the local natives had said they would be.

With *Königsberg* contained, it now remained to overcome the problem of how to destroy her. Gathered intelligence revealed strong German defenses in place along the banks and entrances to the delta to foil any attempts at reaching her. Over the next few days *Chatham* destroyed the German signal post on Mafia Island and made a reconnaissance of the channels up the Rufiji.

On November 1, having ascertained the range of the two enemy ships, *Chatham* took up station off the coast at a point eight miles (13 kilometers) from the *Somali*. As the guns of his main batteries had a range of 14,500 yards (13,258 meters) and *Königsberg* was 14,800 yards (13,533 meters) from his ship, Drury-Lowe had *Chatham's* ballast shifted so that his starboard side lifted by five degrees, giving his guns more range, and opened fire with his main batteries. But his shot fell short. A repeat shoot took place on the 7th, and this time *Somali* was bracketed and was soon being hit by salvo after salvo. She was on fire and by the afternoon, a burned-out wreck. *Königsberg,* however, was just out of range of *Chatham's* guns; having received some splinter damage from Drury-Lowe's first attempt, she had been moved, and to ensure her safety Looff took her further upriver. The next day all three cruisers of the British flotilla bombarded known and suspected enemy posts. That evening *Dartmouth* was ordered back to Mombasa to be coaled, while Looff moved *Königsberg* even further up the Rufiji. That evening Drury-Lowe received a signal sent in clear from the Admiralty. He was to sink or destroy the *Königsberg,* regardless of cost.

Two

Disaster at Tanga

WHILE THE HUNT FOR THE *Königsberg* was being played out, the second expeditionary force was being assembled in India. Designated Indian Expeditionary Force "B," it was placed under the command of Major-General AE Aitken and was formed by two brigades of 8,000 officers and men. The first of these brigades was the 27th Bangalore Brigade, commanded by Brigadier-General Richard Wapshare and comprised of the 2nd Battalion, Loyal North Lancashire Regiment, the 98th Hyderabad Infantry, the 63rd Palamcottah Light Infantry and 101st Grenadiers, Bombay Infantry. The brigade had under command 28th Mountain Battery, 25th and 26th Companies, Sappers and Miners and the 61st King George's Own Pioneers. The second brigade was an Imperial Service Brigade, commanded by Brigadier-General MJ Tighe and comprised of the 13th Rajputs (The Shekhawati Regiment), an Indian Army formation, the 2nd Kashmir Rifles, half battalions of the 3rd Kashmir Rifles and 3rd Gwalior Rifles and the 28th (Faridkot) Sappers and Miners, which were all Imperial Service formations.

Expeditionary Force "B" sailed from Bombay (now Mumbai) on October 16, 1914, in 21 small transports, escorted by the battleship *Goliath* and the light cruiser *Fox*. Of all its fighting units the only ones of undisputed quality were the 2nd Loyal North Lancs and the mountain artillery. The other battalions of the Expeditionary Force had been in garrison or were Imperial Service Battalions, and their field training was deficient, as was their regimental structure (which was also the case with the Indian units of Force "C"); it was of the old eight-companies structure, not the large four-companies structure of the British Army, a situation that would not be addressed until 1916. Not only that, but they had only just been rearmed with the modern Short Magazine Lee-Enfield No. 1 Rifle, and their training with this weapon was still ongoing.

Force "B" reached Mombasa in a poor state after a very stormy crossing from India in troop transports that were unsuitable for the task, something that Captain Richard Meinertzhagen (Royal Fusiliers),

Aitken's intelligence officer—a prolific diarist—noted, "I look with misgivings on any attempt to invade East Africa from the coast. Neither am I enthusiastic about the troops sent with the Force. They constitute the worst in India, and I tremble to think what may happen if we meet with serious opposition. I have seen many of the men and they did not impress me at all, either as men or as soldiers. Two battalions have no machine guns and the senior officers are nearer to fossils than active energetic leaders of men. But it serves no purpose to be critical at this stage. One can only hope for the best and rely on our British battalion, mountain battery, and the element of surprise."[1]

Lieutenant-Colonel Richard Meinertzhagen, General Smuts's Intelligence Officer (Her Majesty's Stationery Office, 1917).

Meanwhile, in the Mount Kilimanjaro area, the Germans had been defeated in an action north of M'zima on the Tsavo River. And a British force of 1,200 men from Indian Expeditionary Force "C" with 360 men from the East African Mounted Rifles had attacked the German position at Longido on November 3. Longido is a steep hill rising to the northwest of Kilimanjaro on the German side of the frontier, on which the *Schutztruppe* had established an entrenched camp halfway up its side. Brigadier-General Stewart had received intelligence reports that it was held by about 200 enemy troops. But this intelligence was flawed, as there were in fact three regular *Schutztruppe* companies—the 10th, 11th and 21st Field Companies—and a volunteer mounted Rifle Company—the 9th Rifle Company—under the command of Major Georg Kraut, numbering in all 686 men holding the position.

The British attack was to be made by two assault columns supported by four guns of the 27th Mountain Battery. The first column, formed by the half battalion of the Kapurthala Infantry and three squadrons of

East African Mounted Rifles, was to mount a frontal assault through the foothills, while the second, comprising the 29th Punjabis—less two companies—and a detachment of the East African Mounted Rifles, would march round the flank of Longido and assault the main camp. A third force of two squadrons of the East African Mounted Rifles was to skirt round Longido to cut the enemy's line of retreat and their communications and to locate and deny them their water supply. Having arrived at the southeast spur of Longido by 1:30 a.m. on the morning of the 3rd, the Punjabis advanced upwards towards the main ridge, which they reached by dawn. The guns of the 27th Mountain Battery, now able to see the German positions, opened fire. A double company of the 29th Punjabis then took the main spur with the bayonet, carrying three of the enemy sangars one after the other. The *Schutztruppe* mounted a counterattack but were stopped and driven off.

During the late morning, between the British camp on the Namanga River and Longido, a mounted patrol from the 9th Rifle Company ambushed a British column of native carriers and mules bringing water, ammunition and supplies to the troops. The mules were stampeded, and some of the native carriers with the column dropped their loads of food and ammunition and bolted, causing desperate shortages to the fighting troops. In the foothills, meanwhile, the frontal assault had been fought to a stand, while the Mounted Rifles sent to cut off the garrison had failed to locate the enemy's water supply but had cut their telephone communications. They were, however, now under attack by a detachment of the 11th Field Company, sent out by Kraut to repair the telephone line. In the skirmish that followed, the squadrons suffered nine killed and six wounded before their commander ordered them to break contact and withdraw.

On the main ridge the 29th Punjabis were coming under increasing opposition from Kraut's askaris. Lieutenant-Colonel AHB Drew, seeing the column in the foothills retreating, ordered his battalion to begin a fighting withdrawal, which they successfully did, supported by the guns of the 27th Battery and two machine guns of the Volunteer Machine Gun Company. The fighting ended at 7:30 p.m., with all the British columns withdrawing to their camp on the Namanga, having lost 312 killed and wounded. As for the *Schutztruppe*, they had sustained losses of 120 killed and wounded in the action and were forced to abandon the Longido position, which was occupied by the British following their withdrawal.

At the same time that the action at Longido was being fought, Indian Expeditionary Force "B" was fighting the disastrous Battle of Tanga, where it was ignominiously defeated. On his arrival in Mombasa on October 31, General Aitken, accompanied by his staff, conferred with the Governor—Sir Henry Belfield—Brigadier-General Stewart and Lieutenant-Colonel BR Graham (Corps of Guides). It was agreed at this meeting that Force "B" would attack and capture Tanga, the seaport and rail terminus of the Usambara Railway to Neu Moshi on the slopes of Kilimanjaro. Intelligence reports indicated that the coastal areas were only lightly defended and that the main body of the *Schutztruppe* was concentrated around Neu Moshi.

Following the fall of Tanga, Aitken planned to advance up the Usambara Railway towards Kilimanjaro, while Brigadier-General Stewart's Force "C" was to march on Taveta from Voi, in conjunction with his advance, and then link up with him. General Aitken then asked Captain Meinertzhagen to brief the meeting about the enemy forces; in his diary he recorded, "I said that perhaps Stewart who had been in East Africa for a month might give us his views. They were nil, beyond that the Germans had occupied Longido and that a 'strong' German force was on the coast, threatening Mombasa.... He knew nothing of the German dispositions, So I spoke, giving my opinion that there was probably very little in Tanga but that there must be a large concentration in the Kilimanjaro area whence troops could be rapidly transported by rail to Tanga within thirty hours,"[2] while Lieutenant-Colonel Graham offered to bring his 3rd KAR to Mombasa and then ship them to Tanga as a covering force for the landing. Aitken disregarded Meinertzhagen and refused Graham's offer. He was then informed by Captain FW Caulfield, RN, of HMS *Fox*, that the navy had a truce with the German authorities at both Tanga and Dar es Salaam and that before operations began, they would have to be notified of the termination of the truce. Despite strong protests from Meinertzhagen that all surprise would be lost, Aitken foolishly agreed, saying, "Tanga by orders of the Admiralty will have to be informed shortly before any hostile act takes place that terms of truce are not ratified." After the conference, Meinertzhagen wrote in his diary that the "plan is bad, for we lay ourselves open to defeat in detail, intercommunication between the two forces being quite impossible, and secondly we would both be operating in thick bush, in terribly unhealthy country and our troops, sad to relate, are rotten."[3]

The British invasion force less one of its escorts, the battleship *Goliath*, which was experiencing engine trouble, sailed from Mombasa at noon on November 1, anchoring 14 miles (22 kilometers) off Tanga the following morning. HMS *Fox* then detached herself and steamed into the outer harbor, where she dropped anchor at 6 a.m. District Commissioner Auracher, the senior civil administrator in the town, went aboard and was informed by Caulfield that the truce was ended and that the town must be surrendered by 8 a.m. or it would be attacked. Auracher said he did not have the authority to surrender Tanga, and he would need to confer with his superiors. Caulfield, therefore, agreed to wait until 9:30 a.m. before opening hostilities.

During these negotiations, the civil population was evacuated, and the 17th Field Company, camped on the outskirts of the town, alerted. Caulfield waited in vain for Auracher's return, as he, as a reserve officer, had changed into his army uniform and joined the 17th Field Company, which had marched from its camp into Tanga. Caulfield, at last realizing that Auracher had been simply stalling for time, upped anchor and returned to the invasion force.

At Neu Moshi, von Lettow-Vorbeck, on being informed by telegraph of the situation, immediately dispatched two and a half companies by rail to Tanga and issued orders for an HQ company and a further two field and two Rifle Companies to follow, while two Field Companies under the command of Captain Paul Baumstark, to the north of the port, were ordered to proceed at once to the town.

It was to be eight hours before the British transports began moving towards Tanga following Caulfield's return. Aitken had decided to land at dusk, a decision that was one of many that would have catastrophic repercussions for the invasion force. Aitken had initially planned to enter the harbor and land his troops at the various jetties, as it was rightly assumed the town was only lightly defended, and these defenders, he felt, would be quickly overcome by his superior force.

Announcing his plan to take the convoy into the harbor to disembark to his commanders at his midday conference, he was interrupted by Caulfield. He refused to lead the transports in until the harbor had been swept for mines. A furious Meinertzhagen angrily declared that there couldn't possibly be mines in the harbor as the navy had been regularly visiting the place since the outbreak of war and that the Germans did not have the means to produce or lay mines. Caulfield would not be convinced and maintained his refusal to enter the harbor until it had been swept. Aitken once again deferred to Caulfield, and a tug was dispatched to sweep for nonexistent mines throughout the night, recovering only logs and debris while an alternative landing place was sought.

The place eventually chosen was the small peninsula of Ras Kasone, two miles (three kilometers) east of Tanga town, which was covered in thick bushland, thorn scrub, rubber plantations and sisal crops. The landing was to take place on three beaches along this peninsula, designated "A," "B" and "C" beaches. "A" was on the east side of the peninsula, "B" on the northwest tip and "C" on the west. The *Official History* recorded, "In the darkness which quickly fell, the unrehearsed loading of lighters took time, and it was not until 9 p.m., after counter-orders to tugs, that the lighters carrying the 13th Rajputs with machine guns at their bows assembled under the lee of the *Karmala*. About 10 p.m., the order to move was given, and in a smooth sea, in bright moonlight which must have shown them clearly to German patrols on the cliffs, the tows drew in. In shallow water about 300 yards off shore the lighters were slipped and drifted shorewards and grounded almost at once. Rifle fire was opened on them from near the Red House, but on this being returned by the machine guns of the 13th Rajputs and the 4.7 guns of H.M.S. *Fox*, it ceased and the landing continued unopposed. The water, too shallow for the lighters, was breast high, too deep for heavily equipped men."[4] The 13th Rajputs, followed closely by the 61st KGO Pioneers, landed on "A" beach. They waded through the 300 yards (275 meters) of chest-deep water and then through mangrove to the beach.

Once ashore they advanced to the Red House opposite their landing place and the Signal Tower opposite "B" beach, their first objectives. They found both places deserted, "but the men both of the 13th and 61st, debilitated by nearly a month of sea sickness and cramped quarters, were thoroughly exhausted."[5] The German 17th Field Company, meanwhile, was establishing a defensive position in depth utilizing a drainage ditch along the west side of the railway cutting that ran from the Customs House on the shore of Tanga Bay in a crescent to the railway station and workshops, three-quarters of a mile to the south and barricading the three bridges over the cutting. In his diary, Meinertzhagen wrote, "So here we are, with only a small portion of our force, risking a landing in face of an enemy of unknown strength and on a beach which has not been reconnoitred and which looks like a rank mangrove swamp. Meanwhile, the convoy except for three ships here, are still ten miles away at sea. We appear to have made a proper mess of today's operation."[6]

At 5 a.m. the next morning (the 3rd) the 16th Field Company reached Tanga, taking up positions to the right of the 17th and south of the railway workshops. At dawn that morning the 13th Rajputs and 61st Pioneers, having taken their first objectives, began advancing towards Tanga town, two companies of Rajputs with two machine guns, under their commanding officer, Lieutenant-Colonel JA Stewart, leading. They moved down a narrow lane that led to the town, and as they reached the railway cutting, they came under heavy fire from the 17th Field Company, which stopped their advance and drove them into cover. The two following companies moved forward and tried to deploy to the left of the leading companies. But the bush was too thick, and they were unable to see where the enemy were. Meanwhile, the 61st too had been stopped by the heavy fire and had begun to fall back. They broke and fled in panic, followed by the Rajputs. Despite heroic efforts by their officers to rally them, they were unsuccessful, and several of these officers were killed or wounded as they desperately tried to stem the flight of their men to the beaches. Meanwhile the 17th Field Company began advancing from its position on the railway cutting, threatening to outflank the British center and right flank. They advanced 600 yards (549 meters), just to the south of the Government Hospital, and then went firm, while on the British left, and newly arrived from Neu Moshi, the 1st (half company) and 6th Field and 6th Rifle Companies, having gone into the line to the right of the 16th and to the south of the railway workshops, were checked in their advance by a double company of the 61st, which, having been delayed getting ashore, had been until then in reserve.

The Rajputs and Pioneers left around 300 casualties behind as they retreated in disorder. They were, however, eventually persuaded by their remaining officers to return to their bivouacs near the Red House. Here they remained throughout the rest of the day, covered by the 2nd Loyal North Lancs, who on landing in the forenoon had dug-in, covering "A" and "B" beaches while the Kashmir and Gwalior Rifles were landed. Of the attack, Meinertzhagen, with some justification, wrote, "We suffered 300 casualties today and our men behaved disgracefully, showing no military spirit or grit. I have never had much faith in our second-rate Indian troops and the bubble of the Indian Army will now burst. I doubt if even half of the Indian Army are really reliable against modern fire."[7] By that evening the Kashmir and Gwalior Rifles were ashore, and Aitken, no longer confident in the reliability of the Rajputs and Pioneers, ordered his remaining infantry to be landed the next morning on "B" and "C" beaches but without the Force's artillery and sappers. They were not to be brought ashore, thus denying the infantry any artillery support.

During the evening, the German commander, von Lettow-Vorbeck, reached Tanga from Neu Moshi. And he, unlike the British commander, immediately carried out a reconnaissance. "Whether Tanga was held by the enemy or not was not certain. Strong officers' patrols were at once pushed forward beyond Tanga towards Ras-Kasone. Luckily Headquarters had brought a few bicycles, and so, in order to satisfy myself quickly by personal observation, I was able to go off at once with Captain von Hammerstein and Volunteer Dr. Dessel to the railway station at Tanga, where I found an advanced post of the 6th Field Company. They, however, could give no accurate information about the enemy, and so I rode on through the empty streets of the town. It was completely deserted, and the white houses of the Europeans reflected the brilliant rays of the

Two. Disaster at Tanga

moon into the streets which we traversed. So we reached the harbour at the further edge of the town. Tanga was therefore clear of the enemy. A quarter of a mile out lay the transports, a blaze of lights, and full of noise: there was no doubt that the landing was about to commence at once. I much regretted that our artillery—we had two guns of 1873 pattern—was not yet up. Here, in the brilliant moonlight, at such close range, their effects would have been annihilating, the hostile cruisers notwithstanding.

"We then rode on towards Ras-Kasone, left our bicycles in the German Government Hospital, and went on foot to the beach, close to which, right in front of us, lay an English cruiser. On the way back, at the hospital, we were challenged, apparently by an Indian sentry—we did not understand the language—but saw nothing. We got on our cycles again and rode back."[8]

By the next morning (the 4th), he had deployed his available troops to meet the next attack. Covering the town, railway station and workshops were a newly raised company of Arab irregulars, the 17th, 6th, 16th Field and 6th Rifle Companies, while in reserve on his right flank he had three companies, the 13th Field Company with four machine guns and the 7th and 8th Rifle Companies with three machine guns, under the command of von Prince. A further two Field Companies, the 4th and 9th, along with his artillery, were en route from Neu Moshi and were expected to arrive at any time.

The landing of the last of the British infantry did not begin until 10:30 a.m., as Atkin had ordered that they should be given a good breakfast. As a result, it wasn't until midday that all his infantry were ashore, and a further three hours elapsed before they were assembled and ready to begin their assault.

Aitkin began his attack at 3 p.m. He had not bothered to send out patrols to locate the enemy defenses or reconnoiter the best approach routes, being overtly confident in a frontal infantry assault without support. Leading his attack on the extreme right, he had the 2nd Kashmir Rifles and the half battalion of the 3rd Kashmir Rifles. On their left was the 2nd Loyal North Lancs. In the center of his line were the 63rd Palamcottah Light Infantry, with the 101st Grenadiers on the left flank. Following in close support were the 13th Rajputs, 98th Infantry and 61st Pioneers. His stores and reserves of ammunition were left on the beaches under the guard of the half battalion of the 3rd Gwalior Rifles, less one company attached to the 3rd Kashmir Rifles.

The advance through the thick scrub, rubber and sisal plantations, in the full heat of the day, took the leading battalions two hours. As they approached the German positions, they came under a heavy and

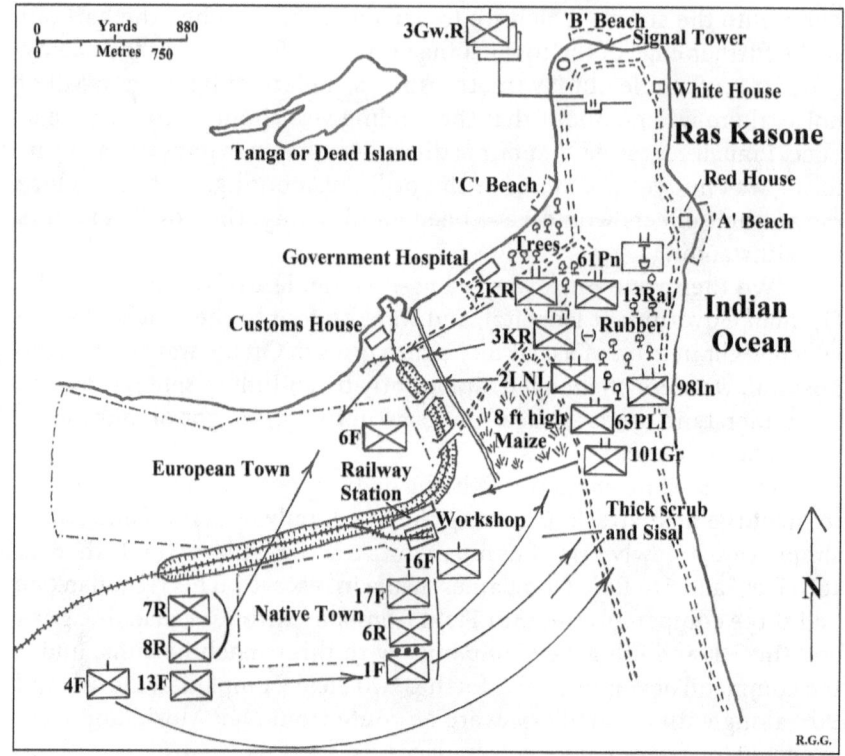

The Attack on Tanga 1914 (map by the author).

sustained fire from the well-situated enemy machine guns. The 63rd Light Infantry began taking heavy losses, and those men not wounded turned and fled into the bush, knocking over their officers as they attempted to rally them. Then the 13th Rajputs, directly behind the 63rd, were caught up in the panic and began to disintegrate. As the men of these battalions ran back through the ranks of the 61st Pioneers, they too broke and ran, carrying with them the men of the 98th Infantry as the panic-stricken rabble burst through them. To add to the terror, confusion and chaos of the fighting, wild African bees, notorious for their savage and painful sting, swarmed as machine-gun bullets smashed their hives. The swarming bees descended in great angry clouds onto the fleeing sepoys, who ran screaming to the beaches and into the sea and attacked and put out of action a German machine-gun position.

The 2nd Loyals, Kashmir Rifles and 101st Grenadiers pushed on into Tanga, where house-to-house fighting began. As the Loyals and Kashmir Rifles doggedly advanced, the askaris of the 6th Field Company, von Lettow-Vorbeck's best-trained unit, began to waver and give ground. Von Prince led his two Rifle Companies to the German left to reinforce the 6th, stopping the advance of the Loyals and the Kashmir Rifles who were on the British right flank and had advanced along the beach to the town. On the British left, meanwhile, the 101st Grenadiers were advancing slowly and steadily, disregarding the heavy casualties being inflicted on them by the Germans. Each time a man fell, his place was immediately taken by another stepping forward from the ranks behind. The askaris of 16th Field Company broke in the face of what seemed an irresistible force, retreating to the Tanga-Pangani road. Von Lettow-Vorbeck committed the last of his reserves, the 13th Field Company with their four machine guns, which opened a continuous fire in a counterattack against the 101st. The badly mauled Grenadiers' morale finally broke; they came to a stop and withdrew in the face of this counterattack.

As the counterattack against the Grenadiers was taking place, von Lettow-Vorbeck received a timely reinforcement. The 4th Field Company had arrived from Neu Moshi and was rushed into the line. Aitken, without establishing the precise positions of his troops and with his entire front crushed, crumbling or stalled, sent an urgent signal to Caulfield to bombard the town but to avoid hitting the railway. For the next half hour *Fox's* main and secondary batteries pounded Tanga, firing 108 rounds of 6-inch and 4.7-inch shells into the town and hospital, most of which fell among the men of the 2nd Loyals. Having suffered severe losses from both the Germans and the naval gunfire, the Loyals and Kashmir Rifles were ordered to withdraw from the town. As the British pulled back, an askaris bugler began sounding the retreat, and the Germans began withdrawing to their camp on the outskirts of Tanga. As they fell back, von Prince was shot through the head and killed.

At Aitken's HQ, his staff officers were convinced that the bugle call was announcing a German attack. Captain Meinertzhagen, familiar with the enemy's bugle calls, told the General that the Germans had blown the retreat, not the attack. But Aitken and his staff were beaten men, and he was ignored. In his diary Meinertzhagen wrote, "I begged him to allow us to collect what we could and go forward, but he would not, for he was tired out and seemed disgusted with the whole business. His one ambition seemed to be to get away."[9] Meinertzhagen, nevertheless, undertook a lone reconnaissance into Tanga as evening fell, confirming that the town was indeed deserted. Despite attempts by Meinertzhagen and the officers of the Loyals to get him to change his mind and let them resume the offensive that night and take the town, all Aitken could think of was re-embarkation and withdrawal, which, he told his staff, would begin the next morning. The officer of the 2nd Loyals sent to HQ to argue for a reconnaissance and a resumption of the attack was bluntly told: "The only information of any value now is that which will help us to get out of this—place as soon as possible."[10]

Throughout the night, the British were subjected to continued panic by the broken Indian regiments who, at the slightest disturbance, would rush in terror into the sea. The only steadfast troops Aitken had were the surviving men of the 2nd Loyals, the Kashmir and Gwalior Rifles and the 101st Grenadiers. These men were deployed in a defensive line about the British position on the peninsula.

At 6 a.m. on November 5, von Lettow-Vorbeck's troops reentered Tanga while he undertook a reconnaissance of the area beyond. He saw the British troops on the beaches and the boats plying to and from the shore. During the morning, Aitken had ordered the re-embarkation of the troops to begin. *Fox* moved inshore to cover the evacuation, as did the transport *Bharata*, carrying the 28th Mountain Battery, who had deployed their guns on the transport's deck.

While the embarkation was in progress, the 2nd Loyals and the 2nd and 3rd Kashmir Rifles were employed as the covering force. As the remaining Indian troops were standing on the shoreline waiting to be taken off, the covering force opened fire on a German patrol that approached their positions; panic gripped the beach as the Indian troops threw away their rifles and ran into the sea up to their necks, some even trying to swim out to the transports. Shortly after issuing his order to begin the evacuation, Aitkin senselessly ordered that all supplies, reserves of ammunition and machine guns were to be left behind. The Loyals were the last unit to be taken off, and they begged for permission to bring their machine guns with them. But this request was refused, and the machine guns were abandoned on the beach.

By 5 p.m., the evacuation was completed. Aitken sent Captain Meinertzhagen ashore under a white flag with a letter for the German commander in which he apologized for the bombardment of the hospital the previous day and requesting a truce so he could remove his wounded. Von Lettow-Vorbeck agreed to observe a truce until 6 p.m. But as midnight approached and the British convoy was still standing off the peninsula, he sent a message to Aitken saying that his artillery had arrived, and if the British did not depart soon, he would be compelled to give the order for them to open fire.

At 4:30 a.m. the next morning, November 6, they finally sailed for Mombasa, arriving there on the 8th. Incredibly, customs officials refused permission for anyone to land until the convoy's remaining stores were examined and any duty paid. Anglo-Indian losses at Tanga were 360 killed, 487 wounded and 148 missing. They abandoned enough modern rifles to allow von Lettow-Vorbeck to reequip three Field Companies (about 700 men), 600,000 rounds of small arms ammunition, 16 machine guns, enough clothing and blankets to last the Germans for a year, and quantities of field telephones and other stores. Of the 1,000 German troops who took part in the battle, 16 Germans and 55 askaris were killed and 76 Germans and askaris wounded.

Following the debacle at Tanga, the War Office in London took over direct control of all operations in East Africa from the Colonial Office, and Major-General Aitken, who had clearly been promoted above his level of capability, was removed from his command and ordered home. He was reduced to the rank of colonel and placed on half pay: "The first offensive against German East Africa completely fell through. It was a serious setback, and for the time placed the British forces in East Africa entirely on the defensive, while it revived the determination of the Germans throughout their territory to resist and not to surrender."[11]

Aitken handed over command of Force "B" to Brigadier-General Wapshare, who was promoted to temporary Major-General. The British forces in East Africa were then reorganized into two commands: Nairobi Area, placed under Brigadier-General Stewart, and Mombasa Area under Brigadier-General Tighe. The various subunits of Forces "B" and "C" were then distributed between these two commands.

Colonel Arthur Aitken spent the rest of his life fighting to clear his name, but his incompetence and lack of initiative at Tanga were undeniable. He had failed to ensure naval-military cooperation, completely disregarded the Field Service Regulations (Part I, Secs 41, 42 and App. II) regarding combined operations, seeming to be in awe of the naval officers when discussing his plans, which lost him surprise and the benefit of naval gunfire support to his infantry commanders. He deferred a second time to his naval colleague Captain Francis Caulfield, his junior in rank, regarding the initial landings. He underestimated his enemy and used a Pioneer battalion, the 61st Pioneers, in his initial assault, despite the fact that FSRs stated that such units should only be used as a last resort or in an emergency. He did not carry out or order any reconnaissance of the landing places or routes of approach into Tanga, let alone the enemy positions. He denied his infantry artillery support, which could have given him success, and to cap it all left huge amounts of weapons, ammunition and stores to the enemy when he withdrew and which were used against British forces during the campaign.

Three

Operations in the Rufiji Delta

A WEEK AFTER THE BATTLE OF TANGA, Brigadier-General Tighe was sent to the Rufiji aboard HMS *Fox* to examine the possibility of a combined operation to destroy the *Königsberg*. It came to nothing, however, as it was decided that to locate the exact position of the German cruiser, air reconnaissance would be required. The British did not have any aircraft in East Africa, but Admiral King-Hall recalled a flying exhibition by two 90-hp Curtiss seaplanes, owned by a Mr. HD Cutler, that had taken place in Durban the previous summer.

The Admiralty authorized the purchase of these seaplanes and commissioned Cutler as a Sub-Lieutenant, RNVR. The aircraft were loaded onto the SS *Kinfauns Castle* and transported to Mafia Island off the Rufiji Delta, arriving there on November 15. While in transit, one of the aircraft was damaged, and the second required work to get her airworthy. Cutler, assisted by Midshipman AN Gallehawk, RNR, cannibalized the damaged aircraft for spares and began work on the second airplane.

While the *Kinfauns Castle* was returning to the delta from Durban, it had been decided to sink the 3,800-ton collier *Newbridge* at the entrance of the Ssimba-Ouranga branch of the Rufiji as a blockship. *Newbridge* was brought south from Mombasa, arriving off the Rufiji on the night of November 9–10. Escorted by the coastal steamer *Duplex* and steam pinnaces from Drury-Lowe's cruiser squadron and the *Goliath*, Commander Raymond Fitzmaurice, RN, with a skeleton crew took *Newbridge* to her designated anchorage across the river mouth. Fitzmaurice then set the scuttling charges and at 6 a.m. fired the fuses. He and his crew were then taken off the *Newbridge* by *Chatham's* pinnace. Fifteen minutes later the charges detonated, and *Newbridge* listed to port before sinking stern first into the mud.

Cutler and Gallehawk, meanwhile, having successfully repaired one of the Curtiss seaplanes with parts from the damaged machine, were ready to begin the hunt for the *Königsberg*. Cutler flew his first

Three. Operations in the Rufiji Delta

The German light cruiser SMS *Königsberg* (Walther Dobbertin, Bundesarchiv, Bild 105-DOA3002).

reconnaissance on the morning of the 19th, taking off from near Niororo Island in the mouth of the Rufiji at 7 a.m. He had a flying time of 55 minutes, and after an hour and no sign of the biplane, search parties were sent out. Six hours later Cutler and his plane were found on Okousa Island, 34 miles (55 kilometers) south of Niororo and 18 miles (29 kilometers) from Mafia Island. Having lost his way, he had tried to retrace his course and had landed near the first island he saw. But he had not located the *Königsberg*.

However, the noise of the biplane's flight had alerted the Germans to the fact that the British were employing aircraft in their search for the elusive cruiser's position. Commander Looff took immediate steps to combat this new threat from the air. Cutler flew a successful mission up the Rufiji on the 24th, and this time he located the *Königsberg*. He informed Captain Drury-Lowe she was 12 miles (19 kilometers) upriver and appeared ready to break out.

On December 6, another flight upriver confirmed that the German cruiser was beyond the range of the guns of the British warships. A further reconnaissance was ordered on the 10th, which revealed that *Königsberg* had shifted her position. Unfortunately, the Curtiss was, by this time, in pretty bad shape; her rigid silk-covered wings were affected by the humid heat, and her radiator was constantly overheating. While undertaking yet another reconnaissance, and only a mile upriver, the Curtiss's engine began to miss. Cutler turned the aircraft and tried to fly to the Kikouya entrance of the Rufiji but was forced to crash-land under the guns of the German shore parties.

Arthur Gallehawk, who had seen the Curtiss come down, headed upriver in a motor launch accompanied by the armed tug *Helmuth*. They reached the site an hour later and found the seaplane in deep water, but it hadn't sunk and was recoverable. Gallehawk, under covering fire from the *Helmuth*, which drove off the Germans on the shore, dragged the plane from the river. Unfortunately, it was damaged beyond repair. Of Cutler there was no sign. He had swum ashore after crashing and had been taken prisoner by the *Königsberg's* shore parties.

On the Ugandan frontier, meanwhile, a detachment of the *Schutztruppe's* 7th Field Company, reinforced with police askaris and Ruga-Ruga, crossed into British territory on November 20. Fort Kyaka on the south bank of the Kagera River was abandoned to them, but all other positions held, and they were eventually repulsed by units of 4th KAR, having lost 60 killed and wounded. At the same time, in the south, an attack was launched against the Northern Rhodesian and Nyasaland frontiers by the 5th Field Company, whose commander, Captain Erich von Langenn-Steinkeller, informed the British that his askaris would massacre any whites captured. The incursion was met by a flying column under Lieutenant-Colonel F Maning, which chased them back across the frontier with a loss of two machine guns, seven German officers and 65 askaris killed. Maning was killed along with four other members of his column.

On the 26th von Lettow-Vorbeck ordered Major-General Kurt Wahle—a retired Saxon general officer who was visiting his son and the colonial exhibition when the war began and who had placed himself at the *Schutztruppe* commander's disposal—his Inspector of Lines of Communication, to move the 10th Field Company into Dar es Salaam and defend it against possible British occupation. Dar es Salaam, along with the coastal towns of Tanga and Lindi, had been left undefended on the orders of the Governor on the outbreak of war. Two days later a British naval squadron led by HMS *Goliath* and *Fox* anchored off the entrance to Dar es Salaam; they had come to inspect all the shipping in the harbor. "On the 28th, two men-of-war, a transport and a tug, appeared off Dar-es-Salaam, and demanded to inspect our ships lying in the harbour. Among others, there was the *Tabora*, of the German East African Line, which had been converted into a hospital-ship. As the English had on a previous occasion declared that they did not consider themselves bound

Three. Operations in the Rufiji Delta

by any agreement about Dar-es-Salaam, fresh negotiations would have been necessary every time we wanted to escape a threatened bombardment. Thus an endless screw was created. I now wired that the entry into the harbour of a pinnace, demanded by the English, was to be resisted by force of arms."[1]

The German civil authorities had, however, immediately displayed white flags and allowed the British inspection parties to enter. The inspection parties were under the command of the First Lieutenant of the *Goliath*, Commander HP Ritchie, RN. They entered the harbor in the steam pinnaces of *Goliath* and *Fox* and aboard the tug *Helmuth*. As they entered, all was quiet. The *Helmuth*, commanded by Lieutenant Patterson, RN, *Goliath*'s Torpedo Officer, drew alongside the *Feldmarshall*. The inspection team boarded her and prepared her for scuttling, while Ritchie, in the *Goliath*'s steam pinnace, drew alongside and boarded the *König*, setting charges under her low-pressure cylinders to immobilize her before moving on to the *Kaiser Willhelm II*. Captain Friedrich von Kornatzki—who had taken over command of the 10th Field Company from 1st Lieutenant von Chappuis—had initially felt bound to comply with the civil authority's decision to allow the British to carry out an inspection. But on observing more than a single pinnace entering the harbor, he decided to comply with his commander's instruction and attack them.

By this time Ritchie had become uneasy; it was far too quiet and the harbor unnaturally so. This unease led him to order two steel lighters lashed to the sides of his pinnace. Shortly after, small arms fire was heard coming from the main anchorage. *Fox*'s pinnace was under fire, and her stoker was mortally wounded. Lieutenant Corson, commanding the pinnace, scrambled forward through the gunfire to stoke the

Commander Henry Peel Ritchie, VC, RN (*Illustrated London News and Sketch*).

boiler and build up a sufficient head of steam to get them out of the harbor. While *Helmuth* was badly holed by the enemy gunfire, it took all the skills of the carpenter to keep her from sinking as they headed out of danger, though without Paterson or Surgeon Lieutenant Holtham, *Goliath*'s medical officer, who were taken prisoner, having been left aboard the *Tabora*.

Ritchie's pinnace pulled away from the *Kaiser Willhelm II* and headed for the harbor entrance under a storm of fire from the houses in the town, the shore, the cemetery and the plantations. The coxswain, Petty Officer TJ Clarke, was wounded. Ritchie took his place, and then he too was hit on the forehead. Over the next 20 minutes, as they desperately tried to regain the warships, he received a further seven wounds: in his left hand, twice in his left arm, in the right arm and right hip and finally twice in the right leg. He eventually fainted through loss of blood, and Able Seaman George Upton took over the wheel, bringing the pinnace alongside *Goliath*.

Goliath opened fire with her main 12-inch batteries, destroying the Governor's residence. She was joined shortly after by *Fox*, and between them they badly damaged all the shipping in the harbor and the town. When the boats regained the squadron, they had with them 14 Germans and 20 native seamen as prisoners. They had lost one killed, 12 wounded and two missing. Commander Ritchie was awarded the Victoria Cross—the British Empire's premier award for gallantry—for his inspiration and leadership during the operation.[2] Lieutenant Corson received the Distinguished Service Cross, Petty Officer Clarke the Conspicuous Gallantry Medal and Able Seaman Upton the Distinguished Service Medal.

In late December 1914 Admiral King-Hall was ordered to tighten the blockade of the Rufiji Delta and to extend his blockade along the entire German East African coast. As part of this tightening of the blockade, Mafia Island was to be occupied, as the local German commander, Reserve Lieutenant Schiller, had been in contact with *Königsberg* via the island's communications tower. He had been keeping Looff informed of all British operations since late October.

On January 8, 1915, a force of four companies of 1st KAR, a company of 101st Grenadiers, and a section of machine guns from 4th KAR, under the command of Lieutenant-Colonel Ward, embarked in the auxiliary cruiser *Kinfauns Castle*. At 6:30 a.m. on the 10th, following a bombardment of the Ras Kisimani area in the southwest by the cruiser *Fox* and the *Kinfauns Castle*, the troops were put ashore unopposed on the western tip of Mafia Island. A defensive perimeter was established by the Grenadier's company and patrols sent out to locate the enemy.

The next morning the 1st KAR companies, commanded by Major

LM Soames (East Kent Regt), advanced towards Ngombeni village, where Lieutenant Schiller had taken up positions with his small German force. The 1st KAR's scouts made contact with the enemy here at 8:30 a.m. Soames, keeping "A" and "C" Companies in reserve, ordered Captain GJ Giffard's (Royal West Surrey Regt) "B" Company to mount a holding attack, supported by 4th KAR's machine guns, against the front of the German position, while Lieutenant LG Murray's (Gordon Highlanders) "E" Company moved around the enemy left in an attempt to turn their flank.

With the hours passing and no progress being made, Soames committed his reserve, ordering these companies to move round the Germans right flank. With both his flanks threatened, Schiller withdrew from the village and across the valley behind under heavy fire. But suffering several casualties in the process, he was forced to surrender. The German garrison of 26 police askaris and three Germans surrendered, having lost two killed and six wounded, one of whom was Schiller; 1st KAR's casualties were one killed, ten wounded, including Soames and Giffard.

Following the surrender, Ward marched to Chole Bay on the southeast coast, having dispatched "C" Company to take the island's main town, Kilindoni, which it did without meeting any opposition, and there it raised the British flag at 2:23 p.m. that afternoon. On the 13th a company of 63rd Palamcottah Light Infantry reached the island to take up duty as its garrison, and the following day Ward's force returned to Mombasa.

Shortly afterwards, HMS *Chatham*, long overdue for a refit, was ordered to Bombay, and Rear-Admiral King-Hall arrived off the delta in *Hyacinth* to take personnel command of the operations against *Königsberg*. He requested the dispatch of further aircraft for bombing and reconnaissance missions and the use of two monitors. He also arranged for the South African big game hunter, Pieter J Pretorius, who had hunted elephant in the delta before the war, to undertake a reconnaissance of the river. Pretorius was to make soundings of the various channels and chart possible routes for an attacking force as well as identify *Königsberg's* precise location. As soon as he landed on Mafia Island from *Hyacinth*, Pretorius established a base camp and then began preparations for his hazardous reconnaissance.

Four

The Action at Jasin and Early Operations in the West and Northwest

As 1914 drew to a close, German forces were still in possession of British territory north of the Umba River. The commander of Mombasa Area, Brigadier-General Michael Tighe, was ordered to begin a limited operation to drive them out. A column of 1,800 men of the 2nd Kashmir Rifles, 101st Grenadiers and the 1st and 3rd KAR with 5,500 porters was dispatched to the Umba Valley. By January 2, 1915, they had cleared the Umba and reoccupied the coastal town of Vanga, which had been in German hands since the opening of hostilities.

From Vanga the column marched over the frontier and took Jasin, 20 miles (32 kilometers) inside German territory. Tighe had Jasin fortified and placed under the command of Lieutenant-Colonel Raghbir Singh, the CO of the 2nd Kashmir Rifles. Two defensive posts were constructed; the larger was garrisoned by three companies of the 2nd Kashmir Rifles and a company of the 101st Grenadiers, supported by a machine-gun section of the KAR, while the smaller post, at the Sisal Factory to the northwest, was held by 40 men of the 2nd Kashmiris.

Von Lettow-Vorbeck, fearing that the British intended to use Jasin as an advanced base for another attempt on Tanga, decided to retake the town. He ordered a reconnaissance in force by the 15th Field and 4th Rifle Companies on January 12. But his troops were beaten off with heavy losses. Reinforcements were ordered up from Neu Moshi by rail, and by the 17th, he had eight Field Companies, two Rifle Companies, 16 machine guns and two field guns assembled just south of Jasin.

It was customary in the *Schutztruppe* for the women to accompany their men on operations, tending their needs, cooking their food and waiting in the rear of the companies when they were in action; they then tended to the wounded once the fighting had ended. The Arab

Four. The Action at Jasin and Early Operations 39

Company, unlike the other companies, had a following of young boys, a situation which von Lettow-Vorbeck accepted. "With these simple people, whose predilection for their ancient traditions and customs is further confirmed by Islam, and who are besides very proud and vain, it is particularly difficult to interfere with such customs."[1] On this occasion, however, because the approaches to Jasin were extremely hazardous and the necessity to conserve supplies paramount, von Lettow-Vorbeck made the decision not to allow the boys to accompany the Arab Company. The company became surly on being informed of this decision and demanded to be released from serving in the *Schutztruppe*. This demand was refused, and the disaffected company moved off with the rest of the force.

On learning of the German attack, Tighe ordered the garrison to be withdrawn, but the orders never reached them. Von Lettow-Vorbeck had ringed Jasin with machine guns and then moved his companies to within 200 yards (183 meters) of the town, hidden by the thick agave that grew all around. His plan was for 4th and 11th Field Companies under Major Arthur Kepler to attack from the right flank, the 15th and 17th Field Companies under Captain Otto Adler from the left, the Arab Company from the northwest, while Captain Ernst Otto with the 9th Field Company was to make a frontal assault, followed in close support by von Lettow-Vorbeck's HQ and his reserve, the 1st, 6th, 13th Field and 7th Rifle Companies. All units were to begin their assault simultaneously.

When the order to begin the attack was given on the morning of the 18th, the Arab Company mutinied; firing their rifles into the air when ordered to engage the enemy, they broke and ran towards the 15th and 17th Field Companies in their rear. Captain Adler immediately ordered his men to open fire on them and shot them down to a man. Despite this setback the attack went on, and fighting raged throughout the day. The Germans launched repeated assaults against the British positions, only to be driven off with steadily mounting losses. But the garrison was gradually being forced to fall back from their outer defenses to the fortifications in the town by these determined attacks … all except the small party in the Sisal Factory two miles (three kilometers) west of Jasin.

A relief force, under the command of Captain George Giffard, comprising "B" Company, 1st KAR and "B" and "D" Companies, 3rd KAR, had been assembled at the Umba River camp, three and a half miles (six kilometers) northeast of Jasin, and was soon marching to relieve the garrison. Early on the 18th Giffard's advance companies were closing on the besieged town. They crossed the Suba River and were in sight of the Sisal Factory when they were attacked by the 17th Field Company. In the fighting that followed the KAR companies were gradually forced back towards the river, and running low on ammunition, they had to recross the Suba. As soon as they were on the north side of the river, they regrouped and replenished their ammunition preparatory to renewing their relief attempt and, while doing so, were reinforced by a further two companies, "A" and "C" Companies, 1st KAR and a section of 28th Mountain Battery. That afternoon, following an artillery barrage, the relief force launched its second attack across the river but was stopped. The Kashmiri detachment in the Sisal Factory, commanded by Subadar[2] Mardan Ali, having run out of ammunition, fixed bayonets and broke out, fighting their way through the encircling Germans to reach the KAR north of the Suba, having lost 19 of their original 40 men. The German companies that had been besieging the Sisal Factory were redeployed to face the KAR relief force. Believing the Jasin garrison could hold out for at least another 24 hours, the relief force rested north of the Suba for the night, resuming their attack at 6 a.m. the next morning.

At dawn on the 19th, the Germans again attacked the town; during this attack, Lieutenant-Colonel Raghbir Singh was killed, and Captain GJG Hanson (69th Punjab Inf) took over command. The garrison had run out of water, and they were nearly out of ammunition; not only that, but the company of the 101st Grenadiers were becoming moody and unmanageable. At 7 a.m., Hanson, unaware of the relief attempt and having decided that he could no longer maintain his defense of the town, surrendered. In his memoirs, the German commander wrote, "Four Indian companies, with European officers and N.C.O.'s, fell into our hands. We all remarked the warlike pride with which our Askari regarded the enemy; I never thought our black fellows could look so distinguished. Both friend and foe had been in an unpleasant situation, and were near the end of their nervous strength."[3] Following the surrender of Jasin, von Lettow-Vorbeck withdrew his forces to the south while the British withdrew to the Mombasa Area, as the Umba River district was extremely unhealthy during the rainy season which was almost on them.

The consequences of the victory at Jasin would, however, influence von Lettow-Vorbeck's strategies for the remainder of the war. "Although the attack carried out at Jassini [sic] with nine companies had been completely successful, it showed that such heavy losses as we also had suffered could only be borne in exceptional cases. We had to economize our forces in order to last out a long war. Of the regular officers, Major Kepler, Lieuts Spalding and Gerlich, Second Lieuts Kaufmann and Erdmann were killed; Captain von Hammerstein had died of his wound. The loss of these professional soldiers about one seventh of the regular officers present could not be replaced. The expenditure of 200,000 rounds

Four. The Action at Jasin and Early Operations   41

also proved that with the means at my disposal I could at the most fight three more actions of this nature. The need to strike great blows only quite exceptionally, and to restrict myself principally to guerrilla warfare, was evidently imperative."[4]

With the loss of Jasin, Major-General Wapshare was ordered to adopt a defensive strategy along the Anglo-German frontier from Lake Victoria Nyanza to the sea. Throughout British East Africa, the troops were split into small detachments and distributed along the frontier and the Uganda Railway, taking up their defensive positions in accordance with the War Cabinet instructions.

Despite the announcement of a complete blockade of the German East African coast by the British on March 1, 1915, the initiative had been handed to von Lettow-Vorbeck. His forces began raiding across the frontier, attacking British outposts and the Uganda Railway, derailing trains and blowing up bridges. In the course of two months his forces derailed 30 trains and blew up ten railway bridges.

Earlier, when von Lettow-Vorbeck had ordered the concentration of the *Schutztruppe* on the Pugu heights in August 1914, some companies were exempted from this, notably those units along German East's land frontier to the west which included not only Lake Victoria Nyanza but also Lake Tanganyika and in the southeast Lake Nyasa. And as the British had mastery of Lake Victoria Nyanza from the very beginning of the war—which meant the various German outposts in the lake area could only communicate by wireless—it had been decided early on that the defense of the frontier with Uganda would be undertaken by Captain Willibald von Stuemer—the Resident at Bukoba—using police askaris and Ruga-Ruga. Captain Bock von Wülfingen would take the bulk of his 7th Field Company based in Bukoba around the south of the lake to Mwanza and reinforce Captain Friedrich Braunschweig's 14th Field Company.

Von Wülfingen arrived at Mwanza in early September 1914; he left again almost at once, marching north to the British frontier with a mixed force from both companies and some Ruga-Ruga and attacked a small British force at Kisii to the east of Lake Victoria Nyanza. His incursion was met by three companies of 4th KAR, commanded by Captain EGM Thorneycroft (Royal Lancaster Regt). Immediately on learning of the attack, "G" Company, 4th KAR marched from the British lake port of Kisumu, followed shortly after by "C" and "D" Companies, advancing on Kisii, 40 miles (64 kilometers) to the southwest. Thorneycroft intended to mount an attack against the German column from the northeast while a detachment of the East African Mounted Rifles—sent by rail from Nairobi to Kisumu—had their horses and mules taken aboard the steamer *Winifred* and a second steamer of Commander GS Thornley, RN's lake flotilla—to be carried to Karungu, from where they would advance on Kisii from the west.

As the British steamers made their way south, they were attacked by the German armed steamer *Muansa*, the only enemy vessel on the lake. *Muansa* opened fire on them with her main armament and machine guns, then escaped into the reedbeds along the shoreline before the British ships could effectively return fire, delaying the landing of the Mounted Rifles. Meanwhile, the three companies of 4th KAR made a surprise attack against von Wülfingen's force early on the 12th. Though taken by surprise, von Wülfingen's askaris returned a heavy rifle and machine-gun fire, killing Captain Thorneycroft, who was leading the attack, almost at once, and Captain HA Lilley (Yorkshire Regt) took over command. The fighting raged for several hours, but by the late afternoon, the KAR were running short of ammunition, and Captain Lilley was forced to break contact and pull back until he was joined by the Mounted Rifles. But by the time the Mounted Rifles had been landed at Karungu and begun closing on Kisii, von Wülfingen, who had taken heavy casualties during the day, had withdrawn south across the frontier and returned to Mwanza. Over the following months there was relative quiet, both sides patrolling and undertaking small raids and minor incursions.

Then in January 1915 the commander of Nairobi Area—Brigadier-General James Stewart—decided to take the German port of Shirati which lay just across the frontier with British East Africa on the eastern side of Lake Victoria Nyanza. He planned to utilize Shirati as a forward base for the lake flotilla and to patrol the border area from the enemy side. The operation was to be undertaken by "B" Company, 2nd Loyals, with a machine gun and two 10-pdr guns of 28th Mountain Battery, who were sent by train from Nairobi to Kisumu, where they boarded Commander Thornley's steamers on the 6th. The steamers arrived off Shirati the next morning with the mountain battery's guns deployed on deck. As the Loyals began their landing, the small defending force of 22 askaris from the 7th Field Company, under the command of 1st Lieutenant Wilhelm von Haxthausen, opened fire on the steamers. Von Haxthausen was forced to abandon his position and retire in the face of heavy gunfire from the ships, taking up a new position from where he could continue to observe the British. Once the port had been secured, General Stewart, who had accompanied the expedition, left in one of the steamers for the west side of the lake. The Loyals were, shortly after, reinforced by "E" and "G" Companies, 4th KAR.

Von Haxthausen, meanwhile, had withdrawn some miles to the

Four. The Action at Jasin and Early Operations

east, and having been reinforced with a further 80 men and a light field gun, he occupied Gurribe Hill, which straddled the frontier. On the 16th the commander of "E" Company, Captain RFB Knox (Royal Dublin Fusiliers), learned of the occupation of Gurribe Hill and marched his company out to drive off the Germans. Knox mounted his attack on the 17th; advancing through the thick bush, he gradually forced the Germans off the hill, capturing their field gun and baggage for the loss of four killed and five wounded. Von Haxthausen quickly rallied his askaris, and having learned where the KAR had left their own baggage column, attacked and took it, capturing a medical officer who was accompanying the KAR, 22,000 rounds of ammunition, a number of abandoned porters' loads and eight pack mules before withdrawing, having lost ten men killed and wounded.

Back at Shirati, Major T McG Bridges, commanding the 2nd Loyals, on learning of the action, marched out to support Knox. His company arrived well after the fight was over, however. Captain Knox, meanwhile, unable to bring away the captured field gun disabled it and left it where it was when they and the Loyals returned to Shirati. On January 30, Shirati was abandoned, as von Lettow-Vorbeck correctly assumed when he wrote, "I believe this withdrawal was a result of the severe defeat sustained by the enemy at Jassini [*sic*] on the 18th. He considered it desirable to re-concentrate his forces nearer the Uganda Railway, where they would be more readily available."[5]

In March the Reserve Company, 3rd KAR and the KAR Mounted Infantry Company, along with a section of 28th Mountain Battery and the scout detachment of the East African Mounted Rifles, were sent to reinforce "E" and "G" Companies, 4th KAR. They were to form a mobile column under the command of Lieutenant-Colonel LH Hickson (Royal West Kent Regt and 3rd KAR) to try and put an end to the German incursions that had been increasing towards the end of February along the frontier. At around the same time, von Lettow-Vorbeck ordered the 26th Field Company to move from Dar es Salaam to reinforce Mwanza.

On the 4th Hickson's column crossed the frontier and advanced on Ikoma, where on arrival the two companies of 4th KAR attacked and forced the detachment of the 14th Field Company from Ikoma Hill. The Germans quickly rallied and mounted a counterattack, which was defeated, and they withdrew to Susuni Hill. The following day the Reserve Company, 3rd KAR, drove them from this position after an eight-hour fight. The column then withdrew back across the frontier.

That same day, March 5, the *Winifred* and *Kavirondo* began an operation to destroy the German steamer *Muansa*. Commander Thornley had worked out *Muansa's* regular patrol pattern and the fact that, when pursued by his heavier draft vessels, the German would escape into the reed-covered shallows along the coast or, when in the extreme-southwest of the lake, into the shallow waters of the Rougesi passage which ran between the islands of Oukenoueoue and Nafouba that lay near the northwest of the Speke Gulf. With this information, he decided it was time to put an end to the German steamer.

When his two ships arrived in the Speke Gulf, Thornley positioned *Winifred* behind Nafouba Island, covering the southern entrance to the Rougesi passage, and put lookouts ashore on the island, while *Kavirondo* took up position covering the northern entrance. As night approached, the lookouts on Nafouba reported that the *Muansa*, towing a laden barge, had passed by and was proceeding towards the north, passing the entrance to Speke Gulf. As the *Muansa* approached the northern entrance to the Rougesi passage, the *Kavirondo* attempted to intercept her, but the *Muansa* turned and headed into the shallow waters of the channel, steaming towards the Speke Gulf. As she exited the southern end of the channel heading for Gouta, *Winifred* steamed out of her hiding place behind Nafouba and immediately opening fire gave chase. *Muansa* tried to outrun the British steamer, heading for the inshore shallows along the north coast of the Gulf under heavy fire. As she closed on the shallows close inshore at full speed, her captain misjudged his approach and ran her aground. Still under fire from the *Winifred*, her crew abandoned her. Thornley continued to fire on the grounded German vessel until he was satisfied she was damaged beyond salvage and then withdrew his force north. *Muansa* was recovered by the Germans, but by the time this had been done and the ship made seaworthy, Thornley's lake flotilla had had their armament increased by being fitted with guns recovered from the *Pegasus*. *Muansa*'s guns were removed, and she was relegated to use as a transport.

Shortly afterwards, 1st Lieutenant von Haxthausen, now commanding the 14th Field Company, advanced towards the frontier and on the 9th ran into Hickson's column at Mwaika Hill, a feature with two parallel ridges along the summit. The scouts of the East African Mounted Rifles were leading the column with the KAR Mounted Infantry in close support. They were on the higher of the two ridges when they saw the Germans advancing from the south. Captain JJ Drought, commanding the scouts, ordered his men to dismount and open fire. Immediately on hearing the rifle fire Captain HH Davis (Royal Welsh Fusiliers) rushed his Mounted Infantry Company forward where they took up position on the right flank of the scouts, while the two 4th KAR companies deployed to the left of the firing line. Captain AM Colville's section of 28th Mountain Battery set up their guns on the highest part

Four. The Action at Jasin and Early Operations

of the ridge alongside the Reserve Company, 3rd KAR, and immediately engaged the Germans.

As soon as the British opened fire, von Haxthausen's askaris took cover on the lower, opposite ridge and began returning fire. There following a number of attempts by both sides to drive each other from their positions by frontal assault, during one of these attacks Sergeant Matakia led his section of the Reserve Company forward to support an assault by the Mounted Infantry, advancing his section while under heavy incoming fire and helping cover their withdrawal. (He was subsequently awarded the African Distinguished Conduct Medal.)

Shortly after, Hickson pulled the Mounted Infantry out of the firing line and ordered them to move around the German right and attack them in the rear. On the British left flank, meanwhile, as the Reserve Company, 3rd KAR and the scouts held the line and the artillery provided supporting fire, "E" and "G" Companies, 4th KAR, attacked the German ridge, capturing a knoll on the right of their position only to be driven off by a counterattack by a detachment of the 14th Field Company. By now the Mounted Infantry were behind and attacking the German ridge, while 4th KAR unsuccessfully attempted to retake the knoll. Heavy fighting followed, and Private M Sullivan of the 2nd Loyals, attached to the Mounted Infantry, on his own initiative, carried much needed ammunition forward to the firing line and then carried a wounded askari out of danger while under heavy fire—for which he was awarded the Distinguished Conduct Medal—but the Germans were able to hold the knoll and the ridge despite the onslaught, and one 50-man detachment attacked the Mounted Infantry mule lines only to be driven off by Corporal Ismail Ibrahim and his seven mule-holders, an action for which he would receive the African Distinguished Conduct Medal. As dusk approached, the KAR withdrew to their ridge.

During the night, von Haxthausen, who had been wounded during the fighting for the knoll, quietly withdrew his company south across the Mara River. His casualties during this encounter action were 12 killed, 28 wounded—including himself—and two missing. Hickson's casualties were 13 killed, 13 wounded and a number of askaris missing. The next morning, finding the German ridge empty, Hickson suspected that the Germans were regrouping before resuming their attack on his exposed position, so he withdrew north into British territory. That same day, the 10th three of Commander Thornley's steamers attacked the lake port of Musoma in Mara Bay, destroying several buildings and the guns located there.

In early November 1914 one of the British armed lake steamers, the *Sybil*, while on patrol in German territorial waters, had struck a submerged rock off the Majita Peninsula, halfway between the German ports of Musoma and Mwanza. Because of the damage to her hull, she was beached. However, with increased German activity along the eastern shore of the lake, there grew a fear among the British that the enemy might try to recover the beached steamer. Following Thornley's successful attack on Musoma on the 10th, the decision was taken to destroy her. He sailed south in the *Winifred* and, on March 30, standing off the beach at Majita, opened fire on the stranded ship with his 4-inch and 12-pdr guns, recording 19 direct hits on the stricken steamer before withdrawing. But still fears persisted that the *Sybil* might still be salvageable, so an operation to try and recover her was mounted. The recovery force, under the command of Major RE Berkeley, 2nd Loyals, was assembled at the southern British lake port of Karungu, just north of the frontier. It consisted of "B" Company, 3rd KAR and 150 men drawn from "C" and "D" Companies, 2nd Loyals. The force sailed from Karungu aboard the steamers of the lake flotilla at 6 p.m. on May 11 and arrived off Majita at dawn the following day. Dug-in above the beach was a small force of Germans, 53 strong. The lake steamers immediately opened fire on the trenches, while the infantry landed to the west of the beach and then began advancing towards the Germans, who withdrew to the south where they attempted to take up positions on some small kopjes. Supported by the naval guns, the Loyals and KAR drove them from the kopjes, and they withdrew to the west to a nearby mission station where they could observe the British. The Loyals and KAR then established a defensive perimeter around the beach, while the naval salvage team began work on the *Sybil*. The repair work took three days, the salvage team and infantry drenched by constant heavy rain and plagued by myriads of mosquitoes, but it was finally completed on the night of the 13th/14th. That night those ashore were hit by a tremendous rainstorm, worse than any they had suffered under so far, and the beached steamer filled with water. It took a further two days to empty the hull, but finally on May 16 she was refloated. The Loyals, KAR and salvage team were taken off the beach and the flotilla; with *Sybil* under tow, they made for Irugwa Island, where they remained for two nights while further repairs were made before she was towed into Karungu. Here she underwent a complete refit before returning to duty as part of Thornley's lake flotilla. The entire 150-man detachment of 2nd Loyals had very soon after come down with malaria, and all were hospitalized as unfit for duty. A period of calm now descended on the eastern and southeastern area of Lake Victoria Nyanza and the Mara Triangle.

On Lake Nyasa the British had also armed their lake steamers, and one of these, the *Gwendolen*, attacked the only German vessel of any size

Four. The Action at Jasin and Early Operations

in the port of Sphinxhaven on the eastern shore of the lake, badly damaging her. A second raid was organized against Sphinxhaven on May 30, 1915. The lake flotilla, under the command of Lieutenant-Commander GH Dennistoun, RN, landed a detachment of 1st KAR under Captain HG Collins, RA, and then bombarded the town before the KAR attacked and cleared it of its defenders, capturing large quantities of arms, ammunition and stores. The flotilla then shelled the damaged German steamer, completely destroying her before the KAR were re-embarked and the expedition returned to British territory.

During April there was another change in command when, on April 5, Major-General Wapshare was ordered to the Persian Gulf to take up duties with the British Forces in Mesopotamia. Brigadier-General Tighe was promoted to Major-General and commander of all British and Colonial Forces in the East African theater.

Five

The Destruction of the *Königsberg*

IN JANUARY 1915, Pieter Pretorius paddled up the Rufiji Delta in a canoe to establish the precise position of the *Königsberg*. Eventually moving to land, he and his party of locally recruited native trackers discovered a path cut through the undergrowth. Moving along this track they saw parties of natives, closely guarded by German sailors, carrying supplies. Pretorius was able to capture two of the native porters, who needed little inducement to lead him to within 300 yards (274 meters) of the German cruiser, where he charted its position before returning to his base camp.

Admiral King-Hall ordered a second reconnaissance, this time to locate and chart the Germans' river defenses. Pretorius disguised himself as an Arab trader to undertake the mission, which he successfully completed without being detected. He and his native trackers also sounded all navigable channels in the delta, using a long pole so as not to arouse the suspicion of the *Königsberg's* shore parties. Pretorius's exact reconnaissance showed that the British monitors, en route to East Africa, would be able to move far enough up the delta to get within sight of the *Königsberg*.[1]

Meanwhile, on February 21, two Sopwith 807 100-hp floatplanes, with their crews of 20 officers and ratings of No. 4 Squadron, Royal Naval Air Service, under the command of Flight-Lieutenant JT Cull, RNAS, had arrived at Niororo. Cull was ordered to bomb the *Königsberg*, but the Sopwith's air-cooled engine could not reach full power in the tropical climate. Shortly afterwards the airframes and propellers became warped by the damp, humid heat. They were write-offs. In April three Short Folder seaplanes arrived in theater, and on the 25th John Cull, now a Flight-Commander, with Air-Mechanic Boggis as his observer, took off for yet another aerial reconnaissance of the delta. The idea of bombing the *Königsberg* had, meanwhile, been shelved as being impracticable.

Five. The Destruction of the Königsberg

Earlier in April, King-Hall was informed by the French in Madagascar that an attempt to resupply *Königsberg* was being made by a blockade runner from Germany. The blockade runner was the 1,600-ton British merchant steamer *Rubens*—which had been interned in Hamburg on the outbreak of the war—she had been renamed *Kronberg* for the mission and was sailing under Danish colors with Danish papers, giving her home port as Copenhagen. *Kronberg* sailed from Wilhelmshaven on February 18, 1915, carrying 1,600 tons of coal for the *Königsberg*, two 60-mm guns and ammunition, 6,500 rounds of mixed artillery ammunition, 1,000 rounds of 105-mm ammunition, 1,000 rounds of 4.1-inch ammunition, six machine guns, 1,800 Model 98 rifles, 4,500,000 rounds of small arms ammunition, medical supplies, stores, clothing, machine tools, canned and fresh food, oxyacetylene equipment and telephone and telegraph equipment.

She had used *Königsberg*'s call sign as she passed up the Mozambique Channel. Unable to weaken his forces covering the delta, which could allow *Königsberg* the opportunity to escape, King-Hall decided to use a single cruiser to intercept her; he moved his flag to *Hyacinth* and steamed to intercept the blockade runner, catching her off Tanga on the 14th. *Hyacinth* fired across her bows, and the *Kronberg* turned, making a run at full speed for Manza Bay with the British cruiser in hot pursuit. The second salvo from *Hyacinth* struck her bows, the shells penetrating her hull and starting a fire in her coal bunker. *Hyacinth*'s captain ordered the cruiser's speed increased. As she increased revolutions, a pin holding a connecting rod to a piston in her starboard engine collapsed. With her starboard engine useless, *Hyacinth* could only watch the blockade runner pull away, despite the thick smoke billowing above her.

Kronberg steamed into Manza Bay where she was run aground. Her captain, Reserve Lieutenant Carl Christiansen, ordered the ship's bottom ventilators and seacocks opened, flooding the engine room to stop the fire in her coal bunker from reaching the munitions stores. He then had fires set along her upper deck to make the *Kronberg* appear a total burning wreck before ordering his crew to abandon ship. Once *Hyacinth* had struggled into the bay at half speed, she sent a boarding party to investigate the apparent wreck. They seized papers and charts from the *Kronberg* and informed King-Hall on their return that she was indeed totally destroyed and beyond salvage.

Before departing, *Hyacinth* opened fire on the blockade runner at close range, ripping open her sides and settling her deeper in the water. *Hyacinth* then put to sea where repairs to her damaged engine were made before she rejoined the squadron off the Rufiji. But over the following weeks the Germans were able to salvage most of the *Kronberg*'s cargo. They impressed hundreds of local natives and recovered nearly all the coal consignment, all 1,800 rifles, four machine guns, all 4,500,000 rounds of small arms ammunition, which though water damaged was broken up and remade, two 60-mm guns, a ton of explosives, 7,500 rounds of mixed artillery ammunition, 200 tents and telephone and telegraph equipment.

With the threat of further attempts being made by blockade runners to reach the *Königsberg*, the British Admiralty ordered more ships to East Africa. *Chatham*, having completed her refit in Bombay, returned to the Cape Squadron followed by the cruisers HMS *Cornwall* and HMAS *Pioneer*, the latter coming from Fremantle, Western Australia. *Chatham* and *Cornwall* had not long been on station, however, when they, along with the battleship *Goliath*, were ordered to sail immediately for the Dardanelles. Just over a month later, early in the morning of May 13 while on station at the entrance of the Dardanelles narrows, HMS *Goliath* was attacked by the Turkish Torpedo Boat *Muavenet-i-Milliye*. She sank within four minutes with the loss of 570 men of her ship's company of 750.

The two monitors HMS *Mersey*, Commander RA Wilson, RN, and *Severn*, Captain EJA Fullerton, RN, arrived off Mafia Island on June 3. And on the 18th the auxiliary cruiser *Laurentic* delivered a cargo of new aircraft to the recently constructed airfield at Chole Bay on Mafia Island. These new aircraft were all land-based planes specially constructed for tropical conditions. There were two Henri Farman HF 27s and two Caudron GIII biplanes. The airfield and No. 4 Squadron, RNAS, were now under the command of Squadron-Commander Robert Gordon, RNAS, who, along with the rest of the squadron members, had accompanied the aircraft to East Africa.

By early June, all was ready for an attack on the *Königsberg*. King-Hall had received the light cruiser *Pyramus* as a replacement for the two cruisers sent to the Dardanelles earlier and had the promise of another, HMS *Challenger*, which was to arrive on station from West Africa at the beginning of July. King-Hall dispatched the *Laurentic* to Dar es Salaam, where, in conjunction with a contingent of Indian troops, she would undertake a diversionary attack on the capital.

This diversion began on July 5, and at 5:20 a.m. the next morning the *Severn* and *Mersey* moved up the Kikunja channel of the Rufiji using the charts prepared by Pretorius. As they made their way upriver, they came under heavy fire from the German shore defenses, returning fire with their 3-pdr guns and machine guns as they passed. As the monitors closed on the *Königsberg*, an aircraft from Mafia Island undertook a bombing sortie, while the cruisers *Pyramus* and *Weymouth* engaged

Five. The Destruction of the Königsberg

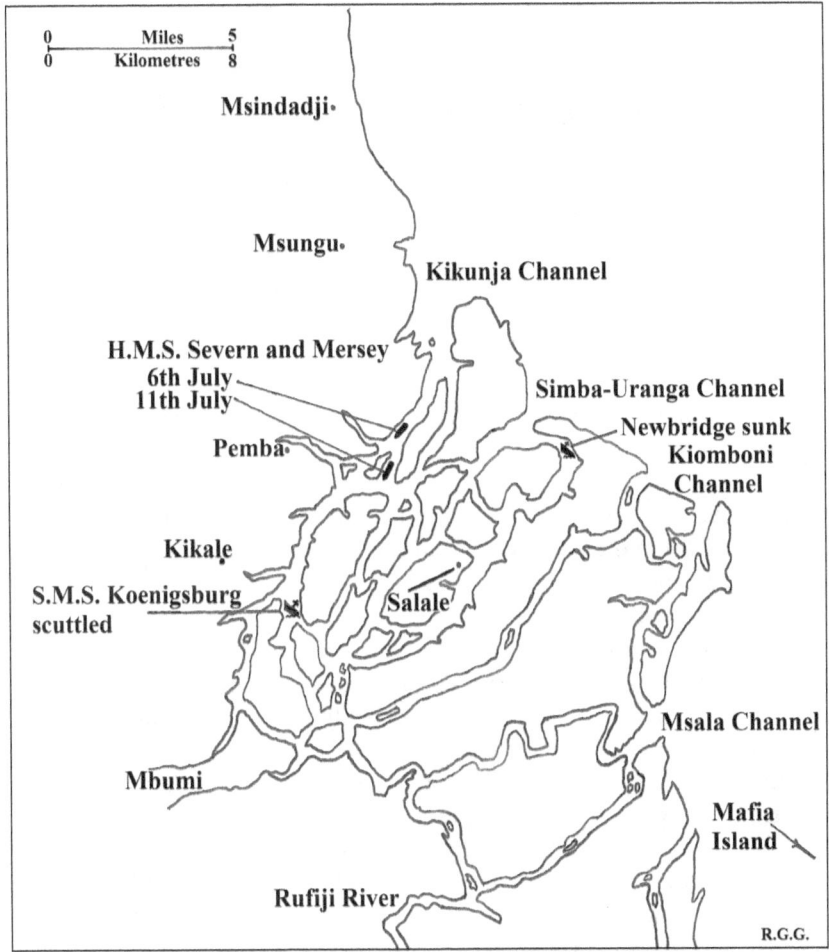

Rufiji Delta (map by the author).

enemy emplacements at the mouth of the Kikunja channel, and *Pioneer* and *Hyacinth* attacked those at the mouth of the Ssimba Uranga channel.

At 6:30 a.m., the monitors anchored downstream of Gengini Island, 11,000 yards (10,058 meters) from *Königsberg*. *Severn* began firing with her two 6-inch guns at 6:48 a.m., her fall of shot closely observed by one of the naval aircraft from Mafia Island. At 7:40 a.m., *Königsberg*, having returned fire immediately, scored a direct hit on the *Mersey*, knocking out her forward 6-inch battery, and shortly after holing her near the water line, forcing her to switch position a further 1,000 yards (914 meters) from the German. *Severn* was faring much better, scoring five hits on the *Königsberg* before she too was forced to withdraw. Throughout the engagement, naval aircraft acted as artillery spotters for the monitors, and at 3:45 p.m., after just over nine hours' action, the monitors retired. They had fired 635 rounds between them, achieving only six confirmed hits.

Five days later, just before noon on the 11th, both *Severn* and *Mersey* again entered the delta, running the gauntlet of fire from the German shore defenses, the *Mersey* sustaining a number of casualties before reaching her designated position. *Mersey's* task was to draw *Königsberg's* fire, allowing *Severn* to close to within 10,000 yards (9,144 meters) before opening fire. Once again, the naval aircraft were aloft to direct their guns.

Königsberg fired for a short time at the *Mersey* before Looff, realizing that she was a decoy, switched her guns on to the *Severn* and quickly bracketed her. At 12:30 p.m., *Severn* opened fire. She found the German's range with the assistance of one of the spotter planes piloted by Flight-Commander Cull and inflicted severe damage on the enemy cruiser. The spotter plane reported eight out of 12 hits on the German before she was shot down.

Just before 1 p.m., *Königsberg* was hit amidships, and shortly after it was noticed that only one of her guns was returning fire. For the next hour *Severn* fired a salvo every 90 seconds. Then, at about 1:30 p.m., seven enormous explosions came from the *Königsberg*, and she listed to starboard, settling in the mud; Commander Looff had ordered the ship's scuttling charges fired. The second spotter plane reported the *Königsberg* ablaze along her entire length, but the monitors continued to fire until 2 p.m. when King-Hall ordered them to break off action and retire. That evening a party of German ratings returned to the wreck, lowered her battle flag and threw the breechblocks of her guns into the river. *Königsberg's* surviving ship's company all volunteered to join the *Schutztruppe*. A hundred and twenty of them were formed into the *Königsberg* Company under the command of the cruiser's First Lieutenant, Lieutenant-Commander Georg Kock, and supplemented by 15 Askaris and 450 porters were marched off to join von Lettow-Vorbeck. "The loss of the Konigsberg, though sad in itself, had at least this advantage for the campaign on land, that the whole crew and the valuable stores were now at the disposal of the Protective Force."[2]

A month after the destruction of the *Königsberg* a salvage party under Reserve Commander Schönfeld recovered the ten breechblocks from the cruiser's 105-mm guns from the river. They then removed these guns, along with a number of smaller pieces and the ship's machine guns left aboard when she was scuttled. These 105-mm guns were mounted on wooden, wheeled gun carriages and became the most powerful artillery in East Africa.

Not long after the destruction of the *Königsberg*, Commander Looff learned that he had been promoted to Captain and had been awarded the Iron Crosses 1st and 2nd Class. His entire ship's company were also awarded the Iron Cross 2nd Class, including his 32 dead. This promotion meant that Looff was now senior to the *Schutztruppe* commander, and the Governor—who was still at loggerheads with von Lettow-Vorbeck—began making overtures to the home government, with Looff's complicity, to have him replace von Lettow-Vorbeck. This intolerable situation, which saw Governor Schnee constantly try to hinder von Lettow-Vorbeck's defense of the colony by blatantly interfering in operational matters that he had no experience or knowledge of, and his efforts to maintain overall control of the *Schutztruppe*, came to a head in December 1915. The exasperated von Lettow-Vorbeck, having previously threatened to write directly to the Kaiser regarding the situation in East Africa, now sent an unprecedented appeal to Berlin; he wrote,

"Most respectfully I report to your Royal and Imperial Highness as follows. On the 4th August 1914 the Governor issued the order not to offer any resistance in the town and port of Dar es Salaam, and on the 8th of August to surrender the town to the enemy without a fight. The execution of this order was out of the question because a landing of enemy forces did not take place. On the 15th August 1914 the Governor also ordered that in the event of the enemy occupying other coastal towns no military resistance was to be offered. When I objected in accordance with para 2c of the Protection Force regulations, on the grounds that

Heinrich Schnee, Governor of German East Africa.

this would constitute a transgression of paras, 58, 62 and 63 of the Military Penal Code, the Governor refuted me. It was therefore necessary to conduct warfare in the Tanga area between the 2nd and 5th November 1914 against the Governor's explicit order. Subsequently the Governor changed his views with regard to coast towns, giving permission of 26th of November 1914 to offer resistance in Dar es Salaam, and on 10th February 1915 also to offer resistance in the other coastal towns. My repeatedly expressed objections to the Governor's interference with the conduct of the war have been ignored. Therefore efficient warfare cannot be carried on, particularly as the Protection Force regulations are based of different premises and do not take into account the action against an exterior enemy. Because of the risk of this report falling into enemy hands I cannot mention any details. Signed, Lettow-Vorbeck."[3]

Governor Schnee, learning of von Lettow-Vorbecks letter, also wrote to the Kaiser to defend his actions. He wrote that in his opinion, and the opinion of other officials, the action at Tanga, though a spectacular success, was a foolhardy risk, which had it failed would have been disastrous for the colony. He claimed, "because of the risk of a native uprising, I have forbidden the Commander to denude of troops those areas of the colony, politically and economically important, inhabited by strong groups of unreliable natives. If in addition to the war we also had an uprising of the natives on our hands, our position would become untenable. Excellent soldier though he is, the Commander does not have a balanced judgement as regards the natives. Despite the serious uprisings of the past (which proved exceedingly difficult to put down using the whole of the Protection Force) the Commander seems to leave this danger out of his considerations altogether. His successful defence of the Colony proves that the misgivings of the Commander with regard to my instructions lack justification. I shall also in future leave the Commander—to whom I am linked with by the common goal of holding on to the Colony—a free hand in the conduct of the war, so long as political factors or native problems do not compel me to take appropriate measures.

"I should also like to point out most respectfully that my views regarding the present situation are fully shared by the Senior officer of the East Africa Corps, Naval Captain Looff (commander of the *Königsberg*.) Signed Schnee."[4]

Both letters reached Berlin at the end of August 1916 and were immediately answered by the Military Department of the Colonial Ministry, supporting von Lettow-Vorbeck and admonishing the Governor: "The Governor should not have issued orders which hampered the conduct of the war. The attachment to completely outdated defence plans

Five. The Destruction of the Königsberg

shows in the clearest possible way the misjudgement of the situation by the Governor, who lacks the background of military training. The correctness of Colonel von Lettow's views has been confirmed by the success at Tanga and the cancellation of the Governor's instructions, which he recognised as inopportune. We may say that the playing off of a naval captain against the Commander of the Protection Force appears highly inappropriate."[5]

Six

The Bukoba Raid and the Action at Saisi

THROUGHOUT THIS PERIOD British Forces in the colony were still being kept under strict restraint by the War Office. A consequence of this inaction was a high sickness rate from blackwater fever, yellow fever and malaria, which sapped morale. But the decision had been taken in London to reinforce East Africa from other theaters of operations. The first to arrive in East Africa were the 25th (Service) Battalion, Royal Fusiliers (Frontiersmen), commanded by Lieutenant-Colonel DP Driscoll, DSO, and the 2nd Rhodesia Regiment, commanded by Lieutenant-Colonel AE Capell.

Unfortunately, the British hadn't yet grasped the fact that their best sources of manpower for the conditions prevailing in East Africa were the Africans themselves, and it would be another year before steps would be taken to increase the size and numbers of the King's African Rifles. The morale of the *Schutztruppe*, on the other hand, was extremely high. And during April, von Lettow-Vorbeck prepared plans for a second incursion into Northern Rhodesia. He dispatched the 18th and 23rd Field Companies to Bismarckburg (now Kasanga) from Dar es Salaam to reinforce the 22nd and 29th, under the temporary command of the recently promoted Major von Langenn-Steinkeller, until Major-General Wahle could arrive to take up overall command in the Bismarckburg area. Von Langenn-Steinkeller, however, was ordered to march to Neu Langenburg (now Tukuvu) with his experienced companies to meet a suspected British attack—which did not materialize—leaving behind the newly raised 29th. Wahle reached Bismarckburg on June 17, bringing with him the 24th Field and 10th Rifle Companies, and immediately prepared to march into Northern Rhodesia with his depleted force.

Major-General Tighe, meanwhile, had realized that the inactivity and defensive mentality that was developing in his troops was detrimental and a threat to their conduct in any future operations. So, having

Six. The Bukoba Raid and the Action at Saisi

received the first of his reinforcements, he decided that they must be used in an offensive capacity in the immediate future if he was to restore their morale and self-respect and regain their fighting edge. Having gained permission from the War Office, he ordered Brigadier-General Stewart to undertake a raid against the German port of Bukoba, a well-fortified garrison town situated in a small marshy plain surrounded by hills and high kopjes on the western shore of Lake Victoria Nyanza. The fort and garrison protected the trade in coffee, bananas and hides and had a high-powered wireless transmitter. The destruction of Bukoba and its wireless station, it was thought, would isolate the northwest part of the colony and disrupt the movement of these goods.

Major-General Kurt Wahle.

The raiding force, comprising the 2nd Loyal North Lancs, the newly arrived 25th Royal Fusiliers, 3rd KAR, 29th Punjabis and a detachment of the East African Regiment, supported by a section of the 28th Mountain Battery, was assembled at Kisumu on the British side of the lake. They embarked on the steamers of Commander Thornley's lake flotilla on June 21 and sailed that same evening.

Early the next morning the 25th Fusiliers—the spearhead of the attack—were put ashore at Kiaya Bay, which had been selected as the main landing place. Meeting no opposition, they advanced towards Bukoba, taking Rwonga Hill then Karwazi Hill, three miles (five kilometers) to the north of the town after driving off a 30-strong German picket. "It was breaking daylight when we began filing up the steep mountain-side, which was cliff-like in places, and the climb to the top proved a stiff one, of close on a mile in distance, and very breathless were we when the summit was reached, while we judged it our great good fortune that this awkward ground had been covered unopposed by enemy."[1] Shortly after, 2nd Loyals, 29th Punjabis and the two guns of 28th Mountain Battery began landing and were all ashore by 10:30 a.m. and advancing on Bukoba, while 3rd KAR, which had landed nearer the town, was closing on Gun Spur about 3,000 yards (2,750 meters) to the north of the settlement, where they linked up with the 29th Punjabis. "Advancing across the summit, south toward Bukoba, some resistance was encountered there in the banana plantations and forest, but the real fighting did not begin until we reached the southern slopes and looked out on the town of Bukoba, some two miles distant, situated on low land that swept back from the shores of the lake to the foot of the hills, and over the intervening bouldered, rocky hill country, and on to the commanding heights, above the town, on the west and south. It was then that serious fighting began, and all day—while the ships shelled from the lake—we fought in attack against the enemy, who, to begin with, held out amongst the rocks and clumps of trees in the broken hills before us, and who, latterly, defended the commanding hills northwest of the town. It was real guerrilla warfare. From rock to rock one could see men dodge, while puffs of smoke puffed in and out from behind scores of rocks, and from many a tree-clump bottom. The enemy were here using the old ·450 rifle and black powder and lead bullets, hence the prominence of the smoke-puffs. On the whole front all was visible, even the enemy's single piece of artillery, which was plainly seen in position by the river-side in the low flat ground north of the town, and which the Mountain Battery guns in a short time knocked out of action, before turning their attention to the enemy machine guns, which were not so easy to deal with."[2]

As they began their final approach, the Loyals advance became slower and slower until it was almost at a stand. General Stewart was informed by Captain Meinertzhagen—who was attached to the force as Major-General Tighe's representative—that the battalion was being held back by its commander, Lieutenant-Colonel CEA Jourdain, who was worried about taking casualties. Stewart ordered Jourdain to either resume his advance or hand over command of his battalion to Meinertzhagen. Jerked out of his overcautious apathy by the threat of being relieved, Jourdain advanced with more vigor. "In the afternoon we worked down the last of the hill-slopes under constant fire of our foes, and, toward evening, gathering our tired limbs under us, a charge was ordered. Across an open meadow we doubled, cheering lustily; through swamp and river, almost neck-high in water, and, finally, up the hill-side opposite, and on to the lower hill-top of the enemy's coveted position commanding the town; there to lie, panting breathlessly, picking off the fleeing enemy that we could see dodging among the rocks in endeavour to reach the higher hill, across a ravine and to the west of us.

Six. The Bukoba Raid and the Action at Saisi

"Meantime the Loyal North Lancashires, who had made a wide flank movement, were advancing in on the higher hill from the west; and ere darkness set in we were in full possession of the chief positions."[3] By nightfall Bukoba was surrounded—the 25th Fusiliers were to the north, 2nd Loyals, having skirted the town, to the northwest, while 3rd KAR were in reserve—and the British went firm for the night.

At dawn the next morning (the 23rd) the advance was resumed: "At daylight a fighting line was formed across the flats, from the hills to the lake; and an advance began toward the town in face of steady rifle and machine gun fire. The river we had crossed yesterday had swung southward and ran parallel with the lake, and here again proved an obstacle, and many of us got thoroughly wet crossing and re-crossing it. Also, in the morning, in the heat of the early fighting, a thunderstorm burst and heavy rains fell, while we lay in the grass drenched to the skin for an hour or two, and rifle locks choked with sand and moisture. For a time firing ceased on both sides; to resume again as it cleared. Bit by bit, we pushed on across the flat, to be held up for a time before the entrance to the town; and then, breaking the opposition down, to enter the town without further resistance on the heels of the fleeing foe."[4]

By the middle of the afternoon, the 25th Fusiliers had entered Bukoba and taken the fort, where Lieutenant WT Dartnell (an Australian serving in the 25th Fusiliers) hauled down the German flag from the fort and raised the Union flag. Captain Willibald von Steumer, the garrison commander, had pulled out, having lost 15 men killed and a large number wounded, returning to Bukoba the evening after the British left. During the raid, British losses were seven killed, 25 wounded; they captured 67 rifles and 32,000 rounds of small arms ammunition. Before the force withdrew back across the lake, the Faridkot Sappers and Miners dismantled the wireless mast and destroyed it and all the wireless equipment, while all houses that had been used to store ammunition were burned, and everything of military value that could not be taken away was destroyed. The results of the raid, "though not far reaching, the success of this well-planned operation, gained at slight cost in casualties, did much to restore and revive the morale of the British forces."[5]

During late June, Wahle, with a column consisting of the 24th and 29th Field Companies, a hundred Ruga-Ruga irregulars and a 12-pdr gun began a second major incursion into Northern Rhodesia. On the 28th this column surrounded the Mount Saisi post in the early morning mist and opened fire with their artillery, while the infantry half-heartedly probed the garrison's outer defenses. The skirmishing and probing of the defenses carried on throughout the day, and as dusk approached,

Wahle withdrew, having lost seven killed and 24 wounded. The Anglo/Belgian garrison's losses were four killed and six wounded.

Major JJ O'Sullevan led a mixed mobile column of 20 British and Belgian Officers and 450 askaris of his own regiment, the Northern Rhodesia Police, and the *1e Bataillon de Marche* with two machine guns and two field guns (a 7-pdr and 4-pdr), in pursuit. O'Sullevan followed the *Schutztruppe* across the border and into German territory, but Wahle evaded him. He did, however, recover 5,000 rounds of small arms ammunition that the Germans had buried, before returning to Mount Saisi.

As he had overall command of Anglo/Belgian forces in Northern Rhodesia, and as he could not exercise that command at Mount Saisi, Colonel Hodson handed over command of the garrison to O'Sullevan on his return. He then departed for Fife with an escort of an officer and 40 men of the Northern Rhodesia Police. O'Sullevan, suspecting that the Germans would soon return, immediately began strengthening his defenses, which now included an outer abattis of thorn trees.

General Wahle was indeed planning a second attack on Mount Saisi, and this time he intended to use his entire force, the 24th and 29th Field Companies, 10th Rifle Company, an Arab Company, two 12-pdr field guns, ten machine guns, and 100 Ruga-Ruga. Wahle's attack began in the early hours of July 25, when the *Schutztruppe* tried to carry O'Sullevan's position by a frontal assault but were driven off. They then surrounded the position, dug trenches and laid siege to the camp, content to bombard the post for the next 48 hours. For the next four days and nights the fighting raged incessantly, and it wasn't long before all the livestock held by the defenders had been cut down by bursting shrapnel, machine-gun and small arms fire. Water was also of critical importance as the garrison normally drew what it needed from the river, but with that source cut off, small groups had to sneak down to the river at night carrying as many water bottles as they could to fill.

Meanwhile, Colonel Hodson, on losing telegraph communication with the post on the 25th, ordered Major de Konick, with 270 officers and askaris of the *1e Bataillon de Marche*—with 50 Northern Rhodesia Police under the command of Captain CH Fair, attached—to the relief of Saisi. The relief column made contact with the *Schutztruppe* to the north of Mount Saisi on the 28th, and this first contact quickly turned into a savage firefight, requiring Wahle to reinforce his troops engaging the Belgians. The following day a detachment of the relief column was able to fight its way through the besieging Germans to reinforce O'Sullevan, while the bulk of de Konick's force continued in its attempts to break through the besiegers to the north of the post.

Six. The Bukoba Raid and the Action at Saisi

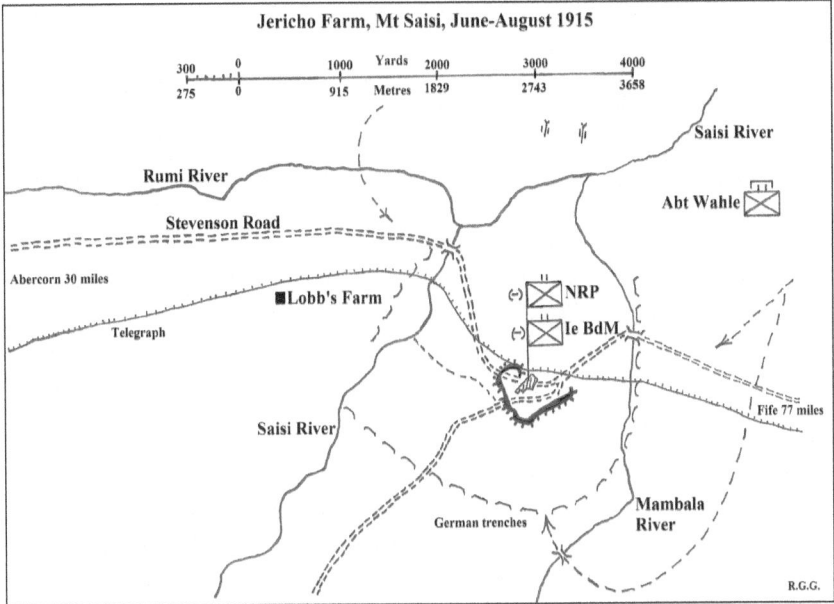

The Defense of Saisi (based on a sketch map by HMSO/Historical Branch 1918).

On the 31st O'Sullevan was called on to surrender, Wahle telling him that the relief force sent to lift the siege had been defeated by his troops. O'Sullevan's reply was that he would not surrender under any circumstances; the Germans must take the position or die in the attempt. That evening the Germans attacked the defenses in force and, like their previous attempts, were beaten back with heavy losses. Then, on August 3, with their supplies all but exhausted, the German column broke contact and withdrew across the frontier. Shortly afterward the camp was relieved by de Konick's Belgian column. Major John O'Sullevan was subsequently awarded the Distinguished Service Order for his defense of Mount Saisi.

Despite the success at Bukoba, General Tighe was deeply concerned about the extremely high sickness rate among his troops and the constant rumors that the Germans were receiving shipments of arms and ammunition. So concerned was he that he informed the chief of the Imperial General Staff that he considered the military situation in East Africa to be critical. On November 25, a subcommittee of the Committee of Imperial Defence made the following recommendations:

1. Steps should be taken to ensure the conquest of German East Africa with as little delay as possible.

    2. That, accepting the general figure of 10,000 already suggested by the CIGS for the reinforcements necessary, a new Army Brigade should be sent to East Africa to make up two complete brigades which, with others already arranged for, would bring the total to 12,600.
    3. That an adequate staff for the large numbers involved should be furnished from England.

The subcommittee also recommended that as the South African government had already, in August, offered to send troops to East Africa, and "since the transport of troops must take time and the rains in the area affected would begin about April, it was desirable to move the Union Government to proffer further assistance to make sure of success during the few weeks available."[6] Consequently, as the campaign in South West Africa had been successfully concluded in early July, the War Cabinet asked the South Africans to provide sufficient troops to bring the East African campaign to an early and successful conclusion. The Union government agreed to this request, and before the year was out, an Infantry Brigade had been formed from volunteers, and by March 1916 there were 20,000 South African troops in or on their way to British East Africa.

Brigadier-General Louis Jakobus (Dirk) van Deventer and Colonel Hughes of the Union Defence Force arrived with the first South African contingent. They were to evaluate the situation in East Africa and to work out a plan for the close cooperation of the British and South African forces. The colonial administration had, meanwhile, introduced compulsory military service throughout British East Africa, primarily to ensure there were sufficient porters to support the fighting troops.

Command of the East African theater was offered to General Jan Smuts. He, however, declined because of his numerous political commitments in South Africa. So Lieutenant-General Sir Horace Smith-Dorrien was appointed in November 1915, while Brigadier-General Edward Northey was made commander of the then assembling Nyasaland-Rhodesia Field Force in Northern Rhodesia.

Northey arrived in Cape Town on December 30, 1915. He traveled directly to Northern Rhodesia to take up his appointment and prepare his command for operations; at the same time, Major-General Tombeur, the Vice-Governor of Katanga, was appointed to the command of all Belgian forces in the Eastern Congo as Military Governor, with instructions to advance into German territory as quickly as possible. Before leaving Katanga, Tombeur sent instructions to Major Olsen in Northern Rhodesia to march his battalions north, but Olsen, wanting clarification of this

Six. The Bukoba Raid and the Action at Saisi

order, was unable to contact Tombeur, who had left on the four-month journey from Katanga to Kivu, so remained where he was to assist the British. While en route to the Cape, Smith-Dorrien was struck down with pneumonia and was so gravely ill when he arrived there that he was forced to resign his new command before he had taken it up.

Once again command was offered to Smuts. This time, aware of the dire consequences of Smith-Dorrien's illness to the successful conclusion of the East African campaign, he agreed to take it. On February 9, 1916, he was appointed a Temporary Lieutenant-General in the British Army and Supreme Commander of British and Colonial Forces in East Africa. The choice of Smuts to command in East Africa was extremely unusual. He was a lawyer, not a professional soldier, and he had only commanded Boer citizen-soldiers like himself in the then Cape Colony during the Boer War of 1899–1902. Though having made a study of military history and held the post of Minister of Defence in South Africa, he had no experience of the logistics of modern warfare or the problems of maintaining and supplying a field army in hostile territory. His whole experience rested on leading small, self-contained, highly mobile commandos through known territories against large forces reliant on lines of communication. These omissions in his military experience would soon become glaringly apparent in East Africa.

Brigadier-General Edward Northey (Her Majesty's Stationery Office).

Seven

The Naval Africa Expedition

BETWEEN OCTOBER 1915 AND January 1916, while these changes and reinforcements were taking place, a Royal Navy detachment destroyed German control on Lake Tanganyika. In April 1915 the First Sea Lord, Admiral Sir Henry Jackson, was approached by Mr. John. R Lee with a daring plan to break the enemy dominance of the lake. Lee, a big game hunter who knew the region extremely well, suggested the employment of a naval detachment with a small, well-armed motorboat which could be transported overland from Cape Town to Lake Tanganyika, where it would destroy all German naval forces. Sir Henry agreed to Lee's audacious plan, which was designated the Naval Africa Expedition.

Admiral Sir David Gamble was given the task of planning the expedition, and he decided to employ two, not one, motorboat. Lee was commissioned as a Lieutenant-Commander, RNVR, and made second-in-command of the expedition, as Gamble decided it must be led by a regular naval officer. He then left for South Africa ahead of the main party, accompanied by Sub-Lieutenant Douglas Hope, RN, to make the necessary arrangements for the transportation of the two motorboats to Lake Tanganyika. Admiral Gamble selected Lieutenant-Commander Geoffrey Spicer-Simson, RN, to command the Naval Africa Expedition—an unlikely candidate for command, as he had been court-martialed for losing his ship, HMS *Niger*, which was torpedoed and sunk in Ramsgate early in the war while he was ashore entertaining. Following the loss of the *Niger*, he had been relegated to a safe job in the Admiralty processing the transfer of merchant seamen into the Royal Navy. His selection to lead the Naval Africa Expedition was primarily due to the fact that there were no suitable officers available at the time and that he had commanded a survey ship on the Gambia River earlier in his career. A team was chosen from volunteers and suitable craft located for the operation. The boats chosen for the expedition were two Thornycroft motorboats built for the Greek Military and commandeered by the Royal Navy from Messrs Thornycroft's Twickenham Yard. These boats measured 40 feet

Seven. The Naval Africa Expedition

British light cruiser HMS *Fox* (Her Majesty's Stationery Office).

(12 meters) in length with a beam of eight feet (2.5 meters) and were powered by two 100-hp petrol engines, which gave them a speed of 19 knots. They were equipped with a 3-pdr bow gun and a machine-gun aft. They were named and commissioned as *Mimi* and *Toutou* by the eccentric Spicer-Simson.

The expedition of four officers and 24 ratings sailed from Tilbury in the SS *Llanstephen Castle*, reaching Cape Town on July 2—shortly after their arrival, Spicer-Simson, with the collusion of Sub-Lieutenant Hope, engineered the dismissal of Lee, and Hope was appointed as 2i/c in his stead. From Cape Town the expedition and their boats were transported to Fungurume in the Belgian Congo by rail, arriving on August 5. Steam traction engines assigned to the expedition reached Fungurume on the 15th and, after an arduous six weeks, had towed the boats to the railhead at Sankisia. From here they were again loaded on a train and carried to Bukama, where the boats were launched into the Lualaba River. From Bukama they were towed upriver to Kabalo, where they were again loaded onto trains and carried to Lukuga on Lake Tanganyika, arriving here on October 28, and much to the embarrassment of his officers and men and the amusement of the Belgians, Spicer-Simson began wearing a khaki kilt.

Towards the end of November 1915, Lieutenant-Commander Zimmer learned that the Belgians were near to completing a replacement for the steamer *Alexandre del Commune*, which had been destroyed in October of the previous year. This new vessel, the *Baron Dhanis* of 1,500 tons, was nearing completion it was reported. Zimmer sent the *Hedwig von Wissmann* and *Kingani* from Kigoma on a reconnaissance of the Congo side of the lake to try and locate where this new ship was being built. It was soon established that the most suitable location was near the mouth of the Lukuga River close by Albertville. But when the *Hedwig von Wissmann* and *Kingani* arrived off the river mouth, they could see no sign of a shipyard and returned to Kigoma. Then a wireless transmission in clear from Albertville by the Belgians, giving what was thought to be a progress report on the steamer's construction, was intercepted by the wireless station at Bukoba and passed on to Zimmer.

Zimmer sent the *Hedwig von Wissmann* across the lake to find the shipyard and report on the progress of the steamer's construction; she was to stand off the river mouth while Sub-Lieutenant Odebrecht went ashore to reconnoiter. On arriving near the Lukuga in the dead of night, Odebrecht was taken by rowing boat with muffled oars and landed just south of the river. He made his way to the river mouth and discovered a small shipyard, but there was nothing on the slips. The *Baron Dhanis* had either not been started, or she had been completed and moved. Over the following nights Odebrecht and Lieutenant Rosenthal—*Hedwig von Wissmann*'s captain—slipped ashore to keep the shipyard under observation, sometimes together but more often than not alone.

Then in the early hours of December 1, Rosenthal took the *Hedwig von Wissmann* to within 220 yards (201 meters) of the mouth of the Lukuga to try and take a photo of the shipyard. Because of the extremely poor light of the approaching dawn, he had to take a time exposure, and as a result the *Hedwig von Wissmann* was soon spotted by the Belgians, who immediately opened fire on the steamer until she pulled away. The following night Rosenthal again snuck ashore but was forced to abort his mission due to the heightened alertness of the Belgian sentries. He returned on the night of December 2 and 3. He was able to slip through the sentries unseen and found, to his surprise, two powerful motorboats—*Mimi* and *Toutou*—which had been here undetected since late October. Eager to return to Kigoma with this intelligence, he quickly made his way back to the rendezvous with his pickup boat, but as dawn approached, he was unable to find her. She had returned to the *Hedwig von Wissmann* when Rosenthal had failed to appear, and the *Hedwig von Wissmann* was steaming back across the lake—he had been given up for lost. Rosenthal made his way two miles (three kilometers) to the south, where he planned to lay up for the day in the hope that the *Hedwig von*

HMS *Toutou* (Her Majesty's Stationery Office, 1918).

Wissmann might return that night, but his luck had run out, and he was captured by a Belgian patrol.

Nearly two months later, on Sunday, December 26, 1915, the German steamer *Kingani* was sighted seven miles (11 kilometers) off Lukuga. She was undertaking a routine patrol and was observed heading south towards Tamboua Bay where such patrols regularly began before they steamed north along the Congo shore. *Kingani's* captain, Lieutenant Schönfeld, unaware of the presence of the two British motorboats, had, on his own initiative, taken the decision to attack and destroy the shipyard while undertaking his patrol. Spicer-Simson finished the church service he was conducting and then put out after her with both his boats. As the range closed, *Mimi* and *Toutou* opened up with their 3-pdr Hotchkiss guns. A direct hit on *Kingani's* foredeck knocked out her forward 6-pdr gun, killing the crew, while another shell hit the wheelhouse, killing all inside, including the captain, and the steamer appeared to go out of control. She stopped and struck her battle flag. Covered by *Mimi*,

The *Graf von Götson*, Lake Tanganyika.

captained by Lieutenant Arthur Dudley, RN, Spicer-Simson, commanding *Toutou*, closed to take the German surrender only to inadvertently collide with the steamer and badly damage his boat. *Kingani* was towed into Lukuga, where, over the following weeks, she was repaired and had two new guns mounted on her decks. She was then renamed *Fifi* by Spicer-Simson, who was shortly after promoted to Commander.

The failure of the *Kingani* to return from her routine patrol was a serious concern for Lieutenant-Commander Zimmer, who could only reflect as to her fate. He eventually learned that she was laid up in the mouth of the Lukuga, and he assumed that she had been caught by the Belgian shore batteries and forced to run aground. In early February 1916, he received intelligence that the *Kingani* had been seen on the lake to the south of the Lukuga. Zimmer decided he would mount a mission to recapture the *Kingani* and destroy the shipyard and whatever else lay concealed in the mouth of the Lukuga. He planned to send the *Hedwig von Wissmann* across the lake on the night of February 8 and 9 to land two of his askari to spy out the target. To disguise his intention the *Hedwig von Wissmann* would be made to appear as if she was undertaking a routine patrol; she would steam along the Belgian shore to a point 40 miles (64 kilometers) to the south of the river, then turn north to arrive off Lukuga at dawn, landing the two askari as close as possible to the river mouth before crossing back to the German shore to rendezvous with the *Graf von Götsen* and a steam-launch. Then at midnight on the night of the 9th/10th the flotilla, having picked up the two scouts, would attack Lukuga, recover the *Kingani* and destroy the shipyard.

At 6 a.m. on February 9, the *Hedwig von Wissmann* was sighted

Seven. The Naval Africa Expedition

The *Graf von Götson*'s forward gun crew practicing drills, Lake Tanganyika, 1915.

steaming towards Lukuga as planned. As soon as she was sighted, however, Spicer-Simson put out with *Mimi* and *Fifi* (*Toutou*, which had developed a problem with her engines, did not take part in the operation) at 7:45 a.m., approaching the German steamer at half speed. At 10 a.m., the first shot was fired, and the *Hedwig von Wissmann*, which had turned at 9:30 a.m., began running for home. *Mimi*, commanded by Lieutenant AE Wainwright, RNVR, much to Spicer-Simson's chagrin, raced ahead of *Fifi* and began firing at her from 3,000 yards (2,743 meters); the action had been raging for half an hour with the *Hedwig von Wissman* trying to come about and engage *Mimi* with her 6-pdr bow gun, circling but unable to hit her, and all the while *Fifi* was closing. When she was within range, *Fifi* began firing her 12-pdr. She was down to her last three rounds when her 12-pdr misfired; as soon as it was safe to do so, the breech was opened and the misfired shell thrown overboard. *Fifi* once more opened fire, her very first round smashing into *Hedwig von Wissmann*'s engine room, killing six men, bursting her boiler and blowing a hole in her side. She was soon burning fiercely and had begun to settle in the water; at 11:15 a.m., her stern rose out of the lake, and she sank. The survivors—her captain, Sub-Lieutenant Odebrecht, 11 German naval ratings and eight native seamen—were picked up by the British boats.

The next day the last of the German vessels, the *Graf von Götson*, was sighted; Zimmer had come to find the *Hedwig von Wissman*. But

Spicer-Simson was conscious of the fact that this ship was far more powerful than his entire flotilla and refused to give chase. Instead he made his way to Stanleyville in an attempt to find a vessel suitable to challenge the *Graf von Götson*. Here he was informed that the British Consul at Leopoldville had a steel boat which met his requirements, the *St. George*; he had this boat dismantled and transported to Lukuga where she was reassembled. But by the time he returned to his base in May, after a three-month absence, the tactical situation on the lake had changed, and shortly after, he received orders to support an attack on Bismarckburg. *Graf von Götson*, meanwhile, returned to Kigoma, where von Lettow-Vorbeck ordered all her guns to be removed for use by the *Schutztruppe*, save a small pom-pom gun, and in July she was filled with concrete and scuttled.

Despite his caution following the destruction of the *Hedwig von Wissmann*, Spicer-Simson and his lake flotilla had destroyed German control on Lake Tanganyika, and this played a significant part in the campaign against the Germans in East Africa. The German commander, Zimmer, had been aware that there was a threat to his dominance on the lake, even though he was unsure of what precisely that threat was. He had a formidable squadron under his command which outgunned Spicer-Simson's little flotilla, and had he brought his superior weight and fire power against the British flotilla, he would have destroyed it. But he underestimated the opposition, failed to properly identify the threat, and as a consequence lost the initiative and the battle to a small force with lighter weapons whose only advantage was daring and the speed of the two Thornycroft motorboats. Spicer-Simson was awarded the Distinguished Service Order for the success of the Naval Africa Expedition.

EIGHT

Operations on the Northern and Northwestern Frontier

By now fresh British units were pouring into East Africa. The first of these to arrive were the 1st South African Mounted and 2nd and 3rd South African Infantry Brigades with five batteries of field artillery. From France there came the 129th (Duke of Connaught's Own) Baluchis, Bombay Infantry, the 130th (King George's Own) Baluchis (Jacob's Rifles), Bombay Infantry, 57th Wilde's Rifles (Frontier Force), and the 40th Pathans, Bengal Infantry, with supporting artillery and armored cars.

Squadron-Commander Robert Gordon's No. 4 Squadron, Royal Naval Air Service, was placed at the disposal of East Africa Command, and at long last preparations were made for the expansion of the King's African Rifles. They would eventually reach a total of 22 battalions—raised by duplicating the units already in existence and reactivating 2nd KAR. Later, in 1917, a further two regiments, the 6th KAR raised in April and the 7th KAR raised in May, would recruit from the askari prisoners of war captured from the Germans.

While Captain Richard Meinertzhagen, following the Battle of Tanga, had been appointed chief of intelligence and was authorized to establish a central intelligence network, he recruited an intelligence unit of primarily Swahili-speaking Africans who were sent behind enemy lines as individual agents and sometimes as fighting patrols. His agents sent information to him through the services of various neutrals such as the Greek and Portuguese merchants residing in the various settlements of German East Africa. Because of their method of obtaining intelligence, his organization was soon known as the "DPM" (Dirty Paper Method). "I found that the contents of German officers' latrines were a constant source of filthy though accurate information, as odd pieces of paper containing messages, notes on enciphering and decoding and private letters were often used where lavatory paper did not exist. By June

1915, I had collected, through captured documents and DPM, the signatures and occupations of almost every German employed in German East. These were reproduced and distributed to every officer, so that when a paper with a signature came into their hands they would know who it was and what his job was."[1]

Von Lettow-Vorbeck quickly came to fear Meinertzhagen and his DPM, constantly warning his officers to be on their guard against him. Meinertzhagen regularly led fighting patrols of the DPM, ambushing German patrols and ruffling the feathers of the commanders of British posts that he found poorly defended. On one such patrol on May 20, 1915, he wrote, "I countered the activity of the German patrols near Kasigau by sending out a party who shot birds and beasts and then laid them round the only pool in the neighbourhood as though they had all died of poison. I also labelled the pool 'poison,' which of course it was not as our men found the pool useful, but every week they went out and rearranged the wild birds and beasts which are supposed to have drunk of the poisoned water. This simple ruse has kept enemy patrols from using the well and it has rendered some eighty miles of railway absolutely secure from attack."[2]

Von Lettow-Vorbeck sent a strong protest to the British stating that the poisoning of water holes was a breach of international law, while his own superiors frowned on the methods he employed. Undeterred, Meinertzhagen simply recorded, "It may be an offense to poison water, but surely there is nothing wrong in labelling water as poison when it is not so treated."[3] Fortunately for von Lettow-Vorbeck, the very precise and, more often than not, accurate intelligence reports issued by Meinertzhagen were regularly disregarded by the senior British commanders. They failed to appreciate that this central intelligence was far more accurate than the locally gathered and random information they gathered. Meinertzhagen's intelligence was, however, not infallible; he overestimated the strength of the *Schutztruppe*, putting their number at 20,000 effectives with 66 machine guns and 60 field guns, way above von Lettow-Vorbeck's actual strength. Such inaccuracies no doubt made commanders skeptical of the Head of Intelligence's reports.

The *Schutztruppe*, meanwhile, had strongly fortified Taveta, covering the only road on which any large British overland expedition would have to advance into the Kilimanjaro area. They established a large entrenched camp at Salaita, 15 miles (24 kilometers) to the east, and a heavily defended outpost at Mbuyuni, 17 miles (27 kilometers) further east of that on the Serengeti Plain.

On the coast, since the action at Jasin, a *Schutztruppe* company was actively operating in the Umba Valley area. It was aggressively patrolling

Eight. Operations on the Frontier

in the vicinity of Mwete, Mdogo, Gazi and the Uganda Railway between Vanga and Mombasa, while operating between Taveta and Mombasa was a mobile column 600 strong whose task was the disruption of the Voi-Maktau and Uganda railways. This mobile column tried several times to destroy these railway lines but was never successful. As a result of this column's activities, a composite Mounted Infantry Company of 150 men was formed at the end of August from men of the 2nd Loyals and 25th Royal Fusiliers, under the command of Captain JS Woodruffe (Royal Sussex Regt attached 2nd Loyals), to protect the railway in this area.

Early on September 3, 1915, Woodruffe was informed by Lieutenant-Colonel Cyril Price, commanding the 130th Baluchis at Maktau, that a large German column about 200 strong had crossed the frontier to attack the railway and that their return route would take them close by Maktau. Woodruffe led a detachment of three troops (66 men) from his Mounted Infantry Company, supported by 50 men of the 130th Baluchis, commanded by Lieutenant AH Wildman, seven miles (11 kilometers) to the south of Maktau to intercept them. Having raced ahead of the Baluch detachment, he set up a firing line on bush-covered high ground overlooking the enemy's line of retreat, No. 3 (25RF) Troop on the right facing to the southeast, 1 (2LNL) Troop on their left facing east and 2 (25RF) Troop in reserve; as this high ground had only limited fields of fire, he then posted pickets forward of his main position. But the *Schutztruppe* had learned of their presence and launched a surprise attack against the picket line at 10:45 a.m., driving them back to the main position. The askaris of the 9th Field Company rapidly closed on the main position, their heavy and deadly accurate rifle fire causing growing casualties among the Mounted Infantrymen who were either lying down or kneeling to return fire. Immediately on first contact Woodruffe ordered 2 Troop to take up positions in the firing line to the left of No. 1, and as Lieutenant Dartnell's 3 Troop was facing away from the enemy, ordered him to swing his line to face east. But in the confusion of the fighting, this order was misinterpreted, and 3 Troop bunched up to the rear of 1 Troop.

With the British position in danger of being overwhelmed, John Woodruffe ordered his men to fix bayonets; moments later he was dangerously wounded in the back; aware that he could no longer hold the position, he ordered the detachment to withdraw. Private Harry Bristow of the 2nd Loyals picked up the captain and carried him to safety while under heavy fire—he was subsequently awarded the Distinguished Conduct Medal. Second-Lieutenant W Parker, commanding 1 Troop, took over command. Parker got every wounded man capable of riding back to the mule lines and mounted, while Lieutenant Wilbur Dartnell,[4] commanding No. 3 Troop, who had been shot through the lower leg, refused to be carried off with the lightly wounded. He insisted on being left behind with the badly wounded men who could not be carried away so that he could try and save them from the enemy askaris, who were known to kill and mutilate all wounded prisoners. When he was finally left, the enemy were within 25 yards (23 meters) of his position, and he was furiously engaging them.

At midday Lieutenant Wildman and his Baluchis were within a mile and a half (two and a half kilometers) of the ambush position and were marching rapidly to link up with Woodruffe when they heard heavy firing to their south. Wildman ordered the detachment to increase their pace. Twenty minutes later riders were seen moving fast to the northwest. It was initially thought that they were the enemy, but it was soon realized that they were in fact the Mounted Infantry withdrawing. At 12:30 p.m., all firing from the vicinity of the ambush site ceased. Taking up a defensive position on a low crest close by the ambush site, Wildman sent forward the six Mounted Infantry that were attached to him to recce the scene of the action. They returned to report that the enemy were gone but that there were a number of bodies lying around. Advancing to the battlefield, the Baluchis found the bodies of Lieutenant Dartnell and the seven Mounted Infantrymen. Dartnell had been unsuccessful in his attempt to save the wounded; after being killed, their bodies were stripped and mutilated. Dartnell sold his life dearly though, as when his body was recovered there lay around him the corpses of seven of the enemy. Lieutenant Dartnell was awarded a posthumous Victoria Cross.

In September 1915 the decision was taken to reoccupy Longido, which had been abandoned in early April when an unprecedented number of troops had been struck down with malaria and dysentery and had to be invalided to hospitals in the rear. It was additionally felt that there would be difficulty resupplying and reinforcing the position from Namanga during the rainy season. Lieutenant-Colonel F Jollie (Indian Army) was given the task. He was allocated a force comprising his East Africa Squadron, 17th Indian Cavalry, a squadron of the East African Mounted Rifles, the KAR Mounted Infantry Company and "A" and "B" Companies, 3rd KAR, A total of 581 officers and men of whom 267 were infantry and 214 Mounted Infantry or Mounted Rifles. Moving south from Namanga, the force arrived near Longido on the 19th, and the East African Mounted Rifles advanced to recce the hill. They found that the former British camp at Longido West was occupied by a detachment of 49 officers and askaris of the 8th Field Company under the command of

Eight. Operations on the Frontier

1st Lieutenant Bauer, who had taken up well-sited defensive positions at the end of a spur running down from the hill and dominating the water holes on the western side of the Longido feature.

Despite being unaware of the enemy's actual strength, Lieutenant-Colonel Jollie decided to assault the position. The KAR Mounted Infantry and East African Mounted Rifles were to establish a firing line on a ridge to the north of and overlooking Bauer's position. From here they were to give supporting fire to the main assault, which would be carried out by "A" Company, 3rd KAR, who were to climb Longido Hill during the night and then attack down the hill from the east at dawn; "B" Company would then advance up the hill from the south to give additional fire support. The 17th Cavalry was to remain on the plain and to cut off any survivors who might escape the infantry assault. Unfortunately, no thought had been given as to how the groups were to communicate so that before they even began their deployment, Jollie had lost all command and control. He had also committed a cardinal error of infantry support by placing his two fire support groups facing directly towards each other.

As darkness came on, "A" Company moved forward from its position in the plain and began climbing the hill to their start line. But insufficient time had been allocated for their climb, and as a consequence they were not in position to begin their attack as scheduled at dawn. As dawn approached, "B" Company began its advance up the hill from the south and walked right into an abatis of thornbushes that had been part of the former British defensive perimeter, unreported when they withdrew in the spring. The company forced its way through the thornbushes, bunching into small packets as they did so. Bauer's detachment was by now fully alert and stood-to. As the bunched groups of "B" Company, 3rd KAR, reached the top of the slope where they were plainly silhouetted, they came under intense rifle and machine-gun fire both from the Germans and the Mounted Infantry on the ridge to their north.

Meanwhile, "A" Company had finally reached its start point and began assaulting down the ridge, but the bulk of the company took a wrong turn as they charged down and ran straight into "B" Company. Only a handful took the right path, led by Lieutenant EAR Gore-Browne (Dorset Regt), but he was severely wounded in the thigh as they closed on Bauer's position from where a heavy fire was directed towards them. Private Mulandi Wamwibi immediately picked up the stricken Lieutenant and carried him to safety. So intense was the rifle fire that Wamwibi's equipment and clothes were riddled with bullet holes. For this act of gallantry, he would be awarded the African Distinguished Conduct Medal.

On the southern slope "B" Company's casualties were mounting. Lieutenant EH Barrett had taken over command after the company commander was wounded, and he brought forward those of his men still down the slope to continue to press the attack. Despite repeated efforts, the attackers were driven back. The company's machine gun was then knocked out by enemy fire, and the section commander, Temporary Lieutenant Thomas Wilson, set to work repairing it and soon got it operating again. Meanwhile, Jollie had given the East African Mounted Rifles—who had lost two killed, one wounded and four missing—and the KAR Mounted Infantry permission to withdraw from the northern ridge. Initially these two units intended to ride around the west of Longido and from there support the two KAR companies. But they discovered that Lieutenant-Colonel Jollie and the 17th Indian Cavalry were withdrawing north to Namanga so abandoned their plans and rode to join them.

On Longido, Lieutenant Barrett and his men were astonished to see the mounted troops withdrawing to the north, but undeterred, they held their positions and continued the fight. An hour later at midday a rider brought orders to the two companies: they were to break contact and withdraw. Thirsty and exhausted, the companies, carrying their wounded, withdrew in good order to Namanga, having lost 15 killed and 32 wounded in this astonishing debacle. The victorious Bauer and his detachment—having had all three officers and 11 men wounded—withdrew from Longido that night, establishing a new position close to Arusha. With them they had the four missing men of the East African Mounted Rifles, three of whom were seriously wounded and who were evacuated to Arusha.

Lieutenant-Colonel Jollie escaped censure as British Headquarters took the decision to keep the details of his incompetent handling of the action and the abandonment of his infantry under strict wraps for fear that should it become common knowledge it would severely damage morale. Particularly since the successful Bukoba raid, British arms had suffered a number of reverses.

For a good part of 1915 the Belgian commander, Major-General Tombeur, was out of touch with his various unit commanders as he made his way to Kivu to take up his post. But by November he had arrived, and Major Olsen received confirmation of his orders to begin moving his two battalions north to the Rusisi River between Lakes Kivu and Tanganyika from Northern Rhodesia—a march of two months' duration—while the other Belgian commanders were instructed to concentrate their units in the Kivu area, where they were to be reorganized into a field army preparatory to operations in German East Africa.

Eight. Operations on the Frontier

To cover his concentration Tombeur had, in December 1915, asked the British to undertake some diversionary actions on the western side of Lake Victoria. To meet this request the British decided to undertake two demonstrations: a crossing of the Kagera River to the south of the Ugandan border and a landing on the Lubembe Peninsula on the southern side of Kemondo Bay to the south of Bukoba. Commander Thornley—commanding the Royal Navy's lake flotilla—was given overall command of the Lubembe operation, while the landing and occupation of the peninsula was to be undertaken by "E" Company, 98th Hyderabad Infantry, commanded by Lieutenant DR Montford and supported by three of Commander Thornley's lake steamers. Lieutenant Montford was instructed to occupy the peninsula for three days. He was to take two of the three hill features on the peninsula—which had been designated "A," "B" and "C," this last the highest of the three. On landing he was to secure hill "B," then advance to and occupy hill "C." Once the latter was secured, he was to dig-in and hold for at least 48 hours and, hopefully, draw off and distract Captain von Steumer's troops—local police askaris and Ruga-Ruga—from Bukoba that were deployed along the Kagera River.

The raiding party sailed from Kisumu in the armed steamers *Nyanza*, *Winifred* and *Kavirondo* on December 2. Having crossed the lake, they anchored in Sango Bay on the Ugandan side for two nights and then headed south. Steaming past Bukoba and Kemondo Bay, the steamers sheltered behind Bukerebe Island. Commander Thornley hoped that these maneuvers would confuse the Germans as to their intentions. Meanwhile, the diversionary attack across the Kagera River was launched on the 4th, the forces here withdrawing the following day, von Lettow-Vorbeck noting unsuccessful "hostile attacks on the lower Kagera on the 4th and 5th December."[5]

In the early hours of the 6th the steamers were again under way and entered Kemondo Bay at dawn, making their way to the north side of the peninsula and to the small cove whose beach at Lubembe Point was chosen for the landing as it was in dead ground. The steamers opened fire on the German defenses spotted above the beach and on a redoubt seen further along the bay, and at 6:45 a.m. "E" Company along with two naval machine-gun sections and 100 porters were ferried ashore from the *Nyanza* and *Winifred* in the ships' boats towed by a motor launch. As they approached the beach, the boats came under fire from the German positions, wounding two men. Immediately on landing, Lieutenant AJ St Leger-Hansard led his section forward to hill "B" held by two platoons of police askaris, part of Reserve Lieutenant Koller's command of 50 men defending Kemondo Bay, who opened fire from their positions on the slopes. Koller fell back to hill "C" as St Leger-Hansard's section advanced to secure the hill.

As Koller fell back, Lieutenant Montford moved around the right flank with the rest of the company and the two naval machine-gun sections to attack hill "C." Pushing through rocky scrub and banana plantations they drove Koller and his men slowly back off the hill. By now Montford and 11 of his men had been wounded, but the Lieutenant remained in command of his company as they closed on the hill, and on gaining the crest he had his men dig-in. The naval machine-gun sections took up positions on the flanks of the defenses. But Lieutenant Koller wasn't prepared to let the British hold the hill if he could help it and launched a counterattack. The attacking police askaris got to within 200 yards (183 meters) of "E" Company before the fire of the naval machine-gun sections and the guns of the steamers forced them to withdraw and take cover in the thick bush on the lower slopes of the hill.

The steamers *Nyanza* and *Kavirondo* then switched their fire onto Koller's men holding the redoubt, while Commander Thornley sent the *Winifred* to the south side of the peninsula to engage any enemy movements around that flank. Meanwhile, the porters had been put to work cutting a path through the scrub from hill "B" towards hill "C" so that the company's reserves of ammunition, personal kit, equipment and rations could be brought forward.

Lieutenant Koller began feeding more of his men forward into the thick bush below hill "C" where they were relatively safe from the naval guns, which could only identify specific targets once an attack began. To ensure that the enemy was kept under pressure Koller sent snipers into the scrub to harass them. At 11 a.m., as his casualties grew, Montford informed Thornley that if he stayed in his present position for the time he was ordered to, his losses would continue to rise and an evacuation would become extremely difficult to execute. Meanwhile Captain Ernst von Brandis, having heard the heavy gunfire and been informed by Koller of the British attack, was marching from Bukoba with 120 police askaris and around 80 Ruga-Ruga to reinforce the defenders. Thornley, having seen the relief column approaching and witnessed the ferocious defenses of Koller's command, was convinced that the objective of the mission had been achieved. He decided that to remain any longer would be a pointless waste of lives, and so he gave the order to begin the withdrawal. *Winifred* was recalled to the north of the peninsula where she took up station just off the beach to cover the evacuation. The first to be taken off were the porters, along with the stores and equipment, all of whom were embarked without incident.

By now, however, von Brandis and his column were approaching

Eight. Operations on the Frontier

hill "C," and Thornley ordered the *Kavirondo* to engage them with shrapnel. As soon as they came under fire the relief column took cover in the thick bush from where they opened fire on the British. Once the porters and stores had been taken off the beach, half of "E" Company withdrew to hill "B," covered by the rest of the company. Here they went firm, and the remaining half company then began retiring from hill "C," withdrawing through them to the beach, where one of the naval machine guns was taken off. The second machine gun and the half company took up covering positions along the edge of the beach while the men on hill "B" fell back and through them. One of Koller's 4.7-cm guns opened fire on the beach, only to be knocked out by *Nyanza*'s 4-inch gun, which scored a direct hit. Then a 6-cm gun situated near the redoubt joined the action, along with heavy rifle fire from von Brandis and Koller's police askaris.

Unfortunately, only three of the six ships' boats were in the cove, and these were quickly filled with the infantry and machine-gun crew. The motorboat which was to tow them to the steamers, however, broke down. Under heavy fire the naval machine-gun crew, Beach Master and two wounded officers split themselves among the remaining three boats and began rowing out to the waiting steamers. As they rounded the end of the cove, they were no longer protected by the dead ground, and the German fire became heavier. The first boat reached *Winifred* having had two men killed and four wounded, followed shortly after by the second boat. The last boat, however, was adrift, all her oarsmen having been hit by enemy fire. *Winifred* and *Kavirondo* moved to within 200 yards (180 meters) of the shore to give covering fire, and as the *Kavirondo* attempted to get a line aboard the stricken boat, Lieutenant Robert Aslin, RNR, was mortally wounded. *Winifred*, meanwhile, received a direct hit from the 6-cm gun above the redoubt, wounding a number of men, but she was able to get a line aboard the boat and tow her to safety. At about 4 p.m., with all the ships' boats under tow by the wounded *Winifred*, the steamers withdrew. During the action, the 98th Infantry's casualties were four killed, 31 wounded and one missing; the naval machine-gun crews had two wounded, while the steamer ship's companies had one killed and a large number wounded.

Von Brandis reported a casualty list of two killed and six wounded; despite British claims that they suffered upward of 100 casualties, "the affair was magnified by the enemy into a German victory."[6] But the facts of the matter were that "E" Company, 98th Infantry had been forced to withdraw after only nine hours ashore instead of the two to three days originally planned for, and the demonstration was only averted from being a complete disaster by the decision to evacuate early.

Before Sir Horace Smith-Dorrien's illness forced him to relinquish his command in East Africa, he had drawn up a plan of operations for the theater, which, as it turned out, was similar to that which Major-General Tighe and his staff had decided on. With German East's north protected for 130 miles (210 kilometers) from the coast to the Kilimanjaro foothills by the Usambara and Pare Mountain Ranges, Tighe's staff quickly realized that the key to a land invasion of German East Africa from the British north was through the gap of four to five miles (seven to nine kilometers) between the northern Pare and the Kilimanjaro foothills in which lay Taveta, Moshi, Himo and Kahe. Tighe had ordered the construction of a water pipeline from the Bura Hills dam to the Kilimanjaro area, along with a branch line running from the main railway. Tighe's plan was to attack the German forces concentrated in the Kilimanjaro area, while a secondary force was to take Dar es Salaam from the sea. No sooner had the construction of the railway branch line begun than news of it reached von Lettow-Vorbeck, who wrote, "The construction of this military line proved that an attack with large forces was in preparation and that it was to be directed against this part of the Kilima Njaro [sic] country."[7] He had also learned of the water pipeline and immediately ordered raids to be mounted against the pipeline and the Bura Hills head works—where the pumps were blown up, putting it out of action for three weeks—and the railway and to cause as much disruption as possible to their construction. He noted, however, "The destruction of the enemy's reservoir by patrols under Lieutenant von S'Antenecai, of the Reserve, only caused him temporary inconvenience."[8]

Acutely aware that his troops could not halt or repel the British invasion when it began and conscious that soldiers being forced to withdraw without knowing the reason why soon lost their morale, von Lettow-Vorbeck informed his detachment commanders, "There is no need to tell your men of the possibilities of the battles of the next few days, but the circumstances should be obvious to you and if they are not I shall not conceal them from you. We face an overwhelming force and it is unlikely that we can secure anything more than local victories against them. Our object is to inflict as much damage as possible against them, but rather to give up territory than risk envelopment. At all costs, we must avoid either being killed or captured, for we must live to fight again another day."[9]

To execute his plan of campaign Tighe reorganized the bulk of his forces into two divisions, the 1st and 2nd East African Divisions, commanded respectively by Major-General JM Stewart and Brigadier-General W Malleson and which included the newly formed 1st and 2nd East African Brigades.[10]

On January 15, 1916, the 1st Division was ordered to reoccupy

Eight. Operations on the Frontier

Longido. Stewart's division advanced north to its start point at Kajiado on the Magadi branch line of the railway, while the 2nd Division began advancing on the German positions to the east of Mount Kilimanjaro, marching from Maktau to Mbuyuni on the 22nd and then on to the Serengeti camp, which they took on the 24th, forcing the Germans to abandon Kasigau. General Tighe then issued orders for the immediate concentration of a large force at Mbuyuni, while his engineers pushed the railway from Maktau to Njoro, halfway between the German positions at Taveta and Mbuyuni. Tighe wanted the railway pushed even further west towards Taveta, but to achieve this he would have to secure Salaita Hill.

On February 3, a brigade strength reconnaissance was made towards Salaita Hill from the Serengeti camp by the 2nd Loyals, supported by the 5th and 6th SA Infantry, while the 130th Baluchis and 2nd Rhodesia Regiment made a demonstration towards the hill to distract the garrison of what appeared to be a strongly entrenched and defended position. Salaita Hill was, in fact, garrisoned by Major Georg Kraut with 900 officers and askaris of the 18th, 27th Field and "W" Companies, along with a battery of field guns.

A second, battalion strength, reconnaissance was undertaken by the 6th SA Infantry two days later, while aircraft of the RNAS and No. 26 (SA) Squadron, RFC, were flying recce missions over the position. During the reconnaissance, shots were traded without any casualties being suffered, until, as the battalion withdrew across the Njoro River, a soldier tripped on a mine and was badly wounded.

On the 9th, the 2nd SA Brigade undertook a demonstration in front of Kraut's eastern defenses, which failed to draw any response, so they burnt off the thick long grass at the foot of the hill and along the side of the main track to Taveta. The 61st Pioneers, meanwhile, constructed defenses at Njoro Drift to their rear, having first checked the approach route and drift area for more mines.

Having been kept abreast of the situation at Salaita, von Lettow-Vorbeck was certain that an attack on the position was imminent. He therefore ordered a further three companies—14th, 15th and 30th Field—be sent to reinforce Kraut.

On February 12, Malleson ordered 1st EA and 2nd SA Brigades, supported by 18 field guns and 41 machine guns, to make a reconnaissance in force towards Salaita from the east of the railway at Njoro Drift. His intention was to take the German position with a surprise attack. Brigadier-General Beves, however, had reservations which he made known to Malleson when being briefed, telling him that the attack would hardly come as a surprise following the repeated demonstrations towards Salaita and the aerial activity by the RNAS and RFC over the hill or the fact that they did not know what the German strength was at Taveta from where the garrison could receive reinforcements. He was also concerned that one of his battalions—the 8th SA Infantry—was not to take part in the attack. Malleson, who had orders from Major-General Tighe to take Salaita, was not about to be dissuaded by Beves's reservations. He told the South African General that his concerns were groundless, the attack by the two brigades with strong artillery support would be quite sufficient to overwhelm the German position. Besides, he told Beves, the intelligence gathered over the preceding week indicated that the hill was held by only around 300 men with two machine guns and no artillery and that a troop of Belfield's Scouts had been detailed to put out a screen to the northwest of Salaita where they would be able to provide sufficient warning of any reinforcements being pushed forward from Taveta.

In the early hours of the 12th the brigades left their camps and made their way to their start lines on the Njoro River. By 6:45 a.m., they were in position. The attack began at 8 a.m., the South Africans advancing on the German trenches from the right flank while 2nd Loyals, 2nd Rhodesians and 130th Baluchis of 1st EA Brigade maintained a defensive line to the east in front of Salaita Hill. The 7th SA Infantry,[11] with the 5th and 6th SA Infantry on their left and right respectively, fought their way through the thick bush to the north of the Serengeti-Salaita track until they reached some open ground 1,000 yards (915 meters) from Kraut's defenses, which found the brigade deployed facing the north of the hill.

At 9 a.m., the British artillery opened fire, and the South African battalions advanced towards Salaita under its covering fire. The 5th and 7th managed to get within 300 yards (275 meters) of the enemy defenses, which were at the foot of the hill, not on its slopes where the artillery bombardment was falling, and here they were pinned down by the heavy enemy fire, while the 6th SA Infantry on the right of the line—having been refused permission to cross the cleared ground in open order and like the other battalions under heavy rifle, machine-gun and artillery fire from the German positions—was able to capture one of Kraut's trenches. The three battalions soon realized, however, that they were taking fire from their rear, where Kraut had placed snipers in concealed positions in advance of his main defensive line.

With casualties mounting in all three battalions, at 11 a.m., Beves ordered the 5th and 7th SA Infantry to withdraw, covered by the 6th. General Malleson, meanwhile, ordered 1st EA Brigade to attack the

Eight. Operations on the Frontier

eastern side of Salaita Hill to try and relieve the pressure on the South Africans. The 2nd Loyals and 2nd Rhodesia Regiment, supported by the 130th Baluchis, advanced towards the German defenses but fared no better than the South Africans, and by the early afternoon, it was clear that this attack was a failure. By this time, Captain Hans Schulz's command (6th, 9th and 24th Field Companies) had advanced to Salaita from their positions halfway between Taveta and Salaita to reinforce Kraut, either unseen or unreported by the troop of Belfield's Scouts to the northwest.

Schulz's companies moved behind the 15th Field Company holding the western defenses, outflanking the 6th SA Infantry, and all four companies then attacked the South Africans. At 1 p.m., 1st EA Brigade was ordered to redeploy to the north to cover the withdrawal of the South Africans. It was only the cover provided by Lieutenant-Commander W Whittall's four armored cars of 10th Armoured Car Battery, the 2nd Loyals' machine guns and the British field guns[12] which stopped the withdrawal from becoming a disordered route. Several attempts were made to rally the South African battalions, but they bolted from the field, abandoning their machine guns, and some men their rifles and equipment, a number of platoons from the 5th and 7th SA Infantry running back through 1st EA Brigade's line. "Men of two broken regiments streamed through our ranks, running to the rear, getting to safety, and yet Rhodesians lay there, quietly shooting when targets offered, quietly enduring a shell-fire that our guns had failed to silence, and then failed to reply to."[13] The 130th Baluchis stood firm as their position came under heavy attack, refusing help from the 2nd Rhodesia Regiment on their flank, who were also being hard-pressed, while the Loyals were able to stop the enemy and even advance a short way against the tide of the German assault. Their actions stopped Schulz's counterattack in its tracks. But with the route of the 2nd SA Brigade, the flanks of 1st EA Brigade were exposed, and the brigade was ordered to withdraw.

They fell back from Salaita Hill to the Serengeti camp in contact with the Germans until they reached Njoro Drift. The South Africans lost 133 killed in the action. Yet despite the severity of the fighting, the battalions of 1st EA Brigade did not suffer any casualties as they covered the South African withdrawal, and the 130th Baluchis were able to recover the abandoned South African machine guns as they retired. The next day the Baluchis sent canvas-wrapped bundles by mule to the South African lines, which, when they were unloaded, were found to contain the brigade's machine guns along with a note which said, "With the compliments of the 130th Baluchis, may we request that you no longer refer to our sepoys as coolies." It was a bloody baptism of fire for the 2nd SA Infantry Brigade and also raised concerns among the 2nd EA Division as to Malleson's ability and competence as a field commander. Shortly afterwards, the 2nd Loyals, having lost 482 officers and men from a total strength of 832 since its arrival in East Africa, was withdrawn from duty and sent to South Africa for rest, recuperation and reorganization.

NINE

The Battle of Kilimanjaro

GENERAL SMUTS ARRIVED in Nairobi on February 22, 1916. On his arrival in theater Major-General Tighe took over command of the 2nd Division, while Brigadier-General Malleson took over 1st EA Brigade. Smuts immediately suspended all operations until a detailed reconnaissance of the German positions could be made, preferring to outmaneuver the enemy rather than outfight him. The Germans were known to be concentrating between the Kitovo Hills and their Salaita strongpoint. Tighe's plan of campaign for the occupation of Kilimanjaro was based on a double thrust: 1st EA Division advancing from Longido while the 2nd EA Division pushed south from Mbuyuni. The objective of both divisions was Kahe. Smuts agreed to the plan in principle, insisting on only a few changes that he considered vital to its outcome.

He did not want to attack the German positions in front of the Mbuyuni and Serengeti camps. Here the *Schutztruppe*, 6,000 strong with 16 field guns and 37 machine guns, were deeply entrenched behind the Lumi River on the Taveta road. They had seven miles (11 kilometers) of thick bush stretching before them, with their right flank protected by the Pare Mountains and the swamps of the Ruwa River and Lake Jipe and their left on the Kilimanjaro foothills. The 1st Division was to march from Longido, cut the *Schutztruppe's* lines of communication and block their line of retreat. Two days later Brigadier-General van Deventer with 1st SA Mounted and 3rd SA Infantry Brigades was to take Chala heights then move against Neu Moshi. On the third day Tighe's 2nd Division was to advance once again against Salaita.

Shortly after assuming command, Smuts visited the lines of advance at Longido and Mbuyuni with General Tighe to finalize his plans. At Longido General Stewart argued that Smuts's timetable for the advance was not realistic considering the difficulties his division would face. He requested an extra two-day headstart over the forces advancing from the east to ensure he could achieve his objective on schedule. Smuts dismissed the difficulties that Stewart presented, regarding

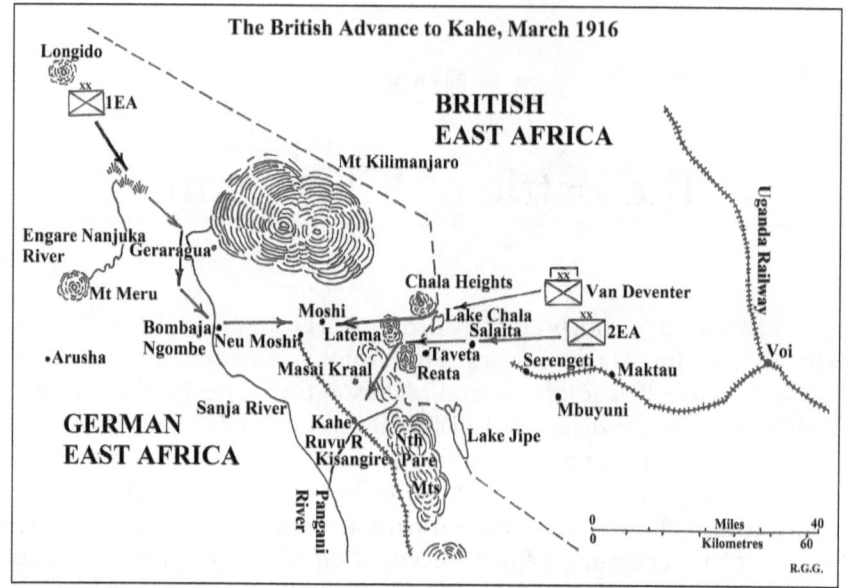

Kilimanjaro Area (map by the author).

his opposition to the timetable as insubordinate and a challenge to his authority. On the 23rd he cabled the War Office to say that he proposed to take the Kilimanjaro area before the rainy season began at the end of March. On the 25th he received a reply from Lord Kitchener giving him permission to proceed with his offensive.

The 1st Division began its advance at dusk on March 5, pushing towards Bombaja-Ngombe. They marched rapidly across the 33 miles (53 kilometers) of barren, waterless waste to the swamps at Engare Nanjuka, crossing the river without incident early on the 6th. But they were exhausted, filthy and desperate for water, and their supply line from Longido was exposed and constantly disrupted by heavy rain squalls. Angus Buchanan, serving in the 25th Fusiliers, wrote, "Marching was unpleasant in the soft, powdered dust which lay ankle-deep underfoot, and was kicked in the air in a hanging cloud to choke both throat and nostrils, and adhere to every visible part of one's clothing."[1] For the first three days of their march there was no opposition, and by the 8th they had reached Geraragua. Here Stewart learned that the road to Bombaja-Ngombe was blocked, all the bridges having been destroyed by the retreating Germans. Mounted patrols were sent forward to search for a passable track. One was eventually found, but it would be a difficult route through the heavily wooded foothills. Stewart ordered his infantry to lead the division, as the going would be difficult for his mounted troops and artillery.

Nine. The Battle of Kilimanjaro

At midday on the 10th, Stewart's infantry, despite their exhaustion, resumed their advance, followed by his mounted troops at 4 p.m. Shortly after, the mounted troops and artillery were attacked by two *Schutztruppe* companies from Major Erich Fischer's command—the 8th and 28th Field Companies, 8th and 9th Rifle Companies and Arusha detachment—and were forced to pull back to the Engare Nanjuka River. The infantry, however, pushed on, reaching the Sanja River on the evening of the 11th where an intact bridge had been found close to Bombaja-Ngombe. Steward sent the 29th Punjabis back to escort his mounted troops and artillery forward before advancing on Bombaja-Ngombe the next day. On the 14th the division rendezvoused with van Deventer's column at Neu Moshi. Here Stewart learned that the companies of Fischer's covering force withdrawing before him had passed through the settlement on the night of the 12th. The 1st Division had been unable to carry out its task and played virtually no further part in this phase of the operations.

Prior to the rendezvous with the 1st Division in the west, van Deventer's column had marched as planned on the evening of March 7. He crossed the Serengeti Plain and reached the northern wall of the extinct volcano of Lake Chala. From here he pushed on to Neu Moshi to affect his link with Stewart.

The next day, the 8th, Tighe's 2nd Division went into action. The divisional artillery bombarded the Salaita positions in preparation for a frontal assault to take place the following morning. But following van Deventer's surprise attack and capture of Lake Chala, and the preparatory bombardment of the Salaita defenses, von Lettow-Vorbeck ordered the withdrawal of his forces from both Salaita and Taveta. The 2nd Division occupied both places on the 10th without opposition, while the *Schutztruppe* fell back towards the Latema-Reata Nek, their rearguard in contact with the pursuing mounted troops and artillery of Tighe's division.

The Latema-Reata Nek was a natural defensive position, but von Lettow-Vorbeck's rearguard—18th and 30th Field and "W" Companies—were too thin on the ground to successfully defend its 12-mile (19-kilometer) length for long. He felt, though, that Major Kraut would be able to decisively defeat at least one of the British columns before being forced off the Nek. Smuts, on the other hand, had no idea if the Germans were holding the Nek in force, but he had to clear this position before he could advance on Kahe.

On March 11 Malleson received orders to take the Nek. He decided to mount a frontal assault against the southern end of the Latema ridge with his 1st EA Brigade supported by the field guns of the 5th SA, 6th,

German East Africa, British Artillery crossing a temporary bridge (Illustrations Bureau).

8th and 9th Field Batteries and 134th (Howitzer) Battery. At 11:45 a.m., the brigade began its advance, 3rd KAR on the left 130th Baluchis on the right and 2nd Rhodesia Regiment in reserve, with the flanks covered by the division's mounted troops—Belfield's Scouts on the right and the Mounted Infantry the left. As they neared the bush-covered slopes of Latema ridge, they came under a devastating fire which checked the brigade's advance.

At 2:30 p.m., Brigadier-General Malleson, claiming to be incapacitated by dysentery, asked to be relieved of his command and left his HQ. Smuts, who considered Malleson an arrogant coward, accepted his resignation; he felt that Malleson's troops had lost their confidence in him, as he certainly had, and he ordered Tighe to take direct control of the attack. The ubiquitous Richard Meinertzhagen, now Smuts's intelligence officer, recorded the affair in his diary, writing, "I felt like shooting the cur, just imagine any general leaving his brigade in the middle of a fight and taking a car as fast as it would carry him back to the rear.... His action has evoked some very disagreeable comments in his brigade and Smuts is quite determined that the man never comes back. He mentioned the affair to me this evening and said it saved him from a very disagreeable task, for the man is a coward. I had to agree, but I dislike a Dutchman calling an English general a coward."[2] On taking command Tighe committed the 6th and 8th SA Battalions, and a general action ensued for the rest of the day. At 6 p.m., the 3rd KAR and 2nd Rhodesians tried to storm Latema ridge but were repulsed, the KAR losing its commander, Lieutenant-Colonel Graham, killed in the fight. Tighe then decided to try and clear the Nek with a night attack by the 5th and 7th SA Battalions, using the bayonet. The attack was led by Lieutenant-Colonel J Byron, CO of the 5th. Byron split his force into three columns, one under Lieutenant-Colonel Freeth of the 7th, to take Latema ridge north of the Nek, the second under Major Thompson, also of the 7th, to take Reata heights to the south, while he led the third against the Nek itself.

The columns moved off at the appointed time. They found the going hard, as the bush they had to penetrate was much thicker than had been anticipated, and the *Schutztruppe* were putting up a dogged defense, their mutually supporting fire inflicting heavy losses on the columns. Freeth fought his way up Latema's steep spur, reaching his allocated objective with only 18 men. Here he was joined by a few surviving Rhodesians and KAR who had been pinned down on the crest since the failure of the earlier attempt to take the position, and here they remained until morning. Thompson's column, 170 strong, also reached their objective, the Reata heights where they dug-in, while Byron's column reached the Nek at midnight. They were only 30 yards (27 meters) from Kraut's main position, from where a heavy fire was being directed at them. They had lost 23 killed during the advance, including the Brigade-Major, Major BW Mainprise, RE. Byron had been wounded in the final stages of the advance and had only 20 men left with him when he gained the Nek, and the German positions commanded the ground that he held. Unable to advance further, and to save what was left of his column from complete destruction, he gave the order to withdraw.

Unaware that the northern and southern positions had been taken, only that Byron had been forced to retire, Tighe ordered the remainder of 2nd Division to dig-in astride the road to await daybreak. During the night a number of attempts were made to try and contact Freeth and Thompson—all of which were unsuccessful. "Neither he nor the Commander-in-Chief were aware that the South African and Rhodesian detachments still stood fast on the ridge."[3] Smuts, on being told of the apparent failure of the attack, ordered Tighe to withdraw his division to a position further back from the Nek. He had decided to rely on his mounted troops outflanking the Latema-Reata positions and had given orders for this flanking march to begin at dawn.

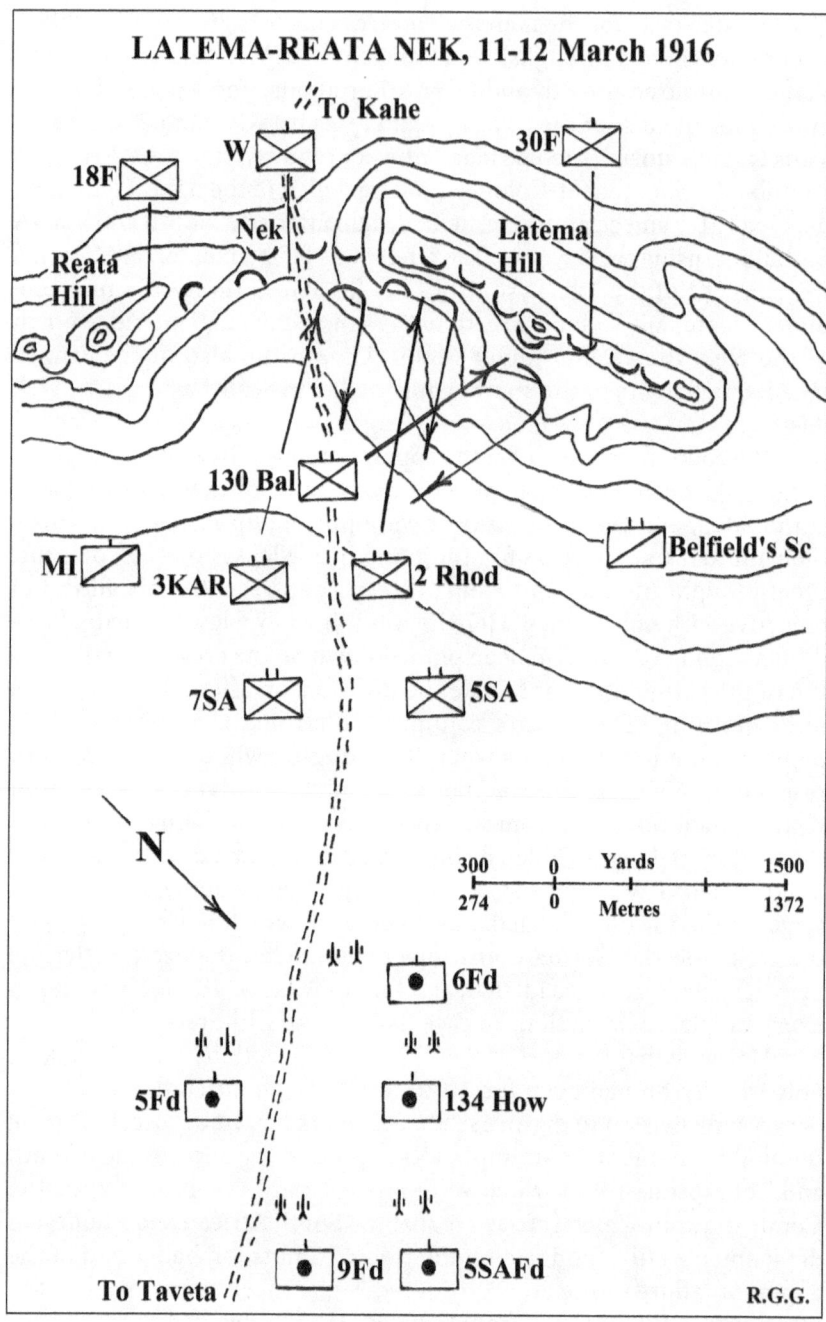

The Action at Latema Nek (based on an official sketch map published by HMSO/Historical Section Military Branch, 1918).

Nine. The Battle of Kilimanjaro

The 2nd Division had begun its withdrawal when patrols sent out to locate the missing flank columns reported that they had, at last, made contact with Freeth and Thompson. Both had taken, and were holding, their objectives, and the Nek itself was clear of the enemy. Von Lettow-Vorbeck, finding his defenses on the Nek vulnerable to these commanding heights, had ordered Kraut to retire on Kahe. He was now in full retreat through the thick forest that stretched from Latema-Reata to Kahe.

Tighe ordered his reserve, the 8th SA Infantry, to secure the Nek; they were followed by the division's artillery, which lay down harassing fire on the withdrawing *Schutztruppe* once they had gained the position. During the Latema-Reata action, the 2nd Division suffered 270 killed and wounded. German losses were 40 killed and 67 wounded.

Meanwhile, the 4th SA Horse and 12th SA Infantry of van Deventer's column, marching from Lake Chala to Neu Moshi, made contact with the *Schutztruppe* on the Taveta–Neu Moshi road, driving them back with heavy losses. The Germans destroyed the bridges along the road as they retired, but despite these obstacles, van Deventer's column occupied Neu Moshi on the 13th and the next day joined hands with Stewart's 1st Division.

Von Lettow-Vorbeck established a defensive line in the thick forest belt along the Ruwa River, covering the railway extension. His artillery now included two 105-mm guns from the *Königsberg*, which had a range of 14,000 yards (12,800 meters). One of these guns was mounted on a railway truck, while the second was positioned south of the river.

As this phase of operations ended, Major-General Tighe, at Smuts's instigation, received orders to return to India as soon as he could be released, while Major-General Stewart, following a heated row with Smuts over his handling of the 1st Division's advance from Longido, resigned. Both Stewart and Malleson returned to India in disgrace, wrongly in Stewart's case as Smuts tried to blame him for von Lettow-Vorbeck's escape to Kahe, when in fact this withdrawal was the result of van Deventer's march to and occupation of Neu Moshi, in line with Smuts's orders and the unrealistic timetable he had to try and meet. Smuts appointed Brigadier-General SH Sheppard, DSO, to the temporary command of the 1st Division.

Having reorganized his command structure, Smuts planned to drive the Germans across the Pangani River before the rains came. The advance on Kahe was ordered to resume on the 18th, following the repair of the road and bridges destroyed by the Germans as they retreated. Van Deventer's column was to make a wide flank march from Neu Moshi to Kahe, while the 1st Division pushed down the Moshi road,

German signal station and askaris of the East African *Schutztruppe* (Topical Press).

and the 2nd Division advanced on Kahe from Taveta. Over the following days Smuts's troops pushed the *Schutztruppe* steadily back, maintaining constant contact with them.

By the 20th, Sheppard, with his mounted troops and 2nd EA Brigade, were camped at Store, four miles (six and a half kilometers) south of Masai Kraal. That afternoon von Lettow-Vorbeck arrived in front of Store. But he did not know the strength of the British or their intentions. "It was quite possible that the enemy was merely making a demonstration in order to attack at some other, more dangerous, spot. Such a manoeuvre would have been very menacing to us, as the close nature of the bush country would prevent us from detecting it until very late, probably too late. I decided to drive the enemy's screen back on his position proper."[4]

That night at 9:30 p.m., a German force 1,000 strong attacked Sheppard's outposts, forcing them back on to 2nd EA Brigade's entrenchments where the 29th Punjabis and 129th Baluchis were in the process of carrying out a relief of the trenches. As the *Schutztruppe* stormed towards the camp, they came under a heavy rifle and machine-gun fire which broke their attack and forced them to withdraw. They quickly rallied, however, and made a further four attacks, which went on until midnight when, having suffered heavy casualties, they broke contact and withdrew. "Leaving patrols out, I withdrew step by step. Our casualties were not inconsiderable, and unfortunately included three company commanders, who were difficult to replace; of the three, Lieutenant von Stosch and Freiherr Grote died of their wounds a few days later, while Captain Augar only became fit for duty again after a long time and when provided with an artificial foot."[5]

Meanwhile, van Deventer's 1st SA Mounted Brigade, reinforced by the 4th SA Horse and field artillery, advanced from Neu Moshi at 2 p.m. on the 20th. Marching through the afternoon and night, they were closing on the Pangani River from the west at daybreak, southwest of Kahe. After a difficult crossing of the Pangani, they took Kahe railway station followed by Bauman and Kahe Hills to the south. Van Deventer then dispatched a mounted section to block the wagon road running from the Ruwa, cutting the Germans' line of retreat. They were unable to achieve their objective, however, as they came under attack from a strong force of *Schutztruppe* (the 9th and 24th Field Companies commanded by Captain Ernst Otto), which drove them off. At the same time, the main body came under fire from one of the Königsberg guns.

As soon as Smuts learned that van Deventer was approaching Kahe, he ordered Sheppard to resume his advance. At 11:30 a.m., Sheppard's brigades marched, 2nd SA Brigade on the right of the Masai Kraal—Kahe road, and 2nd EA Brigade on the left, the road forming the brigades' boundary. At the same time, 3rd SA Brigade pushed down from Euphorbein Hill, intending to operate in conjunction with the 1st Division.

Sheppard planned to envelope the *Schutztruppe's* eastern flank, but the 3rd SA Brigade was hampered by the dense bush country and did not arrive in time to assist his attack. Sheppard drove the Germans back to their main positions, where their flanks were protected on the right by the Soko Nassai River and the left by the Defu River, while to their front was a clear killing ground varying in depth from 600 yards (549 meters) to 1,200 yards (1,097 meters). Here the *Schutztruppe* put up a determined defense.

The British tried several times to cross the clear ground, but on each occasion, they were stopped and driven back by heavy rifle and machine-gun fire. Two double-companies of the 130th Baluchis crossed the Soko Nassai in an attempt to turn the German right flank, but they were brought to a stand by the heavy gunfire, and dug-in. The

27th Mountain Battery was brought into action at the edge of the clear ground but was unable to locate specific targets in the dense bush. The duel across the clearing raged until nightfall when Sheppard, unaware that van Deventer had occupied Kahe station, ordered his troops to dig-in for the night, intending to resume his attack the next day.

At dawn the next morning, the 22nd, Sheppard discovered that the Germans had abandoned their positions during the night and had slipped across the Ruwa, avoiding Kahe, where the South African Horse had been busy looting the station and town, and retired along the main road to Lembeni after destroying their stationary *Königsberg* gun as it was too cumbersome to drag away quickly. During the attack on the Ruwa River position, Sheppard's division had suffered 288 killed and wounded, and it was clear that the Germans had suffered heavy casualties. The 1st Division then marched into Kahe where all they found was the destroyed 105-mm gun.

Though Smuts had cleared British territory of German forces and had occupied the Kilimanjaro area, he had failed to bring the *Schutztruppe* to a general action or to decisively defeat them. Von Lettow-Vorbeck had skillfully carried out a fighting withdrawal in which his troops had inflicted severe losses on the British troops. He continually avoided a full-scale battle, and as a consequence, the British authorities were compelled to dispatch more troops to East Africa. By now General Smuts had become obsessed with the idea of cornering, attacking and annihilating von Lettow-Vorbeck, so much so that his chief of intelligence prophetically recorded, "He is irresistibly drawn towards von Lettow, and if he persists he will lose the initiative and the campaign will end simply in following von Lettow about wherever he may choose to wander."[6]

It was about this time that von Lettow-Vorbeck received news, via a second blockade runner, that the Kaiser, having heard of the exploits of his troops, had awarded him the Iron Crosses 1st and 2nd Class. The blockade runner was the *Marie*, which had slipped through the British blockade and anchored in Sudi Bay just to the north of the Rovuma River, where she put ashore a detachment of artillery specialists and her cargo of four 10.5-cm howitzers, two 7.5-cm mountain guns, ammunition for these guns and for von Lettow-Vorbeck's Königsberg guns, small arms ammunition, medical supplies and other stores needed by the *Schutztruppe*. She also carried dispatches for von Lettow-Vorbeck, including the notification of his awards of the Iron Cross. Once these stores had been unloaded, they were taken to secret supply dumps on the Makonde Plateau in the south of German East Africa. Having unloaded her cargo, *Marie* set sail. She once again successfully evaded the British warships and escaped.

Nine. The Battle of Kilimanjaro

Following the occupation of Kahe, Smuts detached a small mounted column from Neu Moshi to take Arusha on the southern slopes of Mount Meru. This column forced the German garrison out of its position, and it withdrew to the south, leaving the Meru area clear of the enemy with the coming of the rainy season. Having established his HQ at Neu Moshi and ensured that his troops had found reasonably dry, healthy quarters, Smuts reorganized his command, forming them into three divisions.

The 1st Division was to be made up of British, East African and Indian formations and was to be commanded by Major-General AR Hoskins, CMG, DSO. The 2nd and 3rd Divisions were to be entirely South African and commanded by Major-Generals Dirk van Deventer and Coen Brits, respectively.[7] Further reinforcements had also become available from West Africa, following the successful conclusion of operations in the Cameroons, the Gold Coast Regiment, 2nd West India Regiment, 5th Indian Light Infantry and Gold Coast Mountain Battery being the first units transferred from the west to British East. The 5th Indian Light Infantry had deployed to West Africa in early July 1915 under a cloud of suspicion as to its loyalty and reliability, having been sent from Singapore following a mutiny by four of its eight companies. The mutineers murdered 40 British, Indian and Malay soldiers and civilians before the mutiny was put down with the assistance of the State Forces of the Sultan of Jahore and sailors and marines from Russian, Japanese and French warships at that time in Singapore. Two hundred and thirty-one mutineers were court-martialed, 47 were subsequently executed and 184 imprisoned. Following the courts-martial, the under-strength regiment was initially sent to West Africa. Following his reorganization, and as the rains began to fall and the rivers swell until they overflowed their banks, General Smuts and his staff planned the next stage of operations.

TEN

Portugal Enters the War and the Allied Offensive Begins

ON MARCH 9, 1916, the German Imperial government declared war on Portugal, and the Portuguese government began immediate preparations to send an expeditionary force, commanded by Major-General Jose Cesar Ferreira Gil, to their East African colony (Mozambique) on German East's southern frontier. This was the third and largest force dispatched to Portuguese East Africa; the previous two had been sent as a precautionary measure before the German declaration of war. The first, consisting of 1,527 men of the 3rd Battalion, Infantry Regiment 15 (Tomar), 4th Squadron, 10th Cavalry, a mountain battery and supporting units under the command of Lieutenant-Colonel Massano de Amorim, had sailed from Portugal on November 1, 1914. The second force 1,543 strong had followed a year later, in November 1915, and consisted of 3rd Battalion, Infantry Regiment 21 (Penmacor), 4th Squadron, 3rd Cavalry and 2nd Battery, Artillery Group 7, under the command of Major Moura Mendes. Portugal had been in political turmoil since 1910 when King Manuel had been deposed and a republic proclaimed. When the war in Europe began, the Portuguese government was determined to become involved, fearing that its interests would be compromised if they failed to meet their treaty obligations to their old ally, Great Britain. They were also keen to ensure the preservation of their African colonies and announced that they would defend their borders against any German incursions.

Britain, however, made it clear to the Portuguese that it wanted them to neither declare their neutrality nor to declare war but to remain in quasi-neutrality. The political unrest in Portugal continued throughout 1915, and in May that year the government of General Joaquim Pimenta de Castro was violently overthrown, to be replaced by the democrat administration of Afonso da Costa.

Following Germany's declaration of war and the dispatch of General

Ten. Portugal Enters the War and the Offensive Begins 97

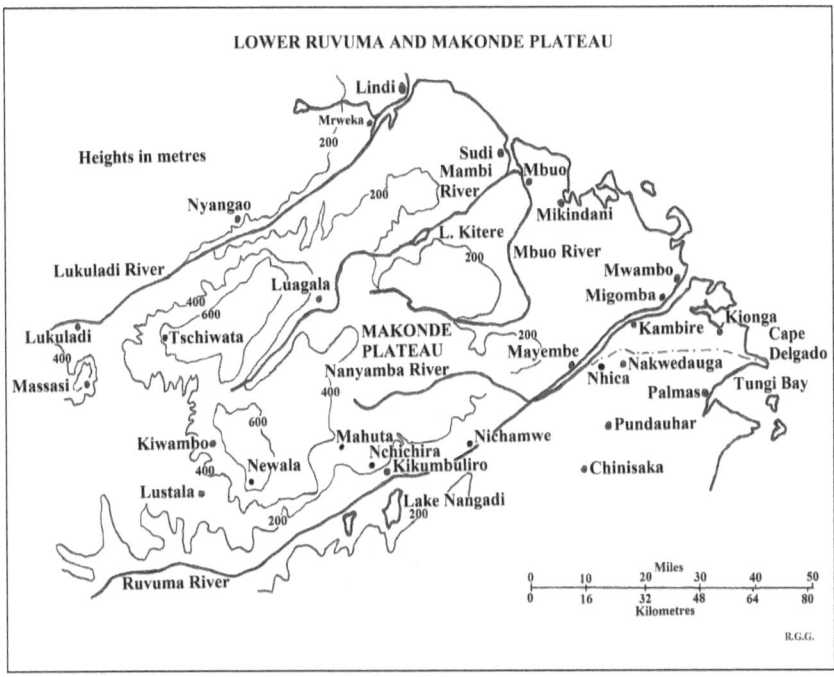

Gil and his command, the da Costa government announced its war aims in Portuguese East Africa. The Portuguese forces were to take the disputed Kionga triangle, an area of 215 square miles (557 square kilometers) on the southern shore of the Rovuma Delta, running from Kionga, south to Cape Delgado, then west to Nhica on the southern bank of the river. The ownership of the triangle had been in dispute with the Germans since they seized it in 1894, and it was now to be reoccupied.

On this frontier Major da Silveira, the senior Portuguese officer in the north of the colony, crossed into the disputed territory on April 6 and occupied the settlement of Kionga just south of the mouth of the Rovuma. Then on the 10th he advanced to and secured the southern bank of the river; shortly after, the *Schutztruppe* began retaliatory nuisance raids across the Rovuma. Da Silveira decided to eliminate this nuisance; he would cross the river and drive off or destroy the Germans.

At the end of May, supported by the cruiser *Adamstor* and the gunboat *Chaimite*, he landed at Mivambo on the northern tip of the river mouth with 400 men. But the Portuguese commander was walking into an ambush. Sub-Lieutenant Leonhard Sprockhoff of the *Königsberg*, with 100 askaris and two machine guns, was in the tree line watching the landing. As the Portuguese began walking up the beach, Sprockhoff's men held their fire until they were almost on top of them, then opened a devastating fusillade. De Silveira and 33 of his men were instantly killed, and a further 24 were wounded. Only eight were captured, including the captain of the *Chaimite*. The remainder of the (now completely demoralized) force was withdrawn to the south of the river, where they went into camp on the swampy south bank of the Rovuma. Here they were decimated by the lack of adequate supplies and the debilitating heat, fever and disease. "The exhausting life on the swampy bank of the Rovuma, with the deleterious effect of an unforgiving climate, the nervous depression caused by the proximity of the enemy, without the compensation of good and regular food drained the strength of almost all the troops, who were reduced to the most abject physical state. By night, in the trenches and posts and lookouts, there was the humidity, the haze of the rainy season, and the cold; by day, shaking with fever, unable to rest because of the searing heat in the tents, everywhere became a veritable hell."[1]

When Gil arrived in Portuguese East Africa, he immediately moved his expeditionary force—numbering 6,985 officers and men and comprising three battalions drawn from Infantry Regiment 23 (Coimbra), Infantry Regiment 24 (Aveiro) and Infantry Regiment 28 (Figueira da Foz), the 1st, 2nd and 4th Mountain Batteries and three field batteries from Artillery Groups 4, 5 and 8—north to secure the frontier, but because of sickness and the poor quality of his troops, he was for the time being unable to undertake any offensive operations. He did, however, cross the Rovuma and occupy the positions along the northern bank of the river, achieving what da Silveira had failed to do with such devastating consequences.

At Neu Moshi, meanwhile, General Smuts had planned a two-pronged attack from Kilimanjaro: one against the Usambara Railway, the other against the Central Railway via Kondoa-Irangi. Simultaneous attacks were to be made by Brigadier-General Northey's Rhodesia-Nyasaland Field Force in the south and by Major-General Tombeur's Belgians in the northwest.

Expectations among the senior officers and staffs were that the offensive would begin at the end of the rains. But Smuts, wrongly as it turned out, was convinced by a local Afrikaner farmer that the worst of the rains would fall in the Kilimanjaro area and that further south and west it would not have much adverse effect on the land. Smuts decided to hold the 1st and 3rd Divisions along the Ruwa River until the end of the wet season but ordered the 2nd south to Kondoa-Irangi and the Central Railway.

Van Deventer concentrated his division at Arusha at the end of March; he had 1,200 mounted troops of Brigadier-General Manie

Ten. Portugal Enters the War and the Offensive Begins 99

Botha's 1st SA Mounted Brigade and 4,088 infantry of Brigadier-General CAL Berrange's 3rd SA Infantry Brigade. Leaving the 10th SA Infantry in garrison, they marched from Arusha on April 4, 1916. The mounted troops pushed ahead to lead the division across the Masai Steppes, driving in the *Schutztruppe* rearguard—the 28th Field Company—in a series of running skirmishes to their stronghold on Lol Kissale Hill, 35 miles (56 kilometers) south of Arusha. The South Africans surrounded the hill, then dismounted and began closing on the German position. After a stiff resistance, the German commander, Captain Paul Rothert, having been seriously wounded, surrendered. The South Africans took 17 Germans and 400 askaris prisoner along with two machine guns. "On this occasion," wrote von Lettow-Vorbeck, "some of the Askari gave evidence of sound military education by refusing to join in the surrender. They, together with the wounded, rejoined our forces near Ufiome, without being interfered with by the enemy."[2]

The road to Kondoa-Irangi was open. Everything appeared to be going relatively smoothly for the South Africans; then, in the evenings the horses of the mounted brigade began to die. They were deep in tsetse fly country. By the 6th the mounted brigade had lost 50 horses. Seven days later they could only mount 800 men. Regardless of this, the brigade struggled southwards through heavy, driving rain and thick clogging mud. They drove the *Schutztruppe* from Ufiome and Umbulu and by the 16th were within seven miles (11 kilometers) of Kondoa-Irangi but had only 650 men mounted. These 650 entered the settlement on April 19 to find it had been abandoned by the Germans and was, in places, on fire. The *Schutztruppe* had destroyed what they could not carry off. The 1st SA Mounted Brigade, with now less than 600 men fit for duty and all their horses exhausted and ill, was at last, however, immobilized.

The rest of the following division was in an equally deteriorating condition. The soldiers were dropping in their hundreds from dysentery and malaria; their transport mules had begun to die in ever increasing numbers, and the divisional artillery had to be manhandled through the deep, thick, clinging mud. They finally joined up with the mounted brigade at Kondoa-Irangi on April 30. Of the 8,600 infantry, artillery and divisional troops that had marched from Arusha, less than 2,500 reached the settlement. "Our capture of Kondoa took the Germans by surprise. They never suspected that we could move so quickly over bad roads in the rains. Neither did they credit Smuts with so bold a move. I doubt whether any British general with British troops could have planned and carried out the move in tropical Africa during the rains. Only South Africans born and bred to long distances and living on the country could have accomplished it. The immediate situation is that von

Lettow has about 3,000 rifles not thirty miles from here and probably more on their way from around the Usambara (Northern) Railway."³

Though the 2nd Division's march had taken the Germans by surprise, von Lettow-Vorbeck immediately began moving troops into the foothills around the town. By May 9 he had concentrated 4,000 men around Kondoa-Irangi: the 9th, 14th and 24th Field Companies under Captain Otto; 15th and 19th Field Companies under Lieutenant-Colonel von Bock; and 18th, 22nd and 27th Field Companies under Captain Friedrich von Kornatzki, along with two 105-mm *Königsberg* guns.

Von Lettow-Vorbeck planned to attack the South Africans early on the 10th, but during the night of the 9th/10th, his forward companies, while probing the enemy's defenses, found that they were easily penetrated. Von Bock, leading these troops, was shot and killed early on; Captain Kornatzki absorbed Bock's two companies into his command and then began pushing his men towards the town. As they pressed their unplanned attack, they were met by two understrength South African battalions, the 11th and 12th, that were changing guard when the assault commenced, and an intense firefight began, which continued through the night. Both sides mounted bayonet attacks of considerable savagery. During one of these hand-to-hand encounters, Captain Kornatzki was overpowered and killed by Captain Meinertzhagen, who disarmed him of a knobkerrie and beat him to death with it. Meinertzhagen carried this knobkerrie with him for the rest of the war. At 3 a.m., the Germans broke contact and withdrew, having lost 50 killed. Of the incident, Meinertzhagen wrote, "All credit to old van Deventer and his South Africans. It is the first real knock von Lettow has had. My God, I should have liked to have caught old von Lettow instead of poor Kornatzky [sic]."⁴

Von Lettow-Vorbeck cancelled his planned attack and withdrew to a defensive position, and both sides began patrolling activities, which lasted until late June. The 2nd Division's mobility was greatly curtailed as they were unable to obtain remounts, and the horses they still had continued to die. Reinforcements were pushed down to the division, and soon the 7th, 8th and 10th Battalions, SA Infantry, 28th Mountain and 10th Heavy Batteries, RA, along with a company of the SA Motor Cycle Corps had reached them.

With van Deventer holding out at Kondoa-Irangi, Smuts, at the end of the rainy season, which had been the worst on record, was preparing to clear the Germans from the Para and Usambara mountain ranges. He formed three mobile-columns from the 1st and 3rd Divisions: a river column, Brigadier-General Sheppard's 1st EA Brigade, which was to push down the left bank of the Pangani River; a center

Ten. Portugal Enters the War and the Offensive Begins 101

column, Brigadier-General JA Hannyngton's 2nd EA Brigade, which was to advance along the Tanga railway; and an eastern column, Lieutenant-Colonel TO Fitzgerald's (Royal Lancaster Regt) 3rd KAR, which was to advance along the eastern edge of the Pare Mountains. In reserve was Brigadier-General Percival Beves's 2nd SA Brigade (less two battalions sent to reinforce van Deventer). The 2nd SA Mounted Brigade, commanded by Brigadier-General Barend Enslin, was retained at Neu Moshi, as they were not considered ready for operational duties. Opposing this advance was Major Georg Kraut with only 2,000 men; he had earlier in May sent part of his command to assist von Lettow-Vorbeck's attacks against van Deventer at Kondoa-Irangi.

Smuts's columns began their advance in the middle of May, meeting only light opposition. Kraut, realizing his position in front of the center column was in danger of being outflanked by the river and eastern columns, discreetly withdrew to Buiko. The British columns, meanwhile, were placed on half rations when their logistical support broke down, and fever began taking a heavy toll on the fighting troops.

Hannyngton's brigade, with orders to clear Usambara, turned east through a pass running between the central and southern Pare Mountains, 40 miles (65 kilometers) south of Kahe, to link up with 3rd KAR. Sheppard, followed by Beves's reserve, continued steadily on down the Pangani. On May 29, 1st EA Brigade made contact with Kraut's force in a heavily defended position at Mikocheni near Buiko. The 2nd Rhodesia Regiment began a holding attack against the enemy's front, while the 130th Baluchis, supported by 27th Mountain Battery, attempted to turn their left flank. As soon as night fell, and having delayed the British advance for 12 hours, Kraut withdrew to Handeni before the flank attack could begin.

Buiko was occupied by Sheppard's brigade on the 31st, where it was ordered to halt by Smuts while the railway and roads were repaired. The bridges destroyed by Kraut's troops were rebuilt by the men of the 25th (Railway), 26th (Railway) and 28th (Faridkot) Companies, Sappers and Miners, while the men of the 61st Pioneers repaired the dirt roads so that vital supplies and equipment could be brought forward to the fighting troops, who had completely outstripped their lines of communication.

Smuts paid a flying visit to van Deventer at Kondoa-Irangi at this time to tell him of his intention to advance on Handeni and attempt to cut off Kraut from the *Schutztruppe* main body. Following the capture of Handeni, van Deventer was to advance, in conjunction with the 1st and 3rd Divisions, to Morogoro and the Central Railway and to try and trap von Lettow-Vorbeck and force him to give battle. Von Lettow-Vorbeck,

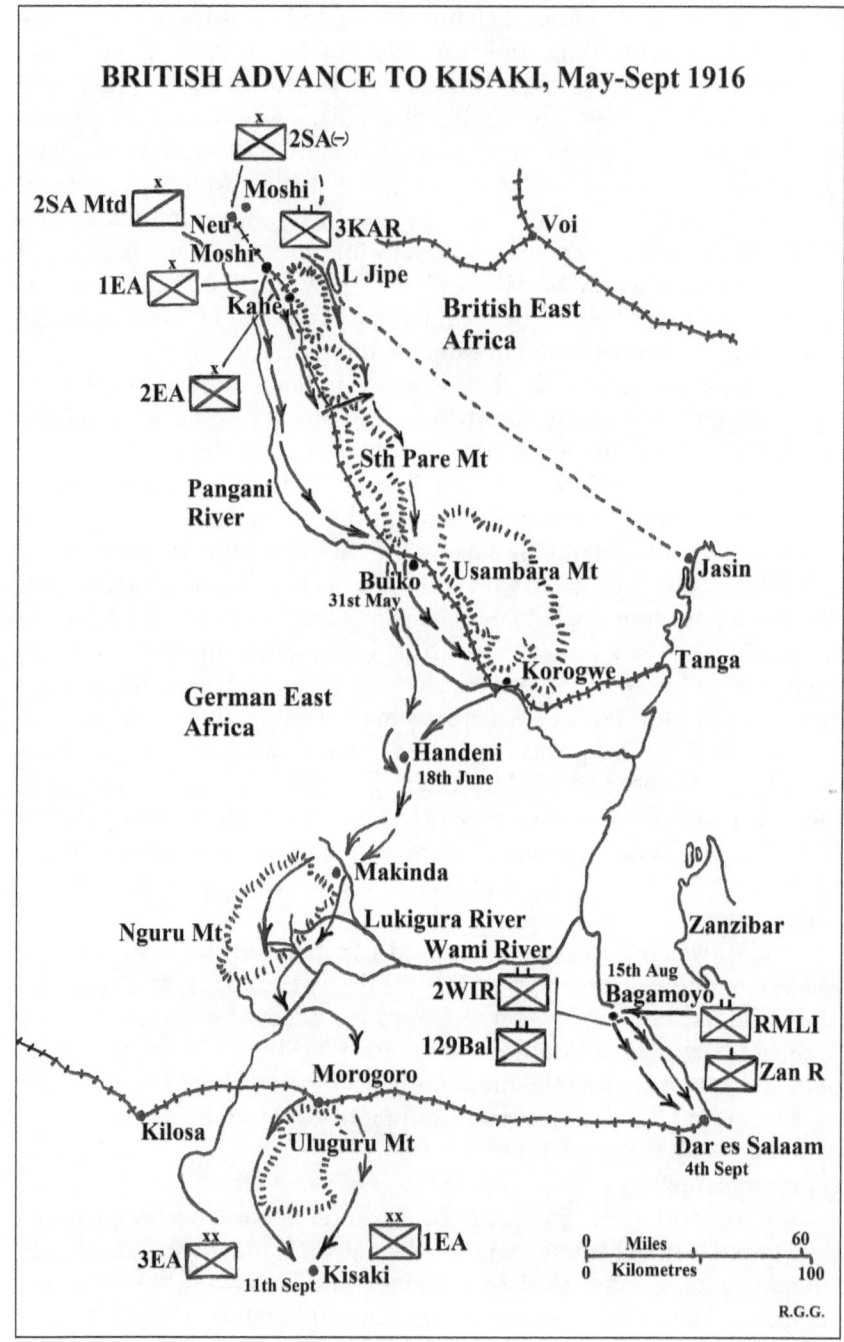

British advance to Kisaki, May–September 1916 (map by the author).

however, was not about to be forced into an action he could not possibly win: "The enemy expected us to stand and fight a final decisive engagement near Morogoro. To me, this idea was never altogether intelligible. Being so very much the weaker party, it was surely madness to await at this place the junction of the hostile columns, of which each one individually was already superior to us in numbers, and then fight with our backs to the steep and rocky mountains."[5]

Arriving back at Buiko on June 7, Smuts ordered the advance on Handeni to begin, having detached Hannyngton's brigade to take Korogwe on the Tanga-Neu Moshi Railway. Hannyngton took Wilhelmstal (now Lushoto) on the 12th and then pushed on to Mombo, which was found to be full of German women and children. These had been left behind by the retreating *Schutztruppe*, who were confident that they would be fed and protected by the British. The brigade then advanced on Korogwe, taking it on the 15th following a spectacular attack on the Zuganatto Bridge by 3rd KAR.

To take Korogwe and then rejoin 1st Division at Handeni, Hannyngton had to find and capture a road or railway bridge over the swollen Pangani River, as the railway bridge at Korogwe had been destroyed by the *Schutztruppe* rearguard under Lieutenant Franz Kempner. Patrols of the KAR Mounted Infantry reported that the bridge at Zuganatto was still intact, so Hannyngton ordered Lieutenant-Colonel Fitzgerald's 3rd KAR to take it. As they marched towards Zuganatto, Fitzgerald's scouts located a crude native footbridge made from tree trunks and rope spanning the Pangani at Mauri, 15 miles (24 kilometers) east of Korogwe.

With the discovery of this crude little bridge, Fitzgerald decided to get his battalion across the river and mount a surprise attack against the Zuganatto Bridge defenses from the rear. He had his men make their way over the footbridge with all their supplies and equipment during the night of the 13th/14th. But as dawn approached, only "A" Company and half of "D" Company had crossed to the south bank of the river. With time at a premium, Fitzgerald could not afford to wait for the remaining companies to cross. He ordered the battalion to carry on along the north bank of the river to the bridge, while he would push on to Zuganatto with those men that had already crossed the river.

At 6 a.m., Fitzgerald's scouts made contact with a small enemy patrol a mile (one and a half kilometers) west of Zuganatto, which was quickly driven off. Shortly after, they came under rifle and machine-gun fire from the German entrenchments protecting the approaches, losing one killed and seven wounded. They continued to advance, taking a small hill 400 yards (366 meters) from the river which overlooked the bridge and the enemy's trenches on the south side of the river.

Soldiers of the King's African Rifles, German East Africa (Her Majesty's Stationery Office, UK Ministry of Information, First World War collection/ Q15409).

From here they opened a heavy return fire, driving the Germans out of these positions. Then at 7 a.m., the advance company of the battalion, approaching from Mauri, closed on the bridge's northern defenses. The *Schutztruppe* abandoned their trenches, crossed to the south and withdrew to Korogwe, leaving the Zuganatto Bridge primed for destruction but untouched. With the capture of the bridge by 3rd KAR, the brigade was able to cross the Pangani and take Korogwe. "This success on which 3rd KAR was warmly congratulated was a good example of the speed and skill with which, under resolute leadership, the African troops were able to work in the bush by night."[6]

Meanwhile Smuts's main force closed on Handeni in contact with Kraut's rearguard (the 1st, 3rd and 16th Field Companies and a detachment of the 5th Field Company) commanded by Captain Robert Döring, which would ambush them, break contact and ambush them again as they conducted their fighting withdrawal. As they neared the Pangani River, a reconnaissance flight from No. 26 Squadron, RFC, reported that the Germans had established a strong defensive position just to the west of the Mkalamo Bridge. The 130th Baluchis were leading the brigade advance, supported by the 29th Punjabis from divisional reserve, a company of the 61st Pioneers and a section of 27th Mountain Battery.

At 11:30 a.m., on June 9, as this column was approaching Mkalamo, they came under German artillery fire. The column commander, Lieutenant-Colonel PH Dyke (Indian Army), led his troops into the bush away from the river to give them cover as they closed on the German position. At 1 p.m., the leading companies of the 130th made contact with the 3rd Field Company, who opened a heavy fire from their trenches. Döring launched a counterattack with the 1st and 16th Field Companies, which was driven back by the Baluchis. With the Baluchis engaged in a savage close-quarter fight with the *Schutztruppe*, Dyke deployed the 29th Punjabis, less one company which he held in reserve, round to the right and left of the 130th to try and get around the enemy's defenses. But the German commander extended his flanks, and the Punjabis flanking companies became engaged in a fierce firefight.

Meanwhile, the main body of the brigade, which had been following two and a half miles (four kilometers) behind Dyke's column, arrived. General Sheppard took over command and had a company of the Kashmir Rifles[7] sent to the left to reinforce the three companies of the 29th fighting there. Shortly after joining the 29th, they helped repulse a fierce counterattack mounted by the 3rd Field Company. As nightfall approached, the *Schutztruppe* broke contact, and General Sheppard ordered his troops to dig-in. During the night, Captain Döring withdrew his force to Handeni. British losses in the action were 17 killed and 34 wounded, while German casualties were about 30 killed, wounded and missing.

On June 18, 1st EA Brigade occupied Handeni, having met only light opposition as it advanced from Mkalamo, followed by Nderema the next day. Kraut had, however, fallen back to the Lukigura River, where he set about preparing a defensive position near Makinda.

As Smuts advanced towards Morogoro, aircraft from No. 26 Squadron discovered and reported the location of the Germans' Lukigura River position. In the hope of forcing Kraut to stand and fight, a flying column was formed from the 25th Fusiliers, 2nd Kashmir Rifles, 5th and 6th SA Infantry and Loyals MG Company under Major-General AR Hoskins, with orders to march round the enemy's flank. (The infantry battalions could only muster between 170 to 200 rifles each due to sickness.) Smuts planned to hold the Germans with the 1st Division while Hoskins mounted a general assault once he was in position.

Hoskin's column began its flank march on the night of June 23–24, crossing the Lukigura and taking up positions straddling the road behind the Germans. The 1st Division then opened its holding attack, pinning the *Schutztruppe* on their front, the heaviest fire being laid down by the armored cars of 1st Armoured Car Battery. At midday the infantry of the 1st Division and the flying column launched a simultaneous

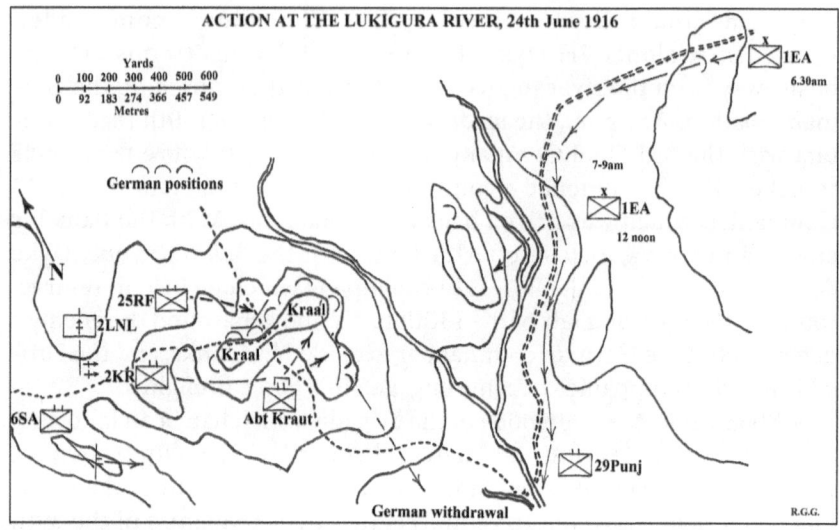

Action at the Lukigura (based on an official sketch map from HMSO/Historical Section Military Branch, 1918).

bayonet attack, advancing on the Germans from three different directions. Kraut's troops were heavily defeated, and those that could escape fled into the thick bush. Smuts halted his advance following the capture of the Makinda position to reorganize his troops and sort out his lines of communication. A large camp was established on the Msiha River, eight miles (13 kilometers) beyond the Lukigura, and here he sat throughout July.

Meanwhile, von Lettow-Vorbeck, having left a small force to oppose the 2nd Division at Kondoa-Irangi, marched his main body to Dodoma, where they were entrained and taken to Morogoro, and then marched north to the Lukiguru area to support Kraut. As soon as they arrived, he deployed his troops, and the 105-mm *Königsberg* gun with his force opened a harassing fire on the British camp. On July 26, the first of the reinforcements from West Africa, the Gold Coast Regiment, reached Mombasa and by August 12 had joined the 1st Division as divisional reserve.

At Kondoa-Irangi, General van Deventer resumed his advance on July 24, sweeping the small German covering force from their positions with an all-out bayonet attack of overwhelming superiority. He then split his division into four columns for the advance on the Central Railway; 1st SA Mounted Brigade marched to the southeast and 3rd SA Infantry Brigade due south, while two smaller units covered the right flank. Throughout their advance, the *Schutztruppe* covering force withdrew

Ten. Portugal Enters the War and the Offensive Begins 107

Pioneers building a river bridge, German East Africa (possibly the Gold Coast Pioneer Company) (Her Majesty's Stationery Office).

in front of them with their usual skill and excellent bushcraft. On the 29th Dodoma was occupied by the SA Motorcycle Company, and van Deventer now controlled a 100-mile (160-kilometer) stretch of the Central Railway, from Kilimatinde to Dodoma. The 2nd Division was then concentrated at Dodoma preparatory to march eastwards to link up with Smuts's main body. While assembling at Dodoma, the commander of 1st South African Mounted Brigade, Brigadier-General Manie Botha, resigned his command, citing personal commitments, and returned to South Africa. Van Deventer's Chief of Staff, Brigadier-General AHM Nussey, DSO, took over command of the brigade.

On the German East African-Belgian Congo frontier in the northwest, Major-General Charles Tombeur had formed five *regiments de marche* into two *Groupes Mobile* (brigades) numbering 15,000 men ready for offensive operations. He moved his HQ from Kibati, north of Lake Kivu, to Bukakata on Lake Victoria Nyanza in preparation for his advance into German territory. He was joined here by Brigadier-General Sir Charles Crewe, sent by Smuts to act as a Liaison Officer between the Belgians and British East Africa Command.

In April 1916, *Group Mobile nord—3e* and *4e Régiments de Marche*—commanded by Colonel Philippe Molitor, advanced from the north of Lake Kivu towards the capitol of Ruanda province, Kigali, which was taken on May 6 without opposition, the German military commander in Ruanda, Captain Max Wintgens, offering only a token resistance to the Belgians. From Kigali, Molitor marched to the southern shore of Lake Victoria Nyanza, taking Biharamuli, Diobahila and St. Michael after short skirmishes with the Germans, while Tombeur's second brigade, *Group Mobile sud—1er* and *2e Régiments de Marche* and *6e Bataillon de Marche*—commanded by Colonel FV Olsen, began advancing into German territory from the south of Lake Kivu.

On Victoria Nyanza a British force commanded by Lieutenant-Colonel DR Adye, supported by Commander Thornley and his lake flotilla, took the large island of Ukerwe, which was to be used as a base for an attack on the German post at Mwanza. Meanwhile, Major-General Wahle with 5,000 men had established his HQ at Tabora, from where he prepared to fight a delaying action against the Anglo-Belgian forces before withdrawing southeast to join up with von Lettow-Vorbeck.

But instead of taking Mwanza, Tombeur, having been ordered to keep his command independent of the British, advanced towards Kigoma on the eastern shore of Lake Tanganyika. Crewe, who had mustered the lake forces—2,000 officers and men drawn from the 4th KAR, 17th Indian and 98th Hyderabad Infantry, Baganda Rifles and the Nandi Scouts—into a single unit under his command in June to fight alongside the Belgians, decided he would operate independently of Tombeur and take Mwanza. He formed his troops into two columns under the commands of Lieutenant-Colonels CR Burgess and HB Towse. As these columns closed on Mwanza, the Germans withdrew, the town falling to the British on July 14.

At the end of the month Olsen's *1er* and *2e Régiments de Marche* of

Ten. Portugal Enters the War and the Offensive Begins

Group Mobile sud took Kigoma then Ujiji before pushing east along the Central Railway and taking Neu Gottorp (modern Uvinza) and advancing towards Tabora, while further south his detached *6e Bataillon* had taken Karema, then begun marching northeast to rendezvous with him at Tabora. Further east Crewe's Lake Force had marched from Mwanza, and it too was closing rapidly on Tabora, while Molitor's *Group Mobile nord* had begun marching south from St. Michael.

As the Belgian brigades closed on Tabora Wahle's troops engaged them. In the savage fight that followed he inflicted a sharp defeat on the Belgians, which stopped their advance long enough for him to break contact and withdraw his forces in three columns towards Neu Iringa and the Mahenge Plateau, taking with him Governor Schnee. Tombeur's troops finally entered Tabora on September 19, where they found 140 German women and children left in the care of the Governor's wife, Frau Ada Schnee, a New Zealander.[8] When Crewe reached the settlement, he turned his troops east and marched along the railway to join up with van Deventer's 2nd Division in late September. Lake Force was then disbanded and its units incorporated into the 2nd Division.

In the southwest Brigadier-General Northey's Rhodesia-Nyasaland Field Force of 3,000 men from the 1st and 2nd SA Rifles, 1st KAR and units of the British South Africa Police and Northern Rhodesia Police (MB) were preparing to advance into German East. Their first objectives were the German frontier forts, which Northey planned to take in a two-pronged advance.

On May 20, Northey dispatched Lieutenant-Colonel Ronald "Kaffir" Murray, DCM—commanding his left—from Abercorn with "A" and "B" Companies of the British South Africa Police and "A," "B," "C" and "D" Companies of the Northern Rhodesia Police (MB), to take the fort at Namema and then push on to Neu Langenburg. Five days later his right wing of three columns would begin their advance. The first under Lieutenant-Colonel George Hawthorne, with two squadrons[9] of 1st SA Rifles and "AR," "CR," "F" and "H" Companies[10] of his 1st KAR, was to take Ipiana fort; while the second under Lieutenant-Colonel TA Rodger with two squadrons of the 2nd SA Rifles and "E" Company of the Northern Rhodesia Police (MB) took Luwiwa; and the third under Major RL Flindt comprising two squadrons of 2nd SA Rifles and "BR" and "D" Companies, 1st KAR took Igamba. The three right-wing columns were to then converge on Neu Langenburg.

Fort Namema, garrisoned by the 29th Field Company, commanded by 1st Lieutenant Gotthold Franken, lay halfway between Abercorn and Bismarckburg; it had been built on high ground with a cleared killing ground 2,000 yards (1,829 meters) wide surrounding it. When Murray's force arrived before Namema on the 28th, his troops quickly encircled the position; his field guns then opened fire on the defenses. The siege went on for five days, until on the night of June 2 the garrison broke out, slipping through the encircling troops in the inky darkness and escaped to Bismarckburg.

Murray, when he realized what had happened, quickly followed up but lost touch with the retreating garrison, and instead of advancing on Neu Langenburg as he was supposed to, once Namema fell, headed for Lake Tanganyika and Bismarckburg. While crossing the deep gorge at the mouth of the Kalambo River, the column came under fire from the German garrison and sustained heavy casualties before clearing the obstacle and closing on the town.

As they neared the town, the garrison abandoned their positions, boarded three dhows and escaped. Murray's troops entered Bismarckburg on the morning of June 9 to find both the town and fort deserted. During the crossing of the Kalambo and subsequent assault on Bismarckburg, Murray was expecting support from Commander Spicer-Simson's lake flotilla, but this was not forthcoming, and the garrison was able to escape.

Meanwhile, on May 25, the remainder of Northey's force had crossed the frontier between Lakes Tanganyika and Nyasa and finding all their primary objectives abandoned had advanced to and taken Neu Langenburg four days later. As soon as the settlement was secured, Northey moved his HQ there before ordering Lieutenant-Colonel Hawthorne to push on and take Neu Iringa with his 1st KAR, less a company, but reinforced by a squadron of the 1st and two squadrons of the 2nd SA Rifles, the KAR Battery, a section of 5th SAMR Battery and 11 machine guns.

The 1st KAR battle group column advanced up the road and across the plateau towards Neu Iringa, picking up abandoned stores and equipment and straggling porters left by the *Schutztruppe* as they retreated. On June 10, while crossing the plateau, they made contact with a force of more than 100 Germans holding a defensive position astride their line of advance. The KAR mounted an immediate attack, quickly overran the position, and carried on their advance to Neu Iringa.

On the 24th, supported by Rodger's column—the detached company of 1st KAR, two squadrons of 2nd SA Rifles, 5th SAMR Battery, less a section (four 75-mm mountain guns), and six machine guns—from Bukhora, they attacked the German rearguard—the 5th and 10th Field Companies, "L" Company and a detachment of 100 officers and men of the *Königsberg* Company, who had elected to fight as infantry with the *Schutztruppe*, a 105-mm *Königsberg* gun and nine machine

Ten. Portugal Enters the War and the Offensive Begins

guns—strongly entrenched on the Malangali ridge around the Pakene rocks, high ground which lay at the eastern end of the ridge. The attack was scheduled to begin at 8 a.m., with Rodger's column attacking from the west and Hawthorne, having marched round the south of the enemy position, attacking from the rear.

Rodger's column began its assault as scheduled, and his companies gained a foothold on the west of the ridge, where they were stopped by heavy fire from the Pakene rocks position. But Hawthorne's march across the rough broken ground on the night of the 23rd/24th had to be halted until dawn, and it was after 11 a.m. before his troops were in position, with a company blocking the Neu Iringa Road.

As soon as his column was in position on their start line, Hawthorne ordered Captain GL Baxter (Cameron Highlanders) to attack the rear of the German position with "CR" Company, 1st KAR and the squadron of the 1st SA Rifles. As they advanced towards the Pakene rocks, the Germans launched a counterattack. Baxter's companies repulsed this attack but were unable to continue their assault as they were pinned down by heavy fire from machine guns and a 105-mm *Königsberg* gun. The two guns of the 5th SA Battery opened fire on the *Königsberg* gun, which quickly returned fire, knocking out both South African guns and killing or wounding their crews.

Before the British attack began, the German rearguard commander, Captain Friedrich Braunschweig, had withdrawn the *Königsberg* Company, which was marching along the road to the northeast. But on hearing firing from their rear, they halted and turned around, marching rapidly towards the gunfire, and attacked "AR" Company of 1st KAR, blocking the road. But coming under heavy rifle and machine-gun fire from this company, and "H" Company on its flank, the attack was repulsed. Shortly afterwards Major Flindt brought forward his squadrons of the 2nd SA Rifles to reinforce the road block.

At 5 p.m., Rodger, still holding on the west of the Malangali ridge, noticed a slackening in the enemy fire. He ordered Captain AC Masters (South Wales Borderers) to advance across the open ground with his "BR" Company of 1st KAR to the Pakene rocks. Masters found the position deserted; the *Schutztruppe* had withdrawn, leaving behind the 105-mm *Königsberg* gun, several machine guns and some of their dead. The KAR had only just entered the position when the mountain guns of 5th SA Battery opened fire on the position, forcing them to take cover. This bombardment led Hawthorne, to the east, to conclude that the enemy still held their position, so he ordered his column to dig-in for the night.

Meanwhile, Rodger moved across the ridge with his remaining

companies to join Masters. The next morning patrols from 1st KAR made contact with Rodger in the Pakene rocks. Braunschweig had evaded the British during the previous evening, withdrawing to the northeast during the night. British losses at Malangali were 20 killed and 27 wounded, while German losses were 32 killed, 68 wounded and eight taken prisoner.

Following the action at Malangali Northey, having outstripped his lines of communication, regrouped his force in preparation for a final push on Neu Iringa, now only 70 miles (113 kilometers) to his northeast, Porters brought up ammunition and supplies for the columns and evacuated the wounded, while Captain Masters's company of 1st KAR, with two sections of the KAR Battery and two machine guns, was deployed to Njombe, 43 miles (69 kilometers) to the south, to protect Hawthorne's right flank from the 2nd Field Company, which was active in the Lupembe area, when the advance resumed. On August 4, however, Masters's company was badly mauled in a skirmish at Lupembe, losing seven killed and 29 wounded. General Northey halted his advance and dispatched Hawthorne's 1st KAR column south to deal with this threat before continuing on to Neu Iringa.

Eleven

Into German East

At his Msiha River camp in the Ngura foothills, General Smuts was busily preparing for his push to the Central Railway. Van Deventer, already holding part of the railway, had moved the 2nd Division to Njangalo, ready to advance eastwards to Mpapua and Kilosa where he would join up with Smuts when he arrived with the 1st and 3rd Divisions. It was estimated that von Lettow-Vorbeck had 20 Field Companies covering the British in the Ngura and Kang Mountains. Smuts planned to hold their front with Sheppard's 1st EA Brigade while a brigade of the 3rd Division undertook a flank march to cut off their line of retreat.

On August 5, Enslin's 2nd SA Mounted Brigade marched from the Msiha River camp to begin this flank march, taking Mhonda on the 8th. But Sheppard's holding action failed, and the *Schutztruppe* were able to break contact and withdraw. Hannyngton's 2nd EA Brigade, meanwhile, was held up for three days at Matamondo by the German rearguard while their main body withdrew to Morogoro. Von Lettow-Vorbeck planned to withdraw to the Rufiji Delta where he believed he would be safe from pursuit for some time. As his forces withdrew towards the railway, they destroyed all the bridges to hamper the British advance. Smuts formed flying columns to hunt down the rearguard, while 2nd SA Mounted and 1st EA Brigades took the Wami River, crossing at Dakawa on the 18th after a short action in which they lost 120 men. Von Lettow-Vorbeck wrote, "In the dense bush it was so difficult to obtain a clear idea of the situation that it did not seem possible to achieve a decisive success. Captain Schulz was chary of putting in the one formed company he had left. I approved his intention of falling back to Morogoro at the end of the action, as the general situation made it desirable for me to concentrate my forces."[1]

Meanwhile, van Deventer's 2nd Division had marched from Njangalo on the 9th, reaching the Tshunjo Pass two days later to find it was strongly held by the Germans. The 2nd Division mounted an

THE ALLIED ADVANCE INTO GERMAN EAST AFRICA, 1916

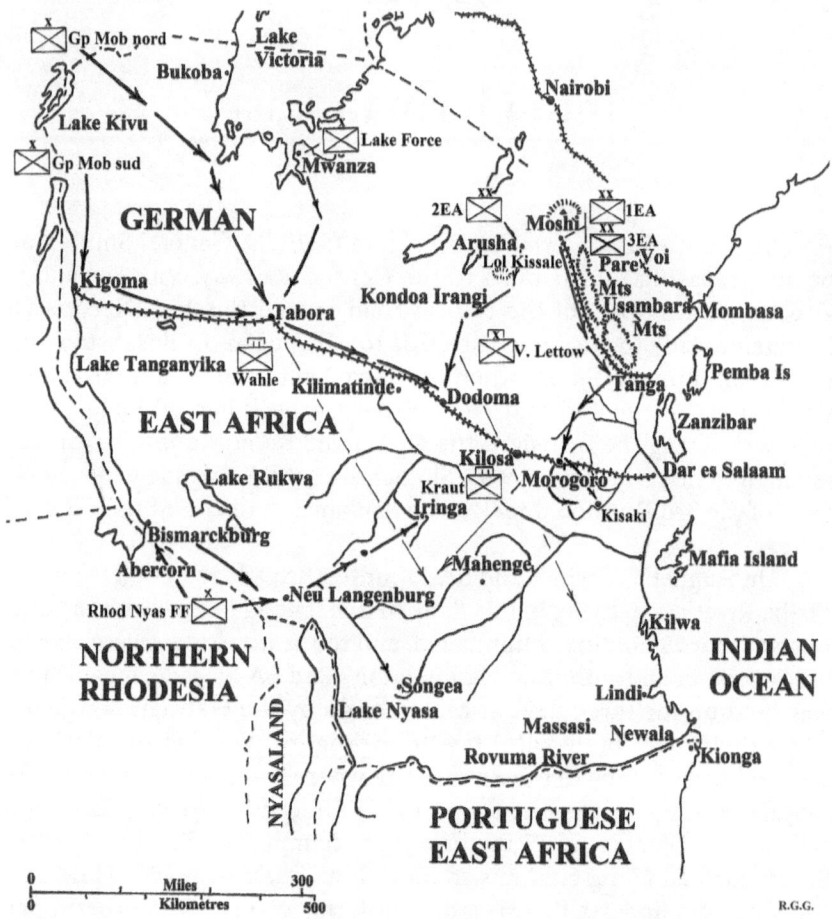

immediate attack in an attempt to force passage but was unsuccessful. The fighting continued throughout the night of the 11th/12th, and as dawn approached, the *Schutztruppe* broke contact, abandoned their positions and withdrew. Van Deventer pursued the retiring enemy until his advance guard ran into well-prepared German defenses near Mpapua, and his main body came under heavy and accurate fire from a 105-mm *Königsberg* gun.

As the 2nd Division deployed, the *Schutztruppe* again broke contact, withdrawing before a general action could develop. They undertook a fighting withdrawal through Kidete to Kilosa, which was tsetse fly country, and virtually all of the 2nd Division's animals became infected

Eleven. Into German East

as they followed in pursuit. Van Deventer took Kilosa on August 22 and here halted his exhausted troops.

Smuts marched from Dakawa on the 23rd, after first dispatching a column to take Ngerengere east of Morogoro. Three days later the 2nd Rhodesia Regiment and two companies of the 130th Baluchis of 1st EA Brigade occupied Morogoro. Smuts then telegraphed van Deventer, ordering him to march south and occupy Kidodi and Kidatu, as it was suspected that enemy forces were at Uleia, 20 miles (32 kilometers) south of the 2nd Division and that these troops had been reinforced by the units withdrawing before Northey's Field Force.

Smuts next planned to envelop the Uluguru Mountains and take Kisaki; his plan called for the 1st Division to push round the east side of the mountains while the 3rd Division moved around the west supported by the 2nd Division. As the 1st Division began its enveloping movement, with 3rd KAR and 57th Wilde's Rifles (FF) from Hannyngton's 2nd EA Brigade leading, they made contact with the German rearguard. This rearguard withdrew in contact as the KAR and Wilde's Rifles pushed through the thick forest north of the Pugu River. The deep waters of the Pugu were crossed by the troops wading through them, assisted by a rope slung between the riverbanks, and on September 1 they began clearing the Uluguru foothills under fire from German artillery.

Matombo Mission Station was taken on September 3, and on the 4th the brigade came under heavy fire from strong German entrenchments on Kikarunga Hill—held by Major Julius von Boemcken with the Tanga *Landsturm* Company and detachments Wilhelmstal and Bahnschutz—which rose 3,000 feet above the road through the mountains. The Gold Coast Regiment was ordered to clear the position. Captain John Butler, VC, DSO (King's Royal Rifle Corps), was detailed to recce forward with his Pioneer Company, and by the evening, he had occupied a kopje to the east of the road and in front of the Germans, with an observation post on a second kopje to his front just beyond a bend in the road.

At 5 p.m., the Pioneer Company came under heavy fire. Butler immediately made his way forward to check on his observation post. As he and his escort made their way along the road, they came under machine-gun fire, and Butler was wounded in the shoulder and lung. With Butler wounded, Lieutenant PVR Bray (Special List) took over command of the company. Shortly after, Captain GS Shaw's (Lancashire Regt's) "B" Company moved forward to reinforce the Pioneers, and both companies dug-in for the night while the wounded were taken back to Matombo mission.

The next morning (the 5th) both companies advanced to and

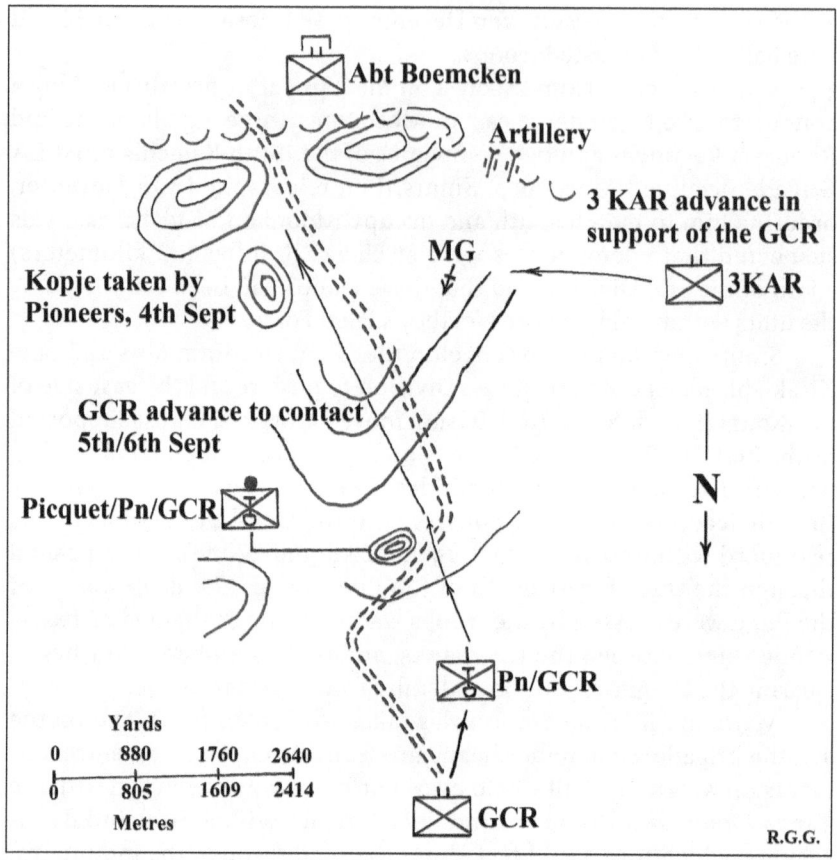

The Action at Kikarunga Hill (based on an official sketch map by HMSO/Historical Section Military Branch, 1918).

cleared a second enemy held kopje with the bayonet, "The charge was sounded, and the men with fixed bayonets rushed up the kopje, which was captured after a few shots had been fired. In this charge Acting-Sergeant Bukari of B Company displayed conspicuous bravery, which was subsequently rewarded by a second Distinguished Conduct Medal,"[2] then fought their way towards the main enemy entrenchments. Late in the afternoon 3rd KAR, supported by a section of the 27th Mountain Battery, began moving to the Gold Coast Regiment's right. Their orders were to turn the Germans' left flank, but nightfall halted operations until the next morning. During the night, Shaw's company was relieved by Captain EG Wheeler's (Hampshire Regt's) "A" Company.

With the coming of daylight, the Gold Coast Regiment continued its frontal attack, while 3rd KAR, supported by artillery fire from the

Gold Coast Mountain Battery and a section of the 5th SA Field Battery, began its flank attack. By 2 p.m., 3rd KAR and the Gold Coast Regiment had linked up and pressed home their assault, and at 4 p.m., the Gold Coast Regiment stormed and captured the summit of Kikarunga Hill. The *Schutztruppe* were forced to withdraw, and 2nd EA Brigade was in possession of the Kikarunga position. During the night, Captain JFP Butler, VC, DSO, died of his wounds.

Having cleared the pass into the mountains, the division advanced into the Uluguru Mountains, heading for the Dutumi River. Which they reached on the 10th, and which was held by a rearguard force of 2,000 *Schutztruppe* with 24 machine guns of Captain Paul Stemmermann's detachment—the 3rd, 14th, 18th, 22nd Field and 4th Rifle Companies—dug-in in an extremely strong entrenched position at Nkessa. The 3rd Kashmir Rifles—supported by artillery and machine guns—tried to storm the German position with a frontal attack but was stopped by the high, dense elephant grass, while 57th Wilde's Rifles advanced and took Kitoho Hill to the north.

At 2 p.m., 3rd KAR was ordered to march around Kitoho, cross the river and attack the Germans' right flank, held by Captain Hans Schultz's detachment—the 4th, 9th, 13th and 21st Field Companies. Early next morning detachments of 3rd KAR began moving down both banks of the river. Those on the right were driven back by enemy reinforcements, led by von Lettow-Vorbeck, marching up from Kisaki, while those on the left were pinned down by heavy machine-gun fire. On the morning of the 12th, 3rd KAR was reinforced by the Pioneer and "I" Companies of the Gold Coast Regiment and a battery of artillery, and at 2:30 p.m., the KAR linked with Wilde's Rifles on the lower slopes of Kitoho Hill, while the two Gold Coast Regiment companies, supported by "G" Company, crossed to the right bank of the river where they were reinforced by the 29th Punjabis.

At 6 p.m., "A" and "B" Companies of the Gold Coast Regiment on the Germans' left flank took up fire positions on a hill overlooking Stemmermann's entrenchments at Nkessa, and at dawn on the 13th, a general advance began. For the rest of the day a battle of attack and counterattack ensued. The fighting stopped at nightfall, and the troops dug-in, only to discover the next morning that the *Schutztruppe* had slipped away during the night. "During the following days the enemy directed his attacks mainly against our left, and was frequently driven back by counter-strokes. But, on the whole, it was evident that success was only possible if the enemy proved very unskilful. On the other hand, our communications, which from now on no longer ran to Kissaki [*sic*], but towards Behobeho in the southeast, were in a great degree threatened by the enemy. I therefore abandoned Dutumi, and withdrew the main body an hour's march to the south, across the Mgeta river, where the Force occupied an extensive fortified camp, which it continued to hold for months. By this move the rich fields of Dutumi were unfortunately given up."[3] The 2nd EA Brigade then led the advance to the Mgeta, crossing that river on the 19th, where they again made contact with the *Schutztruppe* rearguard.

On the western side of the mountains the 2nd SA Mounted Brigade captured a German ammunition depot at Mlali, arriving just ahead of the *Schutztruppe*, and a desperate fight began. Captain WA Bloomfield, commanding the brigade's scouts, was well forward of the main position when the German attack came in and was forced to withdraw his men a quarter of a mile (650 meters) to the main position as the Germans attempted to outflank him. As his men dug-in on their new position, it was discovered that Corporal DMP Bowker was missing; he had been left behind when the scouts withdrew.

William Bloomfield ran forward from cover to try and locate Bowker. When he found him, he discovered that the corporal had been badly wounded in the stomach. He picked him up and carried him the 400 yards (366 meters) to the main position while under a storm of rifle and machine-gun fire, in complete disregard for his own life; he was later awarded the Victoria Cross for this daring rescue. The outnumbered *Schutztruppe*, meanwhile, fell back to the nearby hills, from where they opened a dropping fire onto the South Africans. After 24 hours of continual action, they destroyed their two 105-mm *Königsberg* guns, broke contact and withdrew deeper into the mountains to the Mgeta Mission Station, ten miles (16 kilometers) from Mlali.

Enslin's men left their horses to pursue the Germans on foot, hoping to cut them off. Nussey's 1st SA Mounted Brigade from the 2nd Division arrived to assist Enslin, pushing up the banks of the Mgeta River, while 2nd SA Infantry Brigade arrived at Mlali to reinforce him. But again, the *Schutztruppe* proved elusive, easily evading the South Africans. Nussey's troops continued their pursuit using native porters to carry their ammunition and baggage. They followed the withdrawing Germans southwards through the mountains, picking up vast quantities of abandoned ammunition as they did so.

Brits's 3rd Division, meanwhile, on reaching the Mssongossi River, were unable to get their guns and wagons across and had to retrace their steps out of the mountains and then march around them. They arrived near Kisaki on September 5. Two days later Brits decided to attack the town, even though the 1st SA Mounted Brigade had not yet arrived to support him, and he was unable to communicate with them. His plan

German askari and porters (Bundesarchiv Bild 134-CO25B).

was for 2nd SA Infantry Brigade to push south on a track that ran alongside the Mgeta River into Kisaki, while 2nd SA Mounted Brigade moved around to the right. Once his brigades were in position, he planned to launch simultaneous attacks from the west and southwest.

As the two brigades carried out their approach marches, one of the defending *Schutztruppe* companies, Reserve Lieutenant Volkwein's 11th Field Company, part of Captain von Lieberman's detachment—the 11th and 27th Field and "W" Companies—worked its way through the dense bush between the two forces and attacked them. Their action brought the South African advance to a standstill. The mounted brigade, which was attacked by the larger part of Volkwein's company, were unable to receive support from the infantry, who were hampered by the dense bush, and they were in danger of their left flank being overwhelmed. Enslin moved men from his right to reinforce his left, and Volkwein immediately began pressing his right. Having lost 28 men killed and wounded, Enslin ordered his brigade to withdraw. The infantry too were pulled back, and Brits then retired to Little Nhigu, six miles (nine and a half kilometers) north of Kisaki, where he dug-in to await the arrival of Nussey's brigade.

Next morning, the 8th, Nussey reached Kisaki and was immediately attacked by Captain Theodor Tafel's detachment—the 1st, 17th and 30th Field Companies. Throughout the day the South Africans held against repeated savage attacks, which they were able to drive off. The din of the action was audible at Little Nhigu, from where Brits made several attempts to move up relief units to 1st SA Mounted Brigade, all of which were frustrated by the thick bush.

That evening runners from Brits managed to reach Nussey with orders for him to break contact and retire to the 3rd Division's camp, which he did, having lost 46 killed and wounded in the day's fighting. Von Lettow-Vorbeck, meanwhile, having found that a large dump of ammunition, food and clothing, along with a herd of 2,000 cattle, had built up at Kisaki, issued orders to his detachment commanders,[4] instructing them to undertake a fighting withdrawal to the Rufiji, making it clear to them that no future positions were to be given up before they were contested. "It was not until I arrived at Kissaki [sic] myself that I obtained a proper idea of the abundance of stores and supplies available there. I learned that, contrary to my belief, practically nothing was stored further south at Behobeho or at Kungulio, on the Rufiji. At Kissaki there were large stocks, but notwithstanding the dense native population, it was impossible to get them away. The numerous inhabitants, to whom the war and the many Askari were something quite new, lost their heads and ran away into the bush. The Civil Administration, which enjoyed the complete confidence of the people, proved powerless against the overwhelming influences now bursting in upon them. Even presents of clothing, which were ordinarily so highly valued, failed to hold them. It seemed as if all the evil spirits had conspired together to deprive us of transport. Our column of several hundred pack-donkeys had been driven over the mountains from Morogoro. It arrived at Kissaki late and completely exhausted. Our ox-wagons, which had to go round the east side of the Uluguru Mountains on account of the state of the roads, seemed to be never going to arrive. The head of the Communications Service could not find any other means of carrying away the stocks which were essential to us for continuing the war. And yet it was obvious that we must continue to fall back further south, towards the Rufiji, before the superior numbers of the enemy."[5] He needed to buy enough time to get these valuable stores and cattle south of the river, and to do that his troops must contest every piece of ground. By the 11th, however, the *Schutztruppe* had abandoned Kisaki, and the great herd of cattle along with columns of ox-wagons and pack donkeys were plodding south to the healthier uplands across the Rufiji.

When Smuts's divisions had finally assembled at Kisaki, his lines of communication were stretched to their limit, and his troops were exhausted. The British offensive had come to a stand. Between them the three divisions had lost 33,500 transport animals from a total of 54,000 since leaving the Central Railway, 10,000 horses, 10,000 mules, 11,000 oxen and 2,500 donkeys. Most of these animals had fallen victim to the dreaded tsetse fly. The fighting strength of his divisions had suffered nearly 15,000 casualties to tropical diseases, mainly malaria, while a smaller number of losses in killed and wounded could be attributed to the fighting. Before continuing his operations, it was necessary for Smuts to reform and reorganize his forces. Von Lettow-Vorbeck, meanwhile, began establishing defensive positions along the Mgeta River and the Kisaki-Rufiji Road, where he remained undisturbed for several weeks.

While these events were taking place in the interior, operations had begun in August to take the major German coastal ports. On August 1 Sadani was occupied, and on the 15th Bagamoyo was taken by a combined naval and military force under Rear-Admiral EFB Charlton, CB, RN. His squadron, consisting of the battleship HMS *Vengeance*, the cruiser *Challenger*, the monitors *Severn* and *Mersey* and the armed tug *Helmuth*, anchored off Bagamoyo and provided naval gunfire support to a landing party of 300 Royal Marines Light Infantry and the Zanzibar Rifles. Defending the town was the 1st Rifle Company, commanded by Captain Bock von Wülfingen, and yet another gun from the *Königsberg*, which immediately began firing on the British squadron. Despite the landing being contested, the *Schutztruppe* were quickly forced to break contact and abandon the town.

Following the fall of Bagamoyo, a column comprising the 2nd West India Regiment and the 129th Baluchis was assembled by Brigadier-General WFS Edwards, DSO, Inspector General of Communications, East Africa, and was placed under the command of Colonel CU Price, CMG (Indian Army). Price was ordered to march along the coast and take Dar es Salaam in cooperation with Admiral Charlton's squadron.

Dar es Salaam was taken without opposition on August 4 by the 129th Baluchis, following a grueling march through hot, humid weather by the British column. The German garrison—22nd Field, 1st, 2nd and 3rd Rifle Companies, Dar es Salaam *Landsturm* and *Königsberg* Companies—under the command of the former captain of the *Königsberg*, Captain Max Looff, had withdrawn after it destroyed the railway station and harbor installations.

Realizing that the occupation of the southern ports was vital if he was to shorten his supply routes during the next phase of operations, General Smuts ordered the entire enemy coastal region occupied, beginning with Kilwa. Following discussions with Admiral Charlton, it was agreed that the navy would transport the 2nd West India Regiment to Kilwa and provide support after they had landed. The 2nd West India Regiment was duly landed at and occupied Kilwa without opposition. A detachment, commanded by Major Tyndall, was then sent to take

Mikindani and Lindini. Both places fell after only a token opposition. By the end of September, the entire coast was under British control.

The capture of German East's capital led to the repair of the Central Railway, allowing the British to transport vital stores quickly and directly to their forces in the interior. Though the permanent way was only lightly damaged, the Germans had destroyed 60 bridges between the coast and Kilosa. The SA Pioneers, under Lieutenant-Colonel CW Wilkinson and assisted by Major JW Dobson, were tasked with the repairs to the railway and the rebuilding of the bridges. This work was successfully completed by the end of October 1916, when the railway was opened to traffic from the coast to Tabora.

On the southern frontier of German East in late September, the Portuguese commander, Major-General Ferreira Gil, under continual pressure from his government to begin offensive operations in German East Africa, and at Smuts's suggestion that he march on Liwale, deep inside German territory, which would help in the destruction of the German forces operating on the Mahenge Plateau and cut von Lettow-Vorbeck's line of retreat to the Rufiji, had reluctantly agreed to take the fort at Newala on the edge of the Makonde Plateau and then advance as far as Massasi. On the 25th he ordered a small reconnaissance force of two indigenous companies with two machine guns, under the command of Captain Francisco Curado, to advance towards the Makonde Plateau and Newale. By October 4 the column was approaching Mahuta, where it was ambushed by Lieutenant Sprockhoff's detachment. In the ensuing skirmish Curado's column lost 14 Portuguese and 53 askaris killed, and he was forced to withdraw to Kikumbuliro on the Rovuma River. Major-General Gil immediately reinforced the column, which, now under the command of Major J Pires and comprising two Portuguese and four indigenous companies, a detachment of Mounted Infantry, with seven machine guns and a battery of mountain guns, who marched north from Kikumbuliro on the 18th.

Meanwhile, Sprockhoff had informed von Lettow-Vorbeck that the Portuguese had begun probing towards the Makonde Plateau. Von Lettow-Vorbeck immediately dispatched Captain Max Looff to Utete, where he was to command a force comprising half the 20th Field Company from Lindi and Captain Wilhelm Rothe's detachment (the 4th Rifle and Tanga *Landsturm* Companies with three machine guns and a two-gun artillery detachment) from Kilwa, which was assembling there.

On October 26 Pires's column reached the large stone fort at Newale, which was built atop a steep hill, having been in constant contact with patrols from Sprockhoff's detachment. Pires decided to rest his troops and mount an attack on the fort the next morning. But patrols sent out at dawn found that Newale had been abandoned during the night. He occupied the fort at once, only to discover that the small cistern inside the walls could not supply sufficient water for his force. The nearest adequate supply of water for his column was from wells one and a half miles (two and a half kilometers) from the fort, which required the deployment of a large detachment to guard this, his main water source. Shortly after, Major Leopoldo da Silva arrived by lorry with reinforcements and took over command of the column. Leaving a detachment to hold the fort and wells, da Silva began advancing on Kivambo, where on November 8 he was ambushed by Rothe's detachment. In the fighting that followed da Silva was killed, and command devolved on Major A da Cunha, who ordered a withdrawal to Newala.

In the early hours of November 22 Looff's infantry and machine guns, which now included Sprockhoff's command, had arrived before Newale. Captain Rothe attacked the wells, held by 1,000 Portuguese troops, with the 4th Rifle and Tanga *Landsturm* Companies, at dawn. But the Portuguese troops were well dug-in, in good defensive positions, and it took Rothe's troops 12 hours and an assault with fixed bayonets to finally dislodge them. Leaving behind 60 dead, the garrison fled, some to the fort, others south to the Rovuma River. The next morning the Germans surrounded and besieged the fort, and when his artillery arrived, Looff had them open fire on the fort's walls.

Conditions inside Newale were desperate due to the shortage of water, which came from the single small cistern inside the fort. Da Cunha had his native porters driven out of Newale in an effort to conserve his water supply. As these unfortunates tried to make their way down the hill and through the German lines, they were driven back to the fort, and here they died of thirst and enemy fire beneath the 20-foot-high walls of Newale.

Da Cunha sent ever-more-desperate pleas by wireless to Gil, begging him to break the siege. The first attempt, made by a 100-strong relief column from Mahuta, was repulsed by the *Schutztruppe* outposts to the east of the fort. A second attempt was made by a force of 70 Portuguese and 200 askaris with two machine guns under the command of Captain Benedito de Azevedo. This column was ambushed by the detachment of 20th Field Company, commanded by Lieutenant-Commander Herbert Hinrichs (former navigating officer of the *Königsberg*), who drove them off with the loss of four killed and 23 wounded.

With relief no longer an option, the garrison at Newale broke out in the early hours of the 29th. Hidden by an extremely thick early morning fog, they escaped south and down from the Makonde Plateau to the Rovuma River. At daylight the besieging Germans found the fort abandoned along with four new 7.6-cm mountain guns and ammunition, seven machine guns, a number of unserviceable rifles, 100,000 rounds of small arms ammunition, a wireless station and 45 supply wagons containing an abundance of food and medical supplies, with their teams of horses and mules. Looff ordered a pursuit, but his troops were unable to catch the fleeing Portuguese, arriving at the Rovuma just as the last of them crossed to the south bank of the river.

As the rains set in, the now demoralized Portuguese troops were ordered back to the coast, while their commander, Major-General Gil, was recalled to Portugal. Von Lettow-Vorbeck's southern flank was for the moment secure. Rothe's detachment returned to the Lindi area, while Looff, with the remainder of his force, conducted operations against rebellious tribesmen on the Makonde Plateau to secure it as a possible route of withdrawal for von Lettow-Vorbeck and for the establishment of supply dumps.

In the southwest of German East, meanwhile, Lieutenant-Colonel Rodger's 2nd SA Rifles column from General Northey's Field Force entered Neu Iringa on August 29: forcing Major Kraut's detachment—the 2nd, 5th, 10th, 15th, 16th, 19th, 25th Field 5th and 8th Rifle Companies, "L" Company, 17 machine guns and a field gun—retreating from Smuts's advance to make for Mahenge instead of the healthier Iringa area, while Wahle's retreat from Tabora threatened to cut Rodger off from Northey's HQ at Neu Langenburg. It was proving extremely difficult to reinforce and resupply Northey's command, and he was finding it increasingly difficult to maintain contact with his column at Neu Iringa. His lines of communication were protected by recruits for 1st KAR who were still undergoing training, and they were vulnerable to attack by Wahle's retreating companies.

With this critical development at Neu Iringa, General van Deventer sent Lieutenant-Colonel JM Fairweather, DSO, with a column consisting of the 7th SA Infantry (250 men and six machine guns), a detachment of the SA Motor-Cycle Battalion (70 men), and a section of the 28th Mountain Battery from the Central Railway to reinforce Rodger. When only two days' march from the town, Fairweather learned that Wahle's troops had cut the Field Force's lines, severing communications between Rodger and Northey's HQ. With this sudden development, Smuts ordered van Deventer to take command of the Neu Iringa area and temporary control of Northey's troops there.

To the north of the settlement a detachment of the 4th SA Horse met and defeated part of Major von Langenn-Steinkeller's column, while on October 29, following five days of continuous fighting, Captain Wintgens's column—the 8th, 24th and 26th Field Companies, Ruanda

Eleven. Into German East

"A" and Ruanda "B" Companies, and "C" Company, eight machine guns and two field guns—captured the British supply depot at Ngominji. In August General Northey had ordered Captain CHB Clark (SA Mounted Rifles), commanding the KAR Artillery Section (two 12-pdr naval guns that had been recovered from the wreck of HMS *Pegasus*), to move his section from Neu Iringa to the supply depot that had been established at Ngominji on the Neu Langenburg road.

On arrival at Ngominji Clark took over command of the depot, which consisted of, besides his artillery section, stores staff, a 40-man detachment of 1st KAR for security, a small section of SA Engineers and some invalids. The depot itself contained rations and ammunition laboriously brought forward from Nyasaland by porters and a wireless station run by the engineers.

On October 21 Lieutenant Joseph Zingel, commanding the 26th Field Company, was sent by Wintgens to carry out a reconnaissance of the Ngominji depot, which he planned to take for the ammunition and supplies there. On reporting back to his commander, he was then sent to ambush a small British force, which appeared to be reinforcements, marching from Neu Iringa towards the depot. This column 62 strong was in fact a detachment of the Northern Rhodesia Police under the command of Major Walter Blaxendale, which was marching from Neu Iringa to Malangali via the Ngominji depot, having escorted a section of the 5th SAMR Battery to Neu Iringa. The ambush, which took place on the 23rd, was a success; British casualties were two killed, one of whom was Blaxendale, and 31 wounded.

Having dealt with what he perceived to be reinforcements, Wintgens now turned his attention to the British supply depot. His companies took up position on the high ground surrounding the depot and opened fire. Throughout the following days, the German fire was so intense that the garrison's casualties were forced to remain in their trenches. As the number of wounded grew, Clark sent out a request by wireless for a doctor to try and get through to Ngominji to treat his casualties. On the 28th Wintgens mounted an infantry assault, supported by heavy machine-gun fire from the high ground overlooking the depot, against the British perimeter. The attack was repulsed by the little garrison, using improvised hand grenades made by the SA Engineers to supplement their rifle and machine-gun fire. Wintgens was forced to pull back and regroup his companies. During the night of the 28th/29th, Surgeon Captain EG Storrs of the Northern Rhodesia Medical Service, who had heard Clark's plea for medical assistance, was able to sneak undetected through the enemy lines with aid of a native guide and enter the depot. That same night Clark gave permission for all those who wished to leave the now-doomed depot to do so in small groups. Around 30 of the garrison took up the offer.

At dawn the German assault was renewed with vigor, two of Wintgens's companies—the 8th and 24th Field Companies—charged through the defenses with fixed bayonets. With their perimeter breached, the British rendered the naval guns useless, and the remaining tiny KAR garrison surrendered, but only after their commander, Captain Clark, was killed. Wintgens plundered the depot, then marched south towards Lupemba.

When he learned of the attack on the Ngominji depot, Lieutenant-Colonel Rodger, leaving Major Flindt to hold Neu Iringa with a squadron of the 2nd SA Rifles, marched to the relief of the depot with 80 rifles and two machine guns. As he advanced down the road towards Ngominji, he met some of the survivors of Blaxendale's detachment; then, as he approached Mahansi, nine miles (14 kilometers) northeast of Ngominji, he made contact with part of Wintgens's covering force from the 26th Field Company and was stopped. Meanwhile, Fairweather's column began arriving at Neu Iringa on October 23, and by the next day, the concentration of the entire force was completed. With the town secure, Lieutenant-Colonel Freeth was ordered to march after Rodger with an 80-man detachment of his 7th SA Infantry, two machine guns, and the 28th Mountain Battery.

When Freeth joined Rodger's column on the 29th, they learned that Ngominji had been taken that morning. Suspecting that they would be next to receive Wintgens's attention, they dug-in on the southern end of a ridge near the west of the road. The surrounding country here was thick bushland with swamps to the east of their position and a higher, dominating ridge to their rear. Early the next morning a *Schutztruppe* detachment advanced around the western flank of the British position and took up fire positions on the dominating ridge from where they opened a harassing fire. This was followed by repeated assaults against the British, which were driven off each time by the defenders' accurate small arms and artillery fire. The Germans were also able to bring one of the 12-pdr naval guns, captured at Ngominji and repaired, into action during the day. As night approached, the attacks ceased and the harassing fire lessened.

After a relatively quiet night, the *Schutztruppe* recommenced their harassing fire on the British position at dawn, and though they kept this fire up throughout the day, they did not mount any infantry attacks. Then during the night of October 31–November 1, they broke contact and rejoined Wintgens's main body marching on Lupemba. The action had cost the British force three killed and 16 wounded, while the German casualties were extremely light, one killed and six wounded.

Further north, on the west bank of the Ruhuje River, meanwhile, Lieutenant-Colonel Hawthorne's 1st KAR/1st SA Rifles column, with Lieutenant-Colonel Murray's Southern Rhodesia column under command, defeated the Germans in a sharp action at Mkapira, 40 miles (64 kilometers) west of Mahenge. Hawthorne, following a contact with the *Schutztruppe* column commanded by Major Kraut in late September, had established an entrenched camp on a flat-topped hill surrounded on three sides by thick forest, overlooking the river, Murray's troops covering the southeast and Hawthorne's the northwest, where the hill sloped down to swampy ground along the riverbank, while his artillery, the 5th SAMR Battery, were well camouflaged in the center of the position with the column's wireless station. To compensate for the restricted view from the camp and to give advanced warning of an attack, Hawthorne established an observation post on a dominating hill, named Picquet Hill, one and a half miles (two and a half kilometers) to the west.

On October 21 Hawthorne was informed by his patrols that a large enemy column was closing on his position, and at dawn the following morning, they took Picquet Hill. Major Kraut, the German column commander, had his field gun deployed on the crest of the hill from where it opened fire on the British defenses, while his infantry companies, less "L" Company which he sent towards Mahenge as a blocking force and the 25th Field Company to block the Lupembe road, surrounded the British position with the intention of starving them into surrender. Unknown to Kraut, however, a supply column had reached Hawthorne that very day, and hunting parties had shot an elephant, the meat of which was being dried into biltong in the sun. Even so, Hawthorne ordered food rations to be cut as a precaution.

By 8 a.m., the entire British perimeter was under fire not only from the field gun on Picquet Hill but at least a dozen machine guns. The 5th SAMR Battery, however, was under strict orders not to engage the enemy without specific permission so as not to reveal their location. The first time the battery opened fire was during the midafternoon when the 10th Field Company mounted an attack against the northern defenses. The attack was beaten off, and the guns quickly went silent.

For the next three days the German machine guns and field gun pounded the camp, which Kraut thought contained only four companies. After several days firing, the exact position of the German field gun was plotted by Lieutenant Harold Swifte (SA Mounted Rifles), who had made his way to an exposed position from where he could observe the muzzle flash. The South Africans were given permission to engage it. They scored a hit on the gun-shield which killed the gun commander, Lieutenant Kuhn, and most of the gun crew. The gun was still able to fire, however, but with its replacement crew, it was not as devastatingly effective as it had been.

Determined to break the siege, Hawthorne had been sending out his intelligence officer, Lieutenant HT Barrett, each night to reconnoiter the enemy positions facing his side of the perimeter. During the course of these reconnaissances, Barrett had found routes through the swampy ground along the river and had plotted the enemy defenses opposite, while in front of Murray's perimeter scouts had been actively plotting the enemy positions facing him, and on the night of the 27th two of these scouts, Privates AS Peters and RG Hill, captured a two-man outpost of the 10th Field Company. The intelligence obtained from these prisoners proved invaluable to Hawthorne's plan to break the siege.

Hawthorne planned to mount two surprise attacks. Murray's troops would attack across the open ground to the southeast, while he would simultaneously launch an attack towards Picquet Hill. At the same time, Captain JEE Galbraith's (Royal Fusiliers) "D" Company of 1st KAR, which was guarding the Main Supply Route to Kisinga, would attack the 25th Field Company in position three miles (five kilometers) to the west of Mkapira. Galbraith had been advised of the plan by wireless, and his company was reinforced by Major Charles Fair's "A" Company of the Northern Rhodesia Police and a KAR 7-pdr mountain gun.

On the night of October 29–30 Lieutenant Hugh Barrett[6] guided two KAR companies silently through swampy ground by the river to a point three miles (five kilometers) from the camp and 250 yards (229 meters) behind the 5th Rifle Company. At 5:30 a.m., Captain AH Griffiths's (Duke of Cornwall's Light Infantry) "AR" Company stormed the enemy positions to their front and then advanced on and took Picquet Hill. But on their left Major GL Baxter's "CR" Company was repulsed by the determined defense of the Germans. Baxter withdrew his company a short distance and then assaulted the flank of the enemy position, where a bitter fight developed. Making no headway, Baxter sent Colour-Sergeant Magomera to advise Colonel Hawthorne of the situation. Magomera carried this message to Headquarters under heavy fire, and Hawthorne, on receiving it, committed half of "H" Company under Lieutenant PE Mitchell to the fight, while Magomera returned to his company where he led half the company forward into the German defenses. As a result of this reinforcement, the German position was taken by 7:30 a.m., and the 5th Rifle Company was forced back one and a half miles (two and a half kilometers) onto the 19th Field Company. Colour-Sergeant Magomera was subsequently awarded the African Distinguished Conduct Medal.

Meanwhile, to the southeast, Murray's attack went in. It was led by Lieutenant HT Onyett's reinforced No. 1 Section of 44 men from "A" Company, British South Africa Police, who advanced silently on the positions of the 10th Field Company with fixed bayonets. They were followed closely by Lieutenant JH Vaughan's No. 2 Section and Captain GN Beaumont's company of 1st KAR, who were in close support. While still 600 yards (549 meters) from the German position and advancing in extended order, Onyett's men were seen in the growing light by the enemy's advanced picket, which opened fire and then withdrew to the main position. The section cheered and charged into the German trenches where heavy hand-to-hand fighting erupted. The Germans quickly organized a counterattack, but by this time Vaughan's section had joined Onyett's men, and the Germans were driven out of their position.

Galbraith's and Fair's attack along the Kisinga road against the 25th Field Company had been as equally successful. Their attack was supported by fire from the 5th SA Battery, and this enemy company too was forced to withdraw. By 8:30 a.m., all Kraut's companies had broken contact and withdrawn to a predetermined rendezvous. The *Schutztruppe* left behind 81 prisoners, 42 killed and 158 wounded, when they broke contact and withdrew, along with four machine guns and the field gun. Hawthorne's losses were five killed and 21 wounded.

Two weeks after the lifting of the siege, Colonel Murray's column was dispatched from Mkapira to Malangali, 120 miles (193 kilometers) to the southwest, in lorries and cars. Here Captain T Marriot's (2nd SA Rifles) garrison of 100 men of the Rhodesia Native Regiment had been under siege since November 8 by Wahle's column. Marriot held out for four days against continual attack until Murray's arrival forced the Germans to lift their siege and withdraw eastwards towards Lupembe. Captain Marriot was subsequently awarded the Military Cross for his defense of the post.

Meanwhile Wintgens had already reached Lupemba, where his troops surrounded and besieged the town. The KAR garrison was subjected to continuous attack over the following six days but were able to successfully repulse every effort by the Germans to force the defenses. On the sixth day Wintgens lifted the siege when he learned that a relief force was fast approaching the town. Then, on November 26, at Ilembule Mission Station, which lay between Neu Langenburg and Malangali, Northey's troops isolated Wahle's rearguard. Unable to break through the British cordon, the rearguard surrendered. The total number of troops taken was seven German officers, 47 German other ranks and 449 askaris with three machine guns and a 10.5-cm howitzer.

Wahle's main force had, however, succeeded in getting through to Mahenge, where they joined up with Kraut's companies. From here preparations were made to march to the southeast and link up with von Lettow-Vorbeck in the Rufiji Delta, while Wintgens, following his withdrawal from Lupemba, opted to lead his companies back towards Tabora and not to the Rufiji, a decision which caused consternation to the Belgians and dumbfounded the British and von Lettow-Vorbeck.

With the threat from Wahle lifted, van Deventer, who had moved his HQ to Neu Iringa, made plans to establish a large supply depot in the area. He intended to drive the *Schutztruppe* across the Ruhuje and Ulanga rivers before Smuts renewed the main offensive. But by the middle of December 1916, he had to advise General Smuts that due to the incredible difficulties he faced, and the insecurity of the supply situation, he was not able to build up an adequate reserve of stores and equipment to enable him to supply his division during his planned operations. He thus proposed to move his division back to the Central Railway, less a squadron of mounted troops and three battalions of infantry, who would remain at Neu Iringa until the main offensive began, then rejoin him.

Throughout the period from September to December 1916, the reorganization of the British forces in East Africa was under way. Special Medical Boards were set up, and more than 12,000 South African servicemen were returned home as unfit for further service. Major-General Brits's 3rd Division was disbanded in December, and its officers and staff went home, while all fit men from Enslin's 2nd SA Mounted Brigade were posted to Nussey's 1st SA Mounted Brigade, bringing it up to full strength.

The vacuum left by the repatriation of these troops was filled by the now-expanded King's African Rifles, whose battalions were becoming operational thanks to the new training regime introduced by Colonel EH Llewellyn (6th [Service] Bn, Dorset Regt). Llewellyn had been appointed commandant earlier in the year and had, as a matter of urgency, centralized recruiting and rationalized training. By the time of the British reorganization, 55th Coke's Rifles, 127th Baluchis and 25th Indian Cavalry had arrived in theater, and the KAR had reached five operational regiments of 13 battalions. Brigadier-General FHG Cunliffe, CB, CMG, with his Nigerian Brigade, West African Frontier Force, had also landed at Dar es Salaam from West Africa. This brigade included the 1st, 2nd, 3rd and 4th Battalions, Nigeria Regiment, the Gambia Company and a battery of WAFF artillery; they brought with them their own porters, the Sierra Leone Carrier Corps and the West African and 300th Field Ambulances. The 2nd Loyal North Lancashire Regiment too had returned to East Africa, following a period of recuperation and reinforcement in South Africa, where they had been sent after the battle

Eleven. Into German East

Sierra Leone Carrier Corps of the Nigerian Brigade marching towards the Rovuma River, German East Africa (Her Majesty's Stationery Office, UK Ministry of Information, First World War collection/Q15418).

of Salaita; but during the reorganization, they too were withdrawn and redeployed to Egypt.

On the coast the British forces at Kilwa were strengthened in preparation for a move inland to destroy the few remaining German supply depots situated in the Utete area to the north. A camp was established on Kilwa heights, and by the end of September,[7] four battalions, including the now operational 2nd KAR, had assembled there as the newly constituted 3rd East African Brigade—129th Baluchis, 40th Pathans and 1/2nd and 2/2nd KAR. Brigadier-General Arthur Hannyngton, in command of these troops, had orders to move inland as soon as possible; on October 10 he marched for Kibata, which lay in the center of the Utete area, with 2nd KAR and the 129th Baluchis.

The stone Boma at Kibata, which was ringed by the Mtumbei Hills, was taken on the 14th after a token resistance by the *Schutztruppe* garrison. The commander of the Kibata garrison, Major Julius von Boemcken, had decided to withdraw to and defend the German supply depot at Liwale to the southwest—which he considered to be of more importance to the *Schutztruppe*—rather than to try and hold Kibata.

Leaving 1/2nd KAR[8] and the 129th Baluchis to hold the fort, Hannyngton withdrew to Chemara on the Kibata-Kilwa road with the 2/2nd KAR. Shortly afterwards the 129th Baluchis were ordered to move south to Mitole. On October 28 1/2nd KAR, leaving a machine gun and two platoons at Kibata, marched to Kitambi, approximately six miles (nine and a half kilometers) to the south. At the end of the month, Smuts, following a visit to Kilwa, ordered the 1st Division HQ with 2nd EA Brigade—57th Wilde's Rifles, Gold Coast Regiment and 1/3rd and 2/3rd KAR—now under the command of Brigadier-General H de C O'Grady, there in preparation for his offensive operations to the south of the Rufiji. "General Hoskins assumed command at Kilwa on the 15th November, and the transfer of General O'Grady's brigade by road, rail and sea to the Kilwa area occupied from the 7th to the 29th November."[9] Once assembled, elements of the Gold Coast Regiment were sent forward from Kilwa by O'Grady to reinforce 2/2nd KAR at Chemara.

In early November von Lettow-Vorbeck, learning of the weakness of the Kibata garrison, wrote, "I considered it necessary to transfer strong forces from the neighbourhood of Kissengire towards Kibata. No opportunity had presented itself of fighting a decisive successful battle north of the lower Rufiji; as I had expected, I was obliged to proceed to a prolonged operation in the mountains of Kibata, which offered but little prospect of leading to a decision."[10] He immediately dispatched Captain Hans Schulz with two companies—the 18th and 30th Field Companies—to attack the fort. Learning of this proposed attack, Hannyngton instructed a company of the 129th Baluchis to relieve 1/2nd KAR at Kitambi. Immediately following its relief, 1/2nd KAR undertook a forced march north to Kibata, where, on November 8, following a sharp skirmish with Schulz's companies, they drove them off and secured the position. Communications with General Hoskins's Division HQ at Kilwa were then established by the means of a signals post on a hill to the southeast of the fort and a relay station on Ssongo Ssongo Island just off the coast.

The 129th Baluchis returned to Kibata on the 17th, whereupon its commanding officer, Lieutenant-Colonel H Hulseberg, took over responsibility for the defense of the area. He had the Baluchis construct two stone redoubts near the summit of the hill to the northwest of the fort, which he called Piquet Hill, and strip away all cover in the killing ground on the approaches. Meanwhile, the KAR patrolled the outlying area and skirmished with patrols from Schulz's companies, as well as maintaining outposts on the remaining hills surrounding Kibata fort and the two villages to the north and northeast, called Palm and Coconut villages respectively.

At 1 p.m., on December 6, von Lettow-Vorbeck, having brought nine companies from the Rufiji to reinforce Captain Schulz's two companies, attacked Kibata. The attack drove in the KAR outposts on Ambush Hill, 1,000 yards (915 meters) north of Piquet Hill and Coconut village 1,500 yards (1372 meters) northeast of Palm village. The next morning, at 6:30 a.m., von Lettow-Vorbeck, having crossed the valley from Coconut village in the early hours, opened a diversionary attack against the KAR in Palm village and at Single Palm outpost on the high ground to the northeast of the fort. Shortly afterwards, the main assault, supported by artillery fire[11] from Ambush Hill—where Lieutenant-Commander Hans Apel had sited his guns—was launched against Piquet Hill from the north.

Though this attack stalled, probing attacks continued throughout the day, and the German artillery bombarded the position with heavy harassing fire. Then at 6 p.m., after an intense half hour bombardment, von Lettow-Vorbeck mounted an infantry assault against No. 2 redoubt, covering the west side of the hill. The fighting was fierce, and at the height of the assault, Hulseberg found it necessary to order a detachment of the 1/2nd KAR company forming part of his reserve forward to reinforce the Baluchis. Eventually the Germans were repulsed, but one enemy company had dug-in on the hill's western slope, forming a lodgment within 50 yards (46 meters) of the redoubt. As the light faded, the Baluchis were withdrawn, and the KAR took over the defense of the hill.

There followed a night of intermittent artillery fire against the Piquet Hill positions. The next morning (the 8th) the artillery switched its fire onto Kibata fort, and an assault from the lodgment against No. 2 redoubt was launched in conjunction with flank attacks against the Baluchis positions on Plain Hill and Big Hut Hill protecting Kibata from the west and southwest. All the German attacks were repulsed after heavy fighting, and the garrison dug themselves in as the siege continued. At 2 a.m., in the morning of the 9th, the 2/2nd KAR with a section of the 27th Mountain Battery, reached Kibata. They had been ordered to undertake a forced march to reinforce the garrison by General Hannyngton on the 7th, and leaving Chemara at 4 p.m. that afternoon, they had covered the 36 miles (58 kilometers) to Kibata in driving rain and across the rugged countryside in 34 hours.

Lieutenant-Colonel HSR Filsell (Royal Warwicks) the CO of 2/2nd KAR, as the senior officer now assumed command of the defense. He had one of his companies with a machine gun sent up to Piquet Hill to reinforce this part of the line, while the mountain gun section deployed their guns on Village Hill, just southwest of Big Hut Hill from where they opened fire on the Germans in the lodgment. He then ordered Captain CS Browning to attack the lodgment from No. 2 redoubt at 10 p.m. that night with his company of the 129th and two platoons of the 1/2nd KAR.

Browning's attack went in on schedule, the Baluchis and KAR charging down the slope in the face of extremely heavy fire. They gained the German position, having sustained heavy casualties, including Browning, who was killed on the enemy parapet. With Captain Browning dead, Subadar Sarbiland took over command of the company and continued to press the attack for a further 20 minutes. But the initial success was short lived as the Germans quickly reinforced the defenders and mounted a savage counterattack which drove the Baluchis and KAR back to the redoubt. For his exceptional leadership following the death of his company commander Subadar Sarbiland was subsequently awarded the Indian Order of Merit 2nd Class.

Meanwhile, General O'Grady had been ordered by General Hoskins to concentrate his brigade at Chemara and then advance to the relief of Kibata. O'Grady and his HQ reached Kibata on the night of December 13, bringing with him the machine-gun company of 2nd Loyal North Lancs and a second section of the 27th Mountain Battery. On the 14th, in accordance with O'Grady's orders, the Gold Coast Regiment, supported by the 40th Pathans, began their advance. They were to push through the left of the Mtumbei Hills and turn the Germans' right flank, while the garrison at Kibata began operations from the fort. "Accordingly, at 6 a.m. on the 14th December, B Company, under Captain Shaw, was sent forward along the mountain track which connects Mtumbei Juu with Kibata, to get into touch with the force at Kibata, which a day or two earlier had been reinforced by another battalion of the King's African Rifles, and which was now under the command of General O'Grady. He reported that the road between the two missions was open, and at dusk the rest of the Battalion moved along the road for a distance of two to two and a half miles, and there camped for the night."[12]

Throughout the 15th, the advance of the Gold Coast Regiment and the 40th Pathans was hotly contested by the *Schutztruppe*. The fighting raged until 5:30 p.m., when the flanking battalions on the left, having lost a third of their strength, were halted within two miles (three and a half kilometers) of the fort, held up by the German besiegers dug-in along the ridge to the west of Kibata. "For two and a half more hours the Gold Coast Regiment clung to the position which it had occupied, and in which it had sustained such heavy and continuous losses since 11 o'clock in the morning; but at 5:30 p.m. the 40th Pathans began to relieve it. The relief was effected without serious loss just before darkness fell, and the Gold Coast Regiment took up outpost positions for the night between the hill, which ever since has been known by its name, and the main road from Mtumbei Juu to Kibata."[13]

At Kibata at 11 p.m., Captain HV Lewis, MC, led an assault against the lodgment. Leading his assault group were ten Mahsud pioneers armed with Mills grenades. The Pioneers threw the grenades into the German defenses while the Baluchis tore out the sharpened bamboo stakes forming a protective abattis in the front of the lodgment. The Baluchis then charged in with the bayonet, driving the German garrison out with the loss of 11 killed and four taken prisoner. The Baluchis losses were 13 officers and men wounded. "A" Company, 1/2nd KAR and a machine-gun section of 2nd Loyals relieved the Baluchis in the lodgment, which then became part of the British defensive line. For von Lettow-Vorbeck, however, "the advance of the Gold Coast Regiment had nevertheless been of advantage to the enemy. My force being so weak—we had, all told, about nine companies—I had withdrawn one of the two companies stationed in the immediate vicinity of Kibata in order to employ it against Gold Coast Hill. After I had returned to camp that night I heard the sound of a number of small detonations emanating from the one company left alone to face the enemy. It was only after some time that we recognized this as a grenade attack, a manoeuvre then unknown to us. Several companies of the enemy attacked with such rapidity and skill, that they penetrated the trenches of our weak company by surprise and drove it out. The loss of this position deprived us of the possibility of firing at close range from that very suitable height at hostile troops moving about, or proceeding to their water-supply. Until then I had done so with success, and had even occasionally sent up a light gun to the place, withdrawing it again after it had ceased fire.

"But the loss of this high ground and the casualties sustained in it faded into insignificance beside the success achieved on Gold Coast Hill."[14]

The operations now deteriorated into a battle of attrition, resembling on a small scale the fighting taking place on the Western Front, and it continued in this manner until January 1917, the troops fighting from trenches in heavy rain and mud. On December 18 1/3rd KAR arrived to reinforce the garrison, and on the 26th the 129th Baluchis withdrew to Chumo, where they remained until early January 1917, when they returned to Kibata as Force Reserve. On Christmas Day a British BE2C aircraft, flown by Lieutenant The Honourable Bernard Howard, RFC, with his observer Lieutenant Leo Walmsley, from No. 26 Squadron, Royal Flying Corps, flew from Kilwa to Kibata and dropped a parcel containing a gift of 6,000 cigarettes to the garrison. A much-welcomed gift as they had run out of tobacco two weeks before.

On New Year's Day 1917 two companies of 1/3rd KAR with a section of mountain guns advanced by a circuitous right flanking route the six miles (nine and a half kilometers) to Pangutini and drove off the Germans occupying the village. That same day a detachment of 5-inch howitzers from 14th Howitzer Battery, RA, arrived in Kibata to strengthen 27th Mountain Battery.

Five days later on the night of January 6–7—unaware that von Lettow-Vorbeck had withdrawn six of his companies investing Kibata towards the Rovuma River—Lieutenant-Colonel George Giffard led "A" and "B" Companies, 1/2nd KAR with four machine guns out of Kibata around the right flank to take Mbirikia Hill—just over a mile to the east—from the south. His troops would then overlook Platform Hill, 900 yards (823 meters) to the north. With Mbirikia secured and as dawn approached, "A" Company attacked and drove the Germans from Platform Hill, then informed the artillery at Kibata that the hill had been taken, using a prearranged signal of smoke bombs. Immediately on seeing the signal, the mountain guns and howitzers opened fire on Observation Hill. When the artillery had completed their bombardment, the two companies advanced to and took Observation Hill, while 1/3rd KAR and the 129th Baluchis occupied Coconut village.

On January 8, Lieutenant-Colonel Giffard was reinforced by "C" Company of his battalion, a hundred Baluchis, a machine-gun detachment of 2nd Loyals MG Company and a detachment of 27th Mountain Battery. He then advanced southwest towards Kibata and took Single Palm Hill, where he was relieved by 1/3rd KAR before advancing on and driving the Germans from Ambush Hill. Patrols sent out earlier in the day, however, reported that the *Schutztruppe* were retiring along the Mwengi road, and shortly after, the Gold Coast Regiment finally linked up with the KAR. "At 6.30 on the following morning Major Goodwin began to push forward along the ridge which commanded Gold Coast Hill from the northwest. No opposition was met with, and a patrol which was sent out to reconnoitre Gold Coast Hill reported that it had been evacuated by the enemy. This was later confirmed by Lieutenant Downer, who had reached Gold Coast Hill by the old route from Harman's Kopje, which the Regiment had followed on the 15th December.

"Other patrols were sent forward and reached the Mwengei road, effecting a junction with the 2nd King's African Rifles and the 129th Baluchis, who had been operating from Kibata."[15] Before withdrawing from their positions in the Mtumbei Hills, the *Schutztruppe*, unable to carry away their *Königsberg* gun, destroyed it. The 2nd EA Brigade occupied the abandoned Mtumbei highlands around Kibata, and a brigade camp was established at Kiyombo, 11 miles (18 kilometers) south of Utete, towards the end of the month.

Twelve

The Long Pursuit

THE MAIN BRITISH FORCE, having remained inactive north of the Mgeta River during the period of reorganization, was, in late December 1916, formed by Smuts into four columns for the advance through the German Mgeta River positions to the Rufiji. Three of these columns were to be led by their respective Brigadier-Generals, Sheppard, Beves and Cunliffe, while a fourth smaller column formed by the 2nd Kashmir Rifles and 2nd Nigeria Regiment was to be commanded by Lieutenant-Colonel RA Lyle (Indian Army).

The columns of Sheppard, Cunliffe and Lyle were to smash through von Lettow-Vorbeck's Mgeta River line, while Beves's column carried out a 70-mile (113-kilometer) flank march to the Rufiji River with the objective of capturing the river crossing at Mkalinzo and cutting the *Schutztruppe's* expected line of retreat.

At 10:30 a.m., on January 1, 1917, the British artillery opened fire on the German positions on the north bank of the Mgeta, and an hour later the infantry attack went in. The *Schutztruppe* put up a dogged defense until 3 p.m. and then pulled back to new positions 600 yards (549 meters) south of the river. The British guns switched their fire onto these positions as they were being occupied, and the Germans began a general withdrawal. Lyle's column made contact with the withdrawing *Schutztruppe* and quickly became embroiled in a savage fight, during which the Germans abandoned a howitzer and quantities of stores and ammunition. Von Lettow-Vorbeck mounted a counterattack to retrieve the howitzer at 3:30 p.m., but it was repulsed, and the *Schutztruppe* continued withdrawing.

The next day Cunliffe's Nigerians linked up with Lyle's column at Tsimbe but on the 3rd, due to an acute shortage of supplies, ammunition and transport, were forced to pull back to the Mgeta, while Lyle pushed on to link up with Sheppard's 1st EA Brigade at Behobeho-kwa-Mahinda, 12 miles (19 kilometers) south of the Mgeta. Sheppard's column had been hotly engaged with the German rearguard covering the withdrawal of the main force to and across the Rufiji. Beves's 2nd SA Brigade on the right flank, meanwhile, had cut through the thick bush in driving rain, which made for heavy going to the Rufiji. They crossed the river at Kipenio, 30 miles (48 kilometers) upstream from the crossing point that they expected the Germans to use and dug-in to await the enemy.

As Sheppard's column closed on the Rufiji River, General Smuts sent a personal letter through the lines to von Lettow-Vorbeck. In it Smuts informed the German commander that the Kaiser had awarded him the *Order Pour le Mérite*, Imperial Germany's highest and most prestigious award.

On the 5th Sheppard reached Kimbambabwe on the north bank of the Rufiji. He ordered the 30th Punjabis ferried across the river in small Berthon assault boats during the evening to establish a bridgehead on the southern bank. During the 800-yard (732-meter) crossing of the river, the first wave of boats disturbed a herd of hippopotami, and the Punjabis had to drive them away with their bayonets when the herd attacked. But as the boats could only carry three men and their kit plus an oarsman, by daylight only one company and a machine-gun section was across, and it was under attack by the *Schutztruppe*. The company held on throughout the day, driving off repeated attacks, holding the bridgehead until they were relieved by the rest of the regiment as it was ferried across the river that night. Throughout the 7th, the *Schutztruppe* mounted a series of attacks on the bridgehead, and despite savage hand-to-hand fighting, all were successfully repulsed. That evening Sheppard crossed the river with the advance company of the 130th Baluchis, and the bridgehead was secured.

On the evening of the 15th, Cunliffe's Nigerian column crossed the Rufiji on a bridge built by the Faridkot Sappers and Miners and reinforced Beves. Von Lettow-Vorbeck, whose troops had been in continuous action along the river, broke contact the next day and began withdrawing south towards the Portuguese frontier. With the German withdrawal, the Nigerian Brigade took over the Mkalinzo positions of 2nd SA Brigade, which was pulled out of the firing line preparatory to its return to South Africa. The South Africans had been decimated by tropical disease and were considered no longer combat effective.

In early January 1917, the South African Prime Minister, Louis Botha, informed General Smuts that he had been appointed the South African representative at the Imperial Defence Conference due to take place in London. Botha had become increasingly concerned with Smuts's obsession with the capture or destruction of von Lettow-Vorbeck and his *Schutztruppe*. He instructed him to relinquish his command at once and proceed to England. On January 20, three weeks after resuming his

Twelve. The Long Pursuit

Faridakot Sappers and Miners crossing the Rufiji River (Her Majesty's Stationery Office, UK Ministry of Information, First World War collection/ Q15423).

offensive, Smuts surrendered command in East Africa to Lieutenant-General AR Hoskins, CMG, DSO, and left East Africa consumed by a sense of failure.

Five days later it began to rain in earnest, and by the first week of February, East Africa was subjected to its heaviest rainfall for years. Bridges and roads were washed away or flooded, and all operations were brought to a virtual stand. The military motor roads, built through the Mgeta and Rufiji valleys, could only be traversed by native porters wading through floodwater at times up to their chests. In the west, van Deventer's lines of communication from Dodoma to Neu Iringa were under water, and his porters had to struggle through a deep, wide swamp before and after wading through the flooded Ruaha River. With the rains came tropical disease and the reliance of the opposing armies on columns of porters, which caused a severe shortage in food and essential supplies for the fighting troops. "It is perhaps hard to realise the difficulties which the rainy season in East Africa entailed for a force acting from such widely separated bases, with several different lines of communication running through every variety of difficult country and necessitating in some cases as much as 130 miles of porter transport. In the Mgeta and Rufiji valleys roads constructed with much skill and labour, over which motor transport ran continuously in January, were traversed with difficulty and much hardship a month later by porters wading for miles in water above their waists. The Dodoma-Iringa line of communication crossed the Great Ruaha in the dry weather by an easy ford; when the rain had really set in, supplies had to be transported not only over a flooded river but also a swamp on each side of it 6 feet deep and as many miles wide. Considerable anxiety was caused by this extensive flooding across the Dodoma-Iringa communication, and every effort was made to cope with this. The Iringa Column was kept as small as possible, and special flat-bottomed boats were prepared, but eventually it became necessary to switch on to a new line along the road which runs south from the railway at Kilossa. The valley of the Rufiji and its various tributaries became a vast lake, in which the true courses of the streams were often only discernible with difficulty, if at all. Patrol work had to be carried out for some time in canoes, and the men found themselves making fast to the roofs of houses which had lately formed their quarters."[1]

As the Rufiji Delta flooded, turning into a vast lake, von Lettow-Vorbeck withdrew his main force, 5,000 strong, from the area to new defensive positions in the Matandu Valley west of Kilwa, facing General Hannyngton's brigade, while another column took up position west of Lindi, 100 miles (160 kilometers) south of Kilwa, opposite General O'Grady's troops, and a column of four Field Companies, under Major von Steumer, crossed into Portuguese territory where it was busy raiding in the Mwembe area. The 1/4th KAR was sent by General Northey to Fort Johnson at the beginning of July after it was reported that patrols from von Steumer's command were seen near the southern end of Lake Nyasa. Lieutenant-Colonel WJT Shorthose (South Staffs Regt) commanding the battalion, had orders to attack von Steumer's base at Mwembe, in Portuguese East Africa, which he did, taking it on July 6 after an action lasting for three hours. By August von Steumer had been forced to withdraw back across the Rovuma River. This steady withdrawal of the German troops was closely watched and reported by British patrols.

As the rains continued throughout March and April, von Lettow-Vorbeck was forced to surrender his No. III Field Hospital at Manganza, ten miles (16 kilometers) west of Utete, when the hospital site became flooded and food began running out. The British evacuated 62 Germans and 140 askaris from here to British military hospitals.

In the interior, Wahle, following his linkup with Kraut and Tafel, was still at Mahenge with a combined force of 3,000 men, while Wintgens, with 50 Germans, 500 askaris and 700 porters, was pushing towards the Central Railway. He attempted to avoid the British units operating between Lake Nyasa and Neu Iringa, following an unsuccessful siege of the supply depot at Kitanda, held by 230 men of the 1st Rhodesia Native Regiment, commanded by Lieutenant-Colonel AJ Tomlinson—which had arrived to garrison Songea in November 1916. The siege was lifted on January 30, after two weeks, as a relief column approached.

Then, on February 12, 1917, a detachment of Wintgens's column made contact with a patrol of the 1st Rhodesia Native Regiment operating between Songea and Wiedhafen on the northeast shore of Lake Nyasa at Johannesbruck (now Mabogoro). A company of the battalion was regularly employed in patrolling along the 80-mile (129-kilometer) road to Wiedhafen. This particular patrol was commanded by Sergeant FC Booth of the British South Africa Police attached to the 1st Rhodesia Native Regiment. When the German attack came in, most of Booth's askaris panicked, firing their rifles in the air and running about. Frederick Booth quickly restored order and organized a defense, and seeing his lead scout lying wounded in the open, he dashed out to rescue him, carrying him into his defensive perimeter, where the patrol held out until relief arrived. Following this skirmish, Wintgens called in his detachments, broke contact and withdrew, marching northwest to Lake Rukwa and towards Tabora.

Shortly afterwards Lieutenant-Colonel Tomlinson received orders to join Lieutenant-Colonel Murray's Southern Rhodesia column—Northern Rhodesia Police and two companies of the British South Africa Police—which had been ordered to pursue Wintgens, who was reported to be at Neu Utengule, 30 miles northwest of Lake Nyasa. General Northey deployed 1/1st KAR to Old Utengule with the intention of denying him access to Northern Rhodesia, while Murray's column moved north to Neu Langenburg then on to the Igali Pass, arriving here on March 9. On the 15th Murray engaged Wintgens's rearguard at Neu Utengule, which withdrew following an exchange of fire. But it was quickly established that Wintgens was not heading for Northern Rhodesia, as thought, but was marching westwards towards St. Moritz Mission Station (now Galula) on the south bank of the Songwe River to the southeast of Lake Rukwa, where the only ford across that river was located. But the Songwe was flooded, and the only way across the river was via the bridge at St. Moritz.

Murray immediately ordered Tomlinson's 1st Rhodesia Native Regiment to lead the march to Itaka, just to the south of the mission, where he planned to rendezvous with 1/1st KAR before attacking Wintgens. But somehow Tomlinson misinterpreted his instructions, and when he was joined by an advanced company of the Northern Rhodesia Police, he marched to attack St. Moritz. He made contact with Wintgens's column on the 20th and in the sharp exchange of fire that followed the Rhodesia Native Regiment, taking a number of casualties and losing three of its machine guns, was forced to withdraw. But instead of retiring to the high ground just to the south of the mission, Tomlinson dug-in on the plains where his battalion was quickly surrounded.

Unable to break out, Tomlinson needed to make Murray aware of his precarious situation and have him come to his relief. Sergeant Fred Booth volunteered to carry the news to Murray. Accompanied by one of his askaris, Booth left the perimeter at 7:30 p.m. The two men were able to sneak undetected through the investing *Schutztruppe* and make their way to Itaka, having first informed Tomlinson the next morning of their successful evasion of the enemy, using a signal lamp from the hills to the south. Three days later Murray's column and 1/1st KAR advanced towards St. Moritz, arriving on the 27th, Sergeant Booth leading the advance party of the relief. Despite the arrival of Murray's column and 1/1st KAR, Wintgens continued his investment for a further four days, only breaking contact and withdrawing across the Songwe on the 31st. Sergeant Booth was subsequently awarded the Victoria Cross for this action and the rescue of his wounded scout on the 12th, the last won in Africa. General Northey's troops were unable to catch Wintgens, and he was last seen marching towards St. Boniface Mission on the Saisi River. The British commander asked the Belgians for assistance in hunting down the elusive German. A Belgian column of four battalions—the *4e, 6e, 9e* and *13e Bataillons de Marche*—under the command of Colonel Thomas, was duly dispatched to assist Northey.

Meanwhile, the newly activated 1/6th KAR, commanded by Major HG Montgomerie, MC, marched south from Tabora on March 23 in an attempt to intercept the German column. They reached Kipembawe on May 1 only to find that Wintgens had already passed through. The British C-in-C, Hoskins, ordered the formation of a flying column of 1,700 rifles and 14 machine guns designated "EDFORCE"—3/4th and 1/6th KAR, 30th Punjabis, 1st Cape Corps,[2] 4th Nigeria Regiment, 130th Baluchis, KAR Mounted Infantry and a mountain battery—under the command of Brigadier-General WFS Edwards, to hunt him down.

On May 21, Wintgens, suffering badly from fever and with his health deteriorating, handed over command of his column to 1st Lieutenant Heinrich Naumann. He then surrendered to the pursuing Belgian *6e Bataillon de Marche* near Lukalanka, 61 miles (98 kilometers) southwest of Tabora. While a prisoner of war, Wintgens learned that he had been awarded the *Order Pour le Mérite*.

Twelve. The Long Pursuit

Having left Wintgens to surrender to the Belgians, Naumann continued northwards. He crossed the Central Railway east of Tabora on the 26th and headed towards the frontier of British East. As he crossed the railway, the 4th Nigeria Regiment, deployed to pursue and intercept him in conjunction with the Belgian *4e Bataillon de Marche*, was within 12 miles (19 kilometers) of the crossing point and marching hard to intercept him. Despite their efforts, they arrived at the crossing point two hours after he had passed. Two days later the Belgian *13e Bataillon de Marche* linked up with 4th Nigeria Regiment at Malongwe, and both units, now the Malongwe column under the command of Lieutenant-Colonel J Sargent (Lancashire Fusiliers), took up the pursuit.

Earlier, on May 3, 1917, the Secretary of State for War decided to relieve General Hoskins as Commander-in-Chief East Africa, ordering him to Mesopotamia (now Iraq) to take up command of the 3rd Lahore Division. Hoskins handed over to the newly promoted Lieutenant-General van Deventer, who had just returned from sick leave in South Africa, on May 29.

On taking command van Deventer broke up the 1st EA Division at Kilwa—he felt that the divisional system had proved too unwieldy for operations against a small mobile enemy and that fighting columns, similar to those employed by von Lettow-Vorbeck, would prove more effective and easier to control and direct—and reconstituted it as Kilwa Force. The division's two infantry brigades were redesignated No. 1 column (33rd Punjabis, Gold Coast Regiment, 2/2nd KAR, 22nd Mountain Battery) and No. 2 column (57th Wilde's Rifles, 129th Baluchis, 1/3rd KAR, 2/3rd KAR, 11th [Hull] Heavy Battery, RA, 27th Mountain Battery) under the commands of Colonels GM Orr and H Grant respectively. Brigadier-General Beves had by this time taken over temporary command at Kilwa, as General Hannyngton was sick with fever. Van Deventer ordered him to locate and attack the Germans as soon as his forces were ready to resume operations. Kilwa Force held a line running from the coast to Liwale, 120 miles (193 kilometers) to the southwest, and a light railway had been built as far as Migeregere as part of its main supply route.

Van Deventer also arranged to strengthen the forces at Lindi with a brigade of King's African Rifles (1/2nd, 3/2nd, 3/4th KAR and No. 259 MG Company) under Brigadier-General O'Grady before resuming offensive operations—a two-pronged attack from Kilwa and Lindi towards Massasi to cut off the main German force from Portuguese East Africa. Lindi had been garrisoned till this time by only two companies of the 2nd West India Regiment, who were under constant observation by *Schutztruppe* patrols. O'Grady's orders where to draw off and contain as many German troops from Kilwa as possible by clearing the Germans from the Ngapa—Schaeffer's Farm—Mayani area to the west of Lindi— held by eight *Schutztruppe* companies commanded by General Wahle, who had arrived from Mahenge on June 3 after handing over his command there to Captain Theodor Tafel.

To counter this threat von Lettow-Vorbeck ordered Captain Wilhelm Rothe with three companies (the 19th and 20th Field and Tanga *Landsturm* Companies) to march from Mpotora to Lindi to reinforce Wahle. But he was confounded by heavy rain flooding the Nahungu district and the Matandu Valley. "At Nahungu, on the Mbemkuru, similar conditions hindered Captain Rothe's march. The stream was so strong that the first attempt to cross by the few ferry-boats available failed. Driven out of Nahungu by scarcity of supplies, Captain Rothe marched into the fertile region to the northeast, in this way seriously compromising the plans of Headquarters. It was necessary that this fertile country northeast of Nahungu should be spared to serve as a reserve for the forces south of Kilwa and to provide for a strong reinforcement of these troops should tactical reasons make this necessary. The time that was lost before a message could be got through to Captain Rothe was very vexatious, but finally his division was diverted towards Lindi again in time to take part in some of the fighting."[3]

To carry out his orders Brigadier-General O'Grady formed two columns. The main column, which he would command, consisted of 25th Royal Fusiliers (just returned from R&R in South Africa), 3/2nd KAR, the Machine Gun Section and Trench Mortars of the 2nd West India Regiment, a two-gun section of 3rd South African Field Battery, and a company of the 61st Pioneers. The second or right column, consisting of 1/2nd KAR., the 5th Indian Light Infantry, half the 259th Machine Gun Company, and a section 27th Mountain Battery, was placed under the command of Lieutenant-Colonel Law of the 2nd West India Regiment. O'Grady planned to land his main column eight miles (13 kilometers) up the Lukuledi at Mkwaya Creek on the northern bank of the river where an agricultural trolley line connected all the plantations in the area to the Mkwaya landing stage. From here 3/2nd KAR would move down the Lukuledi toward Narunya then turn northeast towards Schaedel's Farm in the Mohambika Valley where it would rendezvous with the rest of the column advancing from Mkwaya. At the same time, Lieutenant-Colonel Law's column would advance from Lindi to Schaeffer's Farm and Naitiwa.

In the late afternoon and early evening, June 10, the main column began boarding lighters and large open boats lashed together in twos and threes. Once the entire force was embarked the lighters and open

Twelve. The Long Pursuit

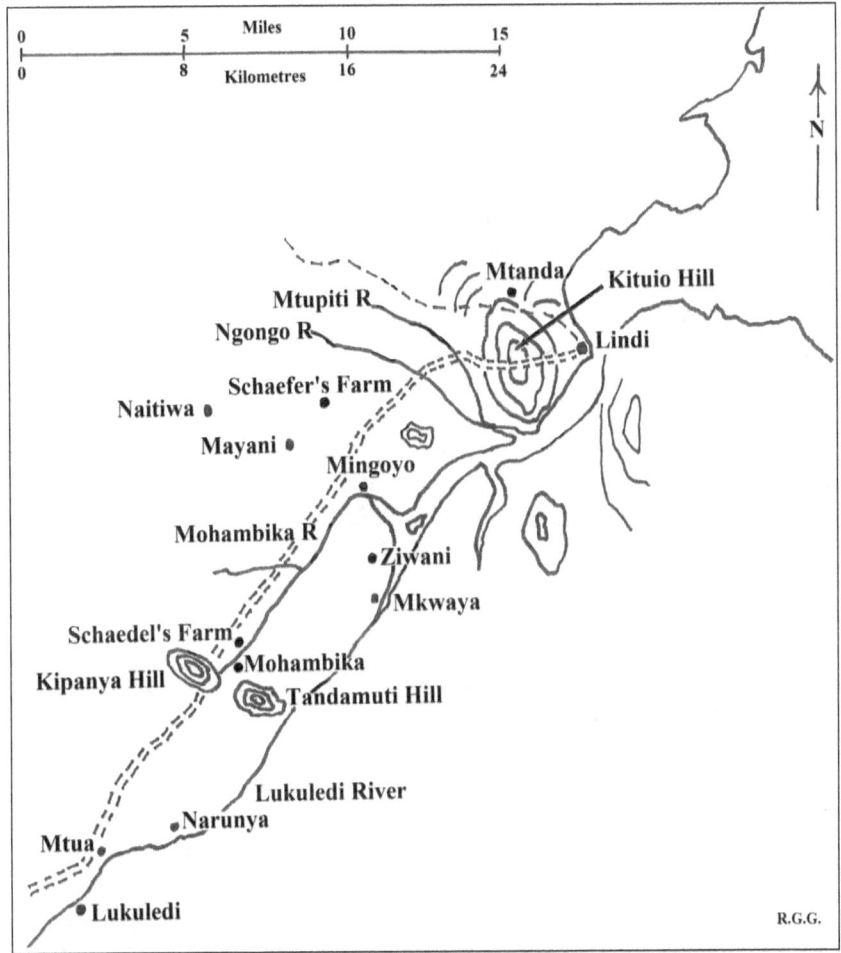

Lindi area (map by the author).

boats were towed by steam-tugs into the mouth of the river to await darkness. Covering them were the cruisers HMS *Hyacinth* and *Minerva*, the gunboat *Thistle* and the monitors *Severn* and *Mersey*, who would provide naval gunfire support to the columns. As soon as darkness fell, the small boat flotilla began moving up the Lukuledi led by armed motor-patrol boats, the lighters and open boats following in their wake; the motorboats towing the lighters and open boats had been armed for added security. The flotilla began landing the first wave just before 11 p.m., the troops wading through thick, knee-deep, cloying mud to the shore. Here they encountered an enemy picket from the 16th Field Company—part of Captain Eberhard von Lieberman's command—which opened fire on the landing force. Captain Spencer Tryon led a platoon of 3/2nd KAR up the muddy riverbank, forcing the picket to quickly withdraw. The 3/2nd KAR were all ashore, formed up and advancing to the southwest along the trolley line by 11 p.m. By 1 a.m., the 25th Royal Fusiliers and the other units of the column had arrived, wet through and plastered in mud. They were formed up on a long, narrow mud-flat just clear of the bush-covered shore, where they were told that there would be no move for at least two hours. Meanwhile Law's column, seven miles (11 kilometers) to the north, had begun advancing from Lindi across Kituio Hill and the Mtupiti and Ngongo rivers towards Schaeffer's Farm, Naitiwa and Mayani. During the night, the monitors *Severn* and *Mersey* took up station in the estuary from where they could provide supporting fire to the columns, and *Thistle* made her way upriver to a position from where her two 4-inch guns could also be of use to the ground forces.

At 3 a.m., the main column, which had been waiting patiently at Mkwaya Creek, began its advance. They moved slowly through the impenetrable darkness where visibility was down to a few yards, along the trolley line to Mkwaya village, arriving at the village just before dawn, while 3/2nd KAR reached the slopes of Tandamuti Hill in constant contact with small parties from the 16th Field Company. With the coming of daylight, Brigadier-General O'Grady altered his original plan and ordered all units of his column to turn north; 3/2nd KAR were to advance on Schaedel's Farm from Tandamuti Hill, while the 25th Fusiliers were to take Ziwani Ridge. Shortly after moving off, artillery fire was heard from the direction of Mingoyo, four miles (six and a half kilometers) to the north. Wahle's artillery had opened fire on *Thistle*, scoring a direct hit on the gunboat, damaging her but not putting her out of action due to the prompt and effective work of her damage control parties. *Thistle* and the two monitors immediately returned fire, and naval aircraft of No. 4 Squadron, Royal Naval Air Service, were aloft to spot for the guns and to try and observe enemy movements through the thick bush. Both *Hyacinth* and *Minerva* by now had maneuvered to positions from where they could add the weight of their firepower to the support of the columns—*Minerva's* captain having the ship's ballast moved to list the cruiser by twelve and a half degrees so that he could give additional range to the nine 6-inch guns of his main batteries.

After a two-hour unopposed advance, the 25th Fusiliers reached the high ground at Ziwani overlooking the Mohambika—an area of almost impenetrable sugarcane swamp—and could see a large number of enemy troops approximately 1,500 yards (1,372 meters) to their front and hear the German artillery in action further down the valley at Mingoyo. On the left, 3/2nd KAR, having only received the change in orders at 11:30 a.m., when they had been dropped to them by a RNAS aircraft, attempted to advance towards Schaedel's Farm but came under heavy fire from the *Schutztruppe*.

The 25th Fusiliers on Ziwani Ridge, meanwhile, had been ordered to dig-in. Covered by intense fire from machine guns positioned on the trolley line, the Germans advanced on O'Grady's position, driving back every attempt to descend into the valley. At 1:30 p.m., Wahle launched a strong infantry assault with 16th Field and Tanga *Landsturm* Companies against the left flank of the 25th Fusiliers. His companies had stealthily pushed forward through the thick bush to within 30 yards (27 meters) of the British position before launching their assault. A hot close-quarter action followed, exacerbated (as at Tanga in 1914) by swarms of angry African bees whose hives had been brought down from the trees by the gunfire. "They inflicted such punishment that many men could barely see through their half-closed eyelids on the following day, while everyone suffered from cruel yellow-poisoned face scars."[4] Reinforcing the Fusiliers with the company of the 61st Pioneers, O'Grady mounted a counterattack, driving the German companies back. The fighting here ended at nightfall, the Germans leaving behind two machine guns as they retired across the valley, while the Fusiliers and Pioneers consolidated their positions.

Meanwhile, 3/2nd KAR were slowly advancing through the thick bush towards Schaedel's Farm, when at 2:30 p.m., they were attacked from the southwest by the 19th Field and "S" Companies of Captain Looff's command. The KAR's No. 1 and 3 Companies immediately counterattacked, forcing the Germans to withdraw. As dusk approached and having been unable to rendezvous with the rest of the column, 2/3rd KAR's commander, Lieutenant-Colonel CG Phillips, MC (West Yorkshire Regt), decided to retrace his steps to Mkwaya. As they began their withdrawal, No. 2 Company, the rearguard, came under attack, and in the confusion of the night they lost two of their machine guns. "One had here a striking example of the difficulties of bush operations; of the disappointments, of the almost impossible task of keeping in touch with each force, across wide areas of dense, untouched, unfamiliar bush miles ahead of the base. One never knows, at the commencement of a day, the full difficulties to overcome; one can never altogether foresee the obstacles that will be encountered to enforce delay, be it an impassable swamp, impenetrable forest, an unbridged river, a loss of direction, or an unknown enemy force. It has been called a difficult campaign; but the difficulties have been so gigantic that the wonder one has is that the men who direct it have not grown old and grey with the weight of the anxieties imposed."[5]

Law's column too had faced heavy opposition as it advanced towards Mingoyo, and by nightfall both columns had to go firm. During the night, Wahle withdrew five miles (eight kilometers) down the valley to the southwest, establishing a defensive line at the village of Mohambika. The next morning Law's column occupied Mingoyo and Mrweka without opposition, and on the 13th the *Schutztruppe* companies begun withdrawing along the Lukuledi River, while O'Grady's Linforce consolidated its newly gained positions. Of the action, von Lettow-Vorbeck wrote, "In the middle of June, 1917, General Wahle had, after several engagements which had brought to light a considerable increase in the enemy's strength, retired so far up the river that the enemy seemed to be incautiously exposing his north flank."[6]

In the interior, Malongwe column, in pursuit of Lieutenant Naumann, reached Mkalama on June 8. The fort here had been under siege by Nauman's companies for the previous four days, but with the approach of the Malongwe column, Naumann lifted his siege and carried on to the north. Sargent's column followed them as far as Tirimo, 50 miles (80 kilometers) south of Lake Victoria Nyanza. On reaching Tirimo, 4th Nigeria Regiment received orders to return to Tabora, and Major Larsen, with his *13e Bataillon de Marche*, carried on the pursuit.

Naumann captured Ikoma on the 28th and the next morning Larsen caught up with him there. Despite being ordered to await the arrival of the *6e Bataillon* and the Nandi Scouts, who were marching to join him, Larsen attacked the fort. It was a trap. The fort was only lightly held, and as Larsen's attack went in, the main body of Naumann's force counterattacked. A sharp action followed in which the Belgians were surrounded, losing 138 killed, 11 wounded and 44 taken prisoner. They also lost their machine guns, 138 rifles and 25,000 rounds of small arms ammunition to the Germans, whose own losses were two killed, three wounded.

Naumann then marched east towards Lake Natron, and van Deventer was compelled to rush troops to the Arusha and Magadi areas to deny entry to the marauding column. So Naumann turned south, marching between Lakes Natron and Eyassi close to the eastern side of Mount Oldeani and headed for Ufiom and Kondoa-Irangi. He continually doubled back on his line of march, and in so doing completely confused the pursuing columns.

At the beginning of August, after a series of night marches through thick bush, Naumann led his troops through the British line stretching from Kondoa-Irangi and Dodoma, marching towards Luita in the east. The *6e* and *13e Bataillons de Marche* broke off their pursuit once the Germans had passed this line, leaving Lieutenant-Colonel Dyke's force to pursue Naumann. Dyke's column consisted of 1st Nigeria Regiment, 1st Cape Corps, KAR Mounted Infantry and the 10th South African Horse. This last unit had been reformed in South Africa at the request of General van Deventer to help in the pursuit of Naumann and was sent to East Africa for that specific purpose.

As Dyke closed on the Germans, Naumann split his column into three smaller groups, and on September 2 one of these groups, consisting of 109 Germans and askaris plus a large number of porters, was surrounded by the British and forced to surrender. Naumann, with the largest group of 14 Germans, 165 askaris and 300 porters, escaped across the Masai Steppe, reaching Geiro on the 15th. Here he found his advance blocked by the 10th SA Horse.

He immediately turned north, closely pursued by the

CSM Belo Akure, DCM, MM. Nigeria Regiment (Her Majesty's Stationery Office, 1919).

South Africans. By late September he had reached Luita Hill, a position of natural strong points surrounded by an abundance of water holes. The South Africans placed pickets on all the water holes then set about containing Naumann on Luita Hill until 3/4th KAR, commanded by Lieutenant-Colonel Harry Lilley, and 1st Cape Corps, under Major CN Hoy, arrived on the 30th and closely invested the German position. Realizing that further resistance was hopeless, Naumann surrendered on October 2. Naumann was subsequently sent to Britain to stand trial for war crimes, having allowed his officers to commit rape and murder. He was charged with cruelty to native women and the murder of Lieutenant Sutherland, who commanded a small group of native levies that assisted Larsen in his disastrous attack on Ikoma and who was killed after he surrendered. He was found guilty on all counts and sentenced to death. This sentence was commuted to seven years, but he was returned to Germany in 1919. The third of Naumann's groups, comprising three Germans and 53 askaris, surrendered to a detachment of the KAR Mounted Infantry from Arusha on October 3, near Lake Eyassi.

Meanwhile, on the coast, von Lettow-Vorbeck had abandoned the Kiturika Hills and fallen back south to the Matandu Valley, where on June 29, Lieutenant-Colonel AL Wilford, DSO, commanding the 5th Indian Light Infantry at Naitiwa, 15 miles (24 kilometers) west of Lindi, was informed of the presence of German units at Lutende, eight miles (13 kilometers) from his post. He immediately moved against them with a detachment of 150 rifles, attacking the camp of the 14th Reserve Company at dawn the next day, taking the enemy by surprise. The German company commander had been criticized by von Lettow-Vorbeck the previous evening for the poor positioning of the camp, which was in the open and surrounded by thick bush and which he had been instructed to relocate to a better defensive site. Unfortunately for Wilford, this was only one of two camps, and the three companies in the second camp—the 3rd, 9th Field and 4th Rifle Companies—counterattacked, surrounding the British force. "Assuming that the enemy had taken advantage of the lie of the ground and was firing on the camp from the surrounding bush, I immediately advanced with the three companies to the right through the bush, so as to strike the road further south and so take the enemy in the rear."[7] Wilford was mortally wounded in the counterattack, and his second-in-command, Captain WD Hall, took over. Following a savage and desperate fight, Hall broke through the surrounding *Schutztruppe* and was able to regain Naitiwa with only 50 men. "In addition to recovering our own ammunition, which had fallen temporarily into the enemy's hands, we captured the enemy's ammunition which he had just brought into the camp, about a hundred rifles and some machine guns. Among the severely wounded whom we took to the English camp at Naitiwi [sic], and there handed over, was the commanding officer of the English regiment. He afterwards died of his wound."[8]

By July 4, General Beves at Kilwa, having been reinforced by the 7th and 8th SA Infantry and 3/3rd KAR, was ready to begin operations. He formed a third column under Lieutenant-Colonel AJ Taylor (consisting of the 40th Pathans, 1/3rd KAR and two companies' 8th SA Infantry), which was to move down the coast to protect the left flank of 1 and 2 columns. Kilwa Force made first contact with a *Schutztruppe* force of eight companies, commanded by Captain Eberhard von Lieberman—the 10th, 11th, 17th, 21st and 27th Field, 14th Reserve, 3rd and 10th Rifle Companies, two field guns and 48 machine guns, and a group of Angoni levies—on July 6 at Mnindi.

Leading the British advance was 2/2nd KAR. The battalion reached a millet field close by Mnindi that had recently been cropped at 8:20 a.m., and here they came under heavy machine-gun fire. No. 1 and 2 Companies opened a holding attack, while No. 4 Company moved round to attack von Lieberman's left flank, and two companies of the 8th SA Infantry deployed to attack the right of his position. A hot firefight followed, and Colonel Orr sent forward the Gold Coast Regiment and two guns of the 22nd Mountain Battery to assist Lieutenant-Colonel Filsell, who held them in reserve. When the flank attacks began at 2 p.m., however, von Lieberman broke contact and withdrew.

Von Lieberman was contacted again the next day by No. 2 column at Mikikama, where the first serious action took place, the British suffering severe losses during the day's fighting. The next morning, the 8th, they were reinforced by the Gold Coast Regiment from No. 1 column, while No. 3 column was executing a wide flank march to cut off von Lieberman's companies, forcing him to break contact again and retire to the Narungombe water holes. "In spite of this success at Unindi [sic], the great superiority of the enemy and the danger from enveloping movements to our supplies in the rear, induced Captain von Lieberman to withdraw gradually south, fighting all the time."[9] Here the *Schutztruppe* set to preparing defensive positions. They strongly entrenched a line stretching for two and a half miles (four kilometers) and consisting of a series of sangars built on the upper slopes of two hills, one on either side of the road, connected by a two-and-a-half-foot-high breastwork. The right flank of the position ended in bushy swamp, while the left was protected by very thick, almost impenetrable scrub; within these defenses von Lieberman had his eight companies deployed four forward and four in reserve, with the forward companies supported by his 48 machine guns.

Beves had little information regarding the German positions at Narungombe but still ordered an attack for July 19. A frontal assault was to be mounted by No. 1 column, while elements of No. 2 and 3 were to undertake simultaneous flank attacks on the German right and left, respectively. "The enemy's main position was reached before 0700 hours. It proved to be a series of breastworks and redoubts, occupying the upper slopes of two hills, one on either side of the road, and extending for a distance of two miles. The Germans had eight companies, two guns and 48 machine guns, and were evidently determined that this time there should be no rapid withdrawal. The three British columns totalled about 1,700 men with 20 machine guns."[10]

As No. 1 column deployed in line, the Gold Coast Regiment in the center, the 33rd Punjabis on the right and 7th SA Infantry (from No. 2

column) on the left, with 8th SA Infantry, minus its detached companies, in support, the Germans opened fire, and by 8:15 a.m., they were heavily engaged. As No. 1 column advanced in extended order, No. 3 column moved against the enemy's left, with the 40th Pathans and 3/3rd KAR leading, while Captain HT Griffiths's (Imperial Light Horse) No. 2 Company of 2/2nd KAR from Force Reserve occupied a hill on the enemy right and opened an enfilading fire on their main positions. No. 3 column advanced steadily against the German left and by noon was in contact with them in the thick scrub. "The 3rd Battalion of the 3rd King's African Rifles and the 40th Pathans had been pushed forward, without any preliminary scouting, into a valley on the British left, where they presently came under a devastating rifle and machine gun fire from both forces. By this time the enemy's fire had grown intense along the whole line; and the 8th South African Infantry, the bulk of whom still formed part of No. 1 Column and occupied ground on the left of the Gold Coast Regiment, attempted to advance, but were enfiladed by machine gun and rifle fire from salients in the enemy's line. They maintained their position for a while, but the troops upon their left failed to make good, and the grass all round them was set on fire by the British shells."[11] No. 2 column had also made contact, and the fighting was becoming increasingly heavier as they pushed through the long grass, which had been set on fire by von Lieberman's field guns and the Stokes' mortars of the British.

The 3/3rd KAR, in action for the first time, lost its commander during a German counterattack, and as a consequence, by 3:30 p.m., No. 3 column began to retire, exposing No. 1 column's left flank to heavy fire. On the enemy's right flank, meanwhile, 1/3rd KAR was, in its turn, subjected to a savage counterattack, but they held firm and drove off the enemy, then fixing bayonets charged forward into the enemy's trenches. The *Schutztruppe* abandoned their left flank positions in the face of the oncoming KAR bayonets.

On the *Schutztruppe's* front, No. 1 column's attack was losing momentum, their advance slowed by the withering fire directed at them. The 2/2nd KAR were sent forward from Force Reserve to reinforce them, and at 4 p.m., they, along with the Gold Coast Regiment and 33rd Punjabis, charged and took the Germans' advance trenches. But they were all running low on ammunition and their left was still exposed. As a consequence, they were forced to fall back 100 yards (91 meters) and dig-in.

During the night, von Lieberman quietly abandoned his positions and withdrew further south. At dawn, when the *Schutztruppe's* withdrawal was discovered, Beves's troops occupied the abandoned defenses. He established a large fortified camp at Narungombe and had a crude airfield constructed, as there was to be no major move by his troops for several weeks. "The occupation of Narungombe practically completed the clearing of the Kiturika Hills, which had been an arduous task for the troops engaged. The effective fighting strength of the Kilwa force had been greatly depleted by malaria and other sickness, and rest and reinforcements were necessary before the advance could be resumed."[12] Of the action, von Lettow-Vorbeck concluded, "At Narungombe, where all the conditions were as favourable as could have been hoped, the decision was finally thwarted by slight mischances, and my belief was strengthened that if I wanted to use different bodies of troops in one operation it was necessary to secure the closest connection first. The engagement at Narungombe brought the enemy at Kilwa to a standstill for a considerable time, and the fighting was confined to patrols, who inflicted losses on the enemy's lines of communication, firing out of the bush on his detachments and motor transport and attacked at close quarters when a favourable opportunity offered."[13]

The *Schutztruppe*, on withdrawing from Narungombe, had dug-in at Mihambia 12 miles (19 kilometers) to the south and Ndessa ten miles (16 kilometers) south of Mihambia, where von Lettow-Vorbeck had one of his principal forward bases and supply depots. Van Deventer planned to drive them off these positions and force them to the south using Hannyngton's Kilwa Force. They were to be driven into the arms of Linforce, which was to cut off their line of retreat. During August he had the Nigerian Brigade, less 3rd Nigeria Regiment which was sent to Lindi to strengthen Linforce, moved from their camp at Morogoro to Kilwa in preparation for this offensive.

The operation began on September 18 with No. 1 column, consisting of 2/2nd KAR, 33rd Punjabis, part of the Gold Coast Regiment and 27th Mountain Battery, closing on Mihambia. The next day 2/2nd KAR advanced on the enemy positions along the main road while "A" Company and half the Pioneer Company, Gold Coast Regiment and the artillery, covering the column's right flank, pushed through the bush, marching on a compass bearing to attack the Germans' left flank. Von Lieberman's companies were dug-in along the crest of a hill on the left of the road which sloped up from the water holes and which dominated them and the Narungombe Road. The flank attack missed its objective, however, and the troops found themselves in front of the *Schutztruppe* defenses. The commander of the flank force, Major GS Shaw (South Lancs Regt), immediately ordered his infantry into the attack, supported by the mountain guns; they were quickly joined by the KAR in pressing their assault. The water holes were easily taken, but when the British moved against the dominating hill—which they thought was unoccupied—they discovered it was held in strength. Throughout the remainder of the day, the column mounted repeated assaults only to be driven back each time, and as night approached, they were forced to break off action and dig-in.

Meanwhile, Lieutenant-Colonel RA de B Rose, with the remainder of the Gold Coast Regiment, marched from their camp at Liwinda Ravine to Nambunjo Hill overlooking the Npingo-Mnitshi Road; reaching the hill at 2:45 p.m., they established a defended camp. Rose had earlier detached two patrols as he closed on Nambunjo, one to cover his right flank, the second to take the German signal station located at Npingo five miles (eight kilometers) from Mnitshi. Both patrols were soon in contact with the *Schutztruppe*; Lieutenant RC Woods—commanding the right flank patrol—was ordered to dig-in and protect the regiment's right flank and rear. Fifteen minutes before reaching Nambunjo, Rose had detached Captain EB Methven, MC (KOYLI), with 90 rifles from "B" Company to pick up Lieutenant SB Smith's patrol at Npingo and then advance to Mihambia to reinforce "A" Company and 2/2nd KAR.

By 5 p.m., Methven was around one and a half miles (two and a half kilometers) south of Mihambia and was in contact with the enemy. Thirty minutes later Lieutenant Smith's patrol, having been located by the Germans and almost surrounded, was able to extricate itself and fall back to Methven's position. As night was fast approaching, any further advance towards Mihambia was out of the question. During the night, von Lieberman's force once again slipped away. "The state of our supplies made it impossible for us to maintain so strong a force in the Mihambia-Ndessa area. As in any case the evacuation of this area could not long be delayed, and as the enemy west of Lindi was at the same time developing increased activity in strong force on General Wahle's front, I decided to join General Wahle with some of the companies from Ndessa and perhaps bring off the operation that had failed at Narungombe; a decisive success by an unexpected reinforcement."[14]

On the 22nd the Nigerian Brigade, operating on Kilwa Force's right flank, became embroiled in an action at Bweho Chini, 30 miles (48 kilometers) southwest of Narungombe and ten southeast of Ndessa. The brigade had bivouacked for the night of the 21st/22nd at Luale Chini. The next morning, leaving the 4th Nigeria Regiment and artillery at Luale, the 1st and 2nd Nigeria Regiments and brigade HQ advanced to Bweho Chini. The lead company of 1st Nigeria Regiment drove in the German picket and entered the hamlet of Bweho Chini at 9:30 a.m., where a defensive perimeter was established and the troops breakfasted.

The Nigeria Regiment advancing through the bush, German East Africa (Her Majesty's Stationery Office, UK Ministry of Information, First World War collection/Q15402).

From here General Cunliffe planned to attack the nearby German position at Mawerenye. He had the two battalions formed up ready to move, following their meal, when he received intelligence from two different sources that indicated that the enemy was still at Bweho Ju and that their line of retreat to Mawerenye was through Bweho Chini. The first came from Sergeant Mafinde Shewa of the 2nd Nigeria Regiment, who, with 2nd Lieutenant F Hobson (4th Northampton Regiment) and a detachment of 16 men, had been ordered to escort the brigade baggage back to the 4th Nigeria Regiment's location before the move began. As the escort was returning to the brigade along the Bweho Carti road, they spotted a party of Germans. Sergeant Shewa immediately led his section in an attack on the enemy party; they captured a German officer and three askaris along with 29 boxes of small arms ammunition, six of which contained British .303 rounds.[15] The second indication came when a picket on the Bweho Ju road captured another German officer carrying documents that showed the enemy's line of retreat was through Bweho Chini. Cunliffe cancelled his attack and had the battalions return to their perimeter positions.

At 12:30 p.m., two companies of 1st Nigeria Regiment were ordered to carry out a reconnaissance towards Mawerenye. They had only advanced 700 yards (640 meters) when they made contact with an enemy force 1,200 strong with 20 machine guns, under the command of 1st Lieutenant Franz Köhl—the 10th, 14th, 17th and 21st Field 3rd and 6th Rifle Companies and detachments Batzner and Haberkorn—which drove them back to the brigade's perimeter. The *Schutztruppe* then invested the Nigerian position, mounting repeated attacks throughout the afternoon and night. The last attack came in at 9:50 p.m., with the German officers reportedly driving their askaris forward with rhinoceros hide whips and rifle butts. Shortly after, Köhl broke off action, having learned that No. 2 column was approaching his rear in an attempt to cut his line of retreat. On the 24th, No. 2 column linked up with the Nigerians, and preparations were made to take Nahungo. Köhl's force suffered 340 casualties in this action, of whom 103 were killed; Nigerian casualties were 134 all ranks. "During the long battle of Bweho-Chini everyone from the General downwards took an active part with rifle and entrenching tool. The men had fought magnificently throughout this day with a coolness beyond praise. Scarcity of ammunition, and urgent need of food and water, rendered pursuit impossible. Further, there were insufficient porters remaining with these battalions even to carry away the wounded, let alone the supplies that would be required to continue the advance."[16]

The advance did resume, however, on the 27th with three assault columns moving down three converging routes. The skirmishing with the enemy rearguard continued until 8 p.m. that evening when the Germans broke contact and withdrew. No. 1 column fought another two minor actions at Kihende on the 30th and Mitonono on October 1, pressing on to Mnero Mission Station, which they took on the 9th and by the 16th had established a camp at Ruponda, where they captured a large supply depot and a base workshop. Linforce's advance, meanwhile, had been vigorously opposed by five companies of Wahle's command who had severely mauled the 2nd KAR on each contact.

Shortly after the British advance began, von Lettow-Vorbeck ordered Wahle to bring the remainder of his companies to reinforce those engaged at Lindi. He then launched a counterattack against O'Grady's leading units, the 25th Fusiliers and 1/2nd KAR at Nrunya,[17] only 20 miles (32 kilometers) from Lindi. His troops were able to get behind the British units undetected in the thick bush, and these, once they realized they were surrounded and cut off, were forced to halt and dig-in; "The enemy were shelling the square and shooting dangerously close, but were unable to locate us exactly, or tell where their shells were landing, in the dense bush."[18] For the next five days von Lettow-Vorbeck's askaris subjected the Fusiliers and KAR to constant and heavy attack: "We lay in the confined square in our shallow trenches, drinking sparingly of foul water, and holding impatiently on, while smaller engagements went on with the enemy, who continued to invest our front closely and right flank. Our porters had a bad time here. In time cooked food was sent up for them from the rear, but on the first two days it was common to see the poor creatures hungrily munching their uncooked ration of hard rice-grains. At the end of the five days, many of them were almost unable to walk, and could not be burdened with an ammunition load,"[19] until, on September 25, the main body of Linforce was able to drive the *Schutztruppe* from their positions with artillery fire and relieve the beleaguered battalions. O'Grady was then able to push as far as Mtua.

On the 28th they attacked the German rearguard on the Nengidi River in a fierce action that lasted throughout the day in the face of stubborn resistance, which only ended with nightfall, the *Schutztruppe* withdrawing to the Nyengedi River, where they again dug-in. Linforce's advanced screen made contact with their patrols at 10 a.m. on the 30th, and the main body deployed into line before advancing against the German entrenchments. Again, the *Schutztruppe* put up a stubborn resistance, forcing O'Grady's troops to dig-in. They were then subjected to two savage counterattacks by the Germans, who were in their turn repulsed, before breaking contact as evening approached.

General van Deventer, meanwhile, moved his HQ to Kilwa in preparation for the junction of Kilwa and Lindi Forces and the subsequent advance south. A large supply dump was built up in preparation for the planned offensive, and the Nigerian Brigade was ordered to march across country from Ruponda to reinforce O'Grady's Linforce near Nyangao, 80 miles (129 kilometers) to their southeast. O'Grady's orders were, once the Nigerians arrived, to make contact with and destroy Wahle's companies,[20] which had arrived in the Lukuledi Valley along with the five companies covering Lindi he had come to reinforce. He was to begin his advance on October 8, linking up with the Nigerians on the 10th.

Thirteen

Mahiwa, Lukuledi Mission and Withdrawal to the Rovuma

THE NIGERIAN BRIGADE BEGAN its cross-country march on October 3, traveling via Mhulu and Nahauga, where they learned of enemy outposts on their line-of-march. To avoid these outposts, and to maintain secrecy, the brigade diverted via the Tschipwada and Nyengedi rivers. On the 8th, heavy gunfire could be heard from the southeast. Linforce had begun its advance from Nyengedi, attacking and driving back the *Schutztruppe* at Nyangao and taking Mtama on the 13th, having driven them from their defenses with a heavy artillery bombardment the previous day and forced them to fall back on Mahiwa.

On the 9th the Nigerians received orders to press on with all haste to Mahiwa to outflank and attack the German force's rear. By the 12th, they were at Narumbego, having crossed the Rondo Plateau. Here a short halt was made while their baggage was cut to the barest necessity, and 283 sick men were evacuated to Mtua.

Meanwhile, von Lettow-Vorbeck had been informed by Wahle of Linforce's attack on his position at Nyangao and Mtama and his withdrawal to Mahiwa. On October 10 he marched with five companies and two mountain guns across the steep, narrow and treacherous paths of the Linkangara Mountains to reinforce Wahle. "On the narrow mountain paths the force got very scattered. The guns were left far behind, and the pack-animals gave trouble. Askari and bearers came to the rescue, and again and again Sergeant-Major Sabath rose superior to the difficulties and brought his guns forward. It surprised me that we were unable to get any information from Mahiwa, but the rifle and machine gun fire indicated that fighting was in progress."[1]

On the 14th the Nigerians reached Namupa Mission Station, three and a half miles (six kilometers) north of Mahiwa. Here they established a baggage camp and left No. 4 Company of 1st Nigeria Regiment and the Pioneer Company as baggage guard. Early on the 15th, 1st Nigeria

Thirteen. Mahiwa, Lukuledi Mission and the Rovuma

Regiment (less No. 4 Company), the Gambia Company and a section of artillery were sent to Nyangao, four miles (six and a half kilometers) to the southeast, with orders to block the Mahiwa road, while the remainder of the brigade marched to attack Wahle's Mahiwa positions. Wahle, meanwhile, had deployed his companies astride the Nyangao-Mahiwa road on a ridge behind the Nakadi River, two miles (three and a quarter kilometers) southwest of Nyangao and two miles southeast of Mahiwa. It was here that von Lettow-Vorbeck joined him on the 15th, deploying his five companies behind those of Wahle. "Before dark I reached Lieutenant Methner's company [4th Rifle Company], which was in reserve behind Wahle's left wing. The enemy seemed to be attacking this company with a view to enveloping it. His fire had the unfortunate effect of causing the disappearance of my bearer, with my dispatch-box, containing most important dispatches and maps: he did not return for two days. The first two companies to come up were immediately thrown against the enemy's enveloping movement, and the enemy was thrown back. The companies then dug themselves in."[2]

The Nigerian's lead companies made contact with the *Schutztruppe's* screen—Captain Karl Göring's detachment, the 4th, 13th, 14th, 17th Field and 8th Rifle Companies—soon after leaving the mission. They were ordered not to engage but to push on. Resistance increased as they approached the Mahiwa River, where they were stopped by heavy fire. A defensive perimeter was established, and by noon the two leading companies were reinforced by a third. At 4:15 p.m., the brigade's temporary commander, Major GD Mann (General Cunliffe was in hospital ill), was ordered by Brigadier-General Beves to keep advancing, to press on in spite of opposition. Mann decided to try and turn the enemy's right flank with a company attack. As this was being executed, the Germans directed a heavy fire on the attacking company's right and left front. Within ten minutes their left was being seriously threatened, and they were in danger of being cut off from the brigade. The company commander ordered them to withdraw to the brigade perimeter on the riverbank, which itself was under heavy attack. These attacks on the Nigerians went on uninterrupted until 7:30 p.m., when the Germans broke contact.

Meanwhile, 1st Nigeria Regiment and the Gambia Company had advanced towards Nyangao in the face of steadily increasing opposition and by 9:30 a.m. were taking heavy casualties. They were within two miles (three and a quarter kilometers) of their objective when the column commander, Major CE Roberts (Northamptonshire Regt), ordered them to halt and establish a defensive perimeter on a small hill overlooking the track leading to the Nyangao-Mahiwa road. The next morning, the 16th, Roberts received orders to withdraw to Namupa and from there reinforce the brigade on the Mahiwa River. Roberts withdrew from his defensive position without opposition, reaching the mission at 11 a.m. and after a short halt to allow his troops to eat, marched for Mahiwa.

At the brigade position, the 2nd and 4th Nigeria Regiments had a reasonably quiet night, and during the morning, they were subjected to only sporadic harassing fire. Then, at 2:30 p.m., the German artillery began bombarding their position and casualties began to mount. "Again and again the 70mm. shelled these unfortunate companies. A sector of 14 Company trenches at one time received three direct hits upon it in succession. There were no alternative trenches to retire to, and no safe 'dug outs' to shelter in. Every direct hit found its human target; the trees above this trench were dripping blood for two days afterwards from limbs and trunks of men that had been blown up and been wedged between the branches."[3] Just before 4:30 p.m., the bombardment stopped, and a heavy infantry assault was launched against the perimeter, which was beaten off, the *Schutztruppe* taking heavy losses from the Nigerian rifle and machine-gun fire. "The Germans in this infantry attack, delivered at 4:30 p.m., must have suffered most heavily. Confident that their guns had so shaken the 4th Battalion, they came on in close formation against 14 and 15 Companies, and must have been mown down by machine gun and rifle fire."[4]

Earlier, at around 2 p.m., Captain Göring, who was opposite the Nigerians' eastern perimeter, withdrew two Field Companies, one from his detachment and one from 1st Lieutenant Walter von Ruckteschell's—the 13th and 21st Field Companies—to intercept Roberts's column, which was reported pushing quickly down from the mission. Göring's attack took Roberts completely by surprise, and by 3 p.m., the column was hard-pressed. The extremely savage fighting raged for an hour, during which time one of the Nigerian guns was taken after its crew were shot down. Roberts withdrew his advance company 250 yards (229 meters), ordering it to dig-in, while the remainder of his force followed suit shortly after. But it wasn't long before he had to abandon this makeshift position, forced out by Göring's determined attacks, and withdraw in contact to the mission, reaching it at 7 p.m.

At Mtama, General O'Grady ordered 3rd Nigeria Regiment to march to and relieve the Namupa Mission, then, following the relief, escort 1st Nigeria Regiment and the Gambia Company plus the brigade baggage to Nyangao, which had been evacuated by the Germans on the night of the 16th. The battalion successfully fought its way to the mission, reaching it at 1 p.m. on the afternoon of the 17th.

Thirteen. Mahiwa, Lukuledi Mission and the Rovuma 161

Lieutenant-Colonel HC Tytler (Indian Army), commanding Linforce's recently formed No. 4 column (3/4th KAR, 25th Fusiliers, 30th Punjabis and No. 259 MG Company) had, meanwhile, occupied Nyangao, while O'Grady, with No. 3 column (1/2nd and 3/2nd KAR and Bharatpur Infantry), was on their right flank. Tytler's column advanced to and attacked the *Schutztruppe* positions on the ridge at dawn on the 17th, with 3/4th KAR gaining a small foothold in the German defenses by 1 p.m.[5] At the same time, No. 3 column, with 1/2nd KAR leading and supported by 3/2nd KAR and the Bharatpur Infantry, were attacking the northern end of the defenses. The 1/2nd KAR's machine-gun company lost all its gun crews to heavy and accurate German fire during the attack as they attempted to cover the advance of "A" and "B" Companies, the two leading Rifle Companies, who, after taking heavy losses, were forced to retreat. "C" Company was sent forward, passing through them with fixed bayonets, to stabilize their front. Lieutenant-Colonel George Giffard, the battalion commander, then brought forward his fourth company, "D" Company, to reinforce the line while the first two companies were being regrouped. The battalion was then able to form and hold a defensive line. Shortly after midday, the battalion came under heavy attack, and later in the afternoon two companies of 3/2nd KAR had to be sent forward to help Giffard's men hold their position. At 8 p.m. that evening, the *Schutztruppe* broke contact. Giffard's battalion lost half its British officers and SNCOs and more than a third of its Africans in the attack.

Von Lettow-Vorbeck deduced that the British would now use the same frontal assault tactics that they had employed at great cost at Reata Nek in March the previous year. He had Wahle's companies moved to strengthen the center of his position, from where they would be able to inflict maximum damage on the British. Beves did just as von Lettow-Vorbeck had expected him to, throwing his men again and again at his positions. They failed to take the German defenses, being driven back repeatedly by strong counterattacks: "Every available company was withdrawn from the left wing to stiffen General Wahle's front. In this way we not only succeeded in holding our ground, but, by immediately taking advantage of the enemy's moments of weakness to make heavy counter-attacks with our reserves, we were able to inflict a real defeat."[6]

The 3rd Nigeria Regiment, on its return to Nyangao, was ordered to rejoin No. 3 column, which it did in time to take part in the attacks of the morning of the 18th, taking up position in a gap between No. 3 and No. 4 columns. Early that afternoon O'Grady ordered his forces to break contact. And at 3 p.m., No. 3 column, covered by 3rd Nigeria Regiment, withdrew to a position just north of Nyangao. At 5:15 p.m., the *Schutztruppe* launched a counterattack against 3rd Nigeria Regiment which lasted until 6:30 p.m. Though the Nigerians stoutly resisted this determined attack, they sustained heavy losses before the Germans withdrew, ending the hardest fighting of the campaign, which, like every other action fought in East Africa, was indecisive.

British losses at the battle of Mahiwa were 579 killed, 1,072 wounded and 250 missing. German losses were also heavy, 95 killed and 400 wounded, casualties that von Lettow-Vorbeck was unable to replace.

Six hours after the British retirement von Lettow-Vorbeck withdrew from his position and marched his companies back over the Linkangara Mountains, taking with him a field gun, nine machine guns and 200,000 rounds of small arms ammunition abandoned by the British. He left behind Wahle, who had withdrawn to Mkwere, to reorganize his badly mauled companies and to observe Linforce.

The day after the battle General Cunliffe arrived back from sick leave and assumed command of Linforce. He immediately began preparations to attack Wahle at Mkwere, a mile (one and a half kilometers) from Mahiwa settlement, having been reinforced by the return of Dyke's column following their successful operations against Naumann.

Over the following days, however, a number of patrol encounters occurred, and Wahle reoccupied his former Mahiwa positions. On November 6, O'Grady's No. 3 column, strengthened by the addition of 1st Cape Corps, attacked and drove Wahle back to Mkwere. "This was the severest day's fighting the battalion had experienced to date, and the magnificent conduct of the men under heavy shell and machine gun fire at close range was a source of much gratification to all concerned. Desultory fighting continued until 3 a.m. on the 7th and, after a couple of hours break, began again and continued all day. The enemy had failed to surround us as they had apparently hoped, and for the next thirty-six hours appeared to be irresolute whether to attack again vigorously or to retire. Their searching shell fire was, however, very accurate, dropping into our trenches on both right and left flanks. Shelling continued all day and two attacks from the west were beaten off."[7] The Nigerian Brigade, having unsuccessfully attempted to link up with No. 4 column and cut the enemy's line of communications, was ordered to make for Mkwere to assist O'Grady.

The Nigerians joined No. 3 column in front of Mkwere early the next morning, the 7th. O'Grady then attacked the German position, and following a savage action involving 1st Cape Corps and the Nigerians that lasted until the evening of the 8th, Wahle withdrew, abandoning large quantities of weapons and supplies. He made another stand at

Hatia but was driven from here by a heavy artillery bombardment and withdrew steadily down the Lukuledi from then on, making only token stands at Ndanda, Nangoo and Chiwata.

In the north, Lieutenant-Colonel Orr's No. 1 column from Kilwa Force—with the 25th Indian Cavalry (Frontier Force) less a squadron, two armored cars of 7th Light Armoured Car Battery, and the 1/3rd KAR and 129th Baluchis from No. 2 column, under command—was ordered to move from Ruponda against Major Kraut's three companies at Lukuledi Mission. The column halted just over half a mile north of the Lukuledi River on the morning of October 18, and here a defended base camp was prepared by 2/2nd KAR. Orr planned to attack the mission frontally that afternoon with the Gold Coast Regiment, while 1/3rd KAR, having marched through the bush to the west, simultaneously attacked the enemy's left flank. The 129th Baluchis and 2/2nd KAR were to protect the camp and baggage and form column reserve.

The attack began as scheduled with Captain Methven's "B" Company, Gold Coast Regiment, supported by the armored cars, advancing down the Ruponda Road from the camp and across the river. Methven deployed his company into line as they approached the Ndanda Road junction, 250 yards (229 meters) north of the mission, with his machine-gun section on the road and one armored car in support, the second vehicle having broken down on the approach. Meanwhile, Lieutenant RC Woods's platoon continued forward up the slope leading to the mission. Unbeknown to Woods, he was entering Kraut's pre-prepared killing ground, the Germans having burnt away all the scrub protecting the approaches to the mission from the north and south. With no sign of the enemy reported by Woods, Methven ordered the rest of the company forward.

Once the entire company was in the killing ground, Kraut ordered his companies, concealed in the mission compound and fort, to open fire. "The position in which Captain Methven's little force found itself was desperate, no less; but, as usual, the courage, the discipline and the steadfastness of the men were beyond praise. Hugging the bare ground as closely as they might they returned the enemy's fire; but save the boma, they had no target at which to aim, while the Germans were firing upon them, as the accuracy of their marksmanship proved, at ranges which had been carefully ascertained in advance."[8]

Methven's company, taking heavy casualties from the Germans' devastating fire, desperately sought whatever cover they could find. "Captain Methven brought his machine gun into action, and Colour-Sergeant Cuneen,[9] who was working it, was immediately killed. Sergeant-Major Mama Juma, who took his place, was instantly hit, and

Soldiers of the Gold Coast Regiment in marching order; their hats are typical West African styles of the period.

though it was now evident that the enemy had the position of this gun 'taped,' as it is called, and that it was practically certain death for any one to touch it, the gun-team continued to try to serve it until every man among them had been killed or wounded."[10] And the armored car was immobilized when its tires were shredded by the heavy incoming fire. In the advanced platoon Lieutenant Richard Woods had been killed along with a number of his askaris, and his platoon sergeant, Sergeant Yessufu Mamprusi, MM, though himself wounded, took command, directing the remainder of the platoon to return fire.

The guns of 27th Mountain Battery[11] quickly came into action in support of Methven's beleaguered company once the ambush had been sprung, engaging all likely targets in and around the mission compound, while the second armored car, once again mobile, moved forward to join its companion. The remainder of the Gold Coast Regiment took up fire positions on the north bank of the river from where they opened fire on the mission, while the Gold Coast Pioneer Company was ordered forward to support Methven.

When the Pioneer's commander conferred with Methven, however, it was agreed that his company could do little to improve the situation and would only sustain heavy casualties if they attempted to move forward. Methven would hold his position until nightfall and then withdraw. Lieutenant R de B Saunderson, though, was sent forward from the Pioneer Company to take over command of Woods's platoon from Sergeant Mamprussi, who had taken a further two bullet wounds. On

Thirteen. Mahiwa, Lukuledi Mission and the Rovuma

taking over, Robert Saunderson attempted to charge forward to the mission, only to be killed along with a number of the platoon. Mamprussi again took command and withdrew the survivors back to their former fire positions.

Meanwhile, Lieutenant-Colonel Fitzgerald's 1/3rd KAR were still deep in the bush, marching towards the sound of the guns. They had taken too wide a swing to the west in their flank march, and the leading platoons were only just approaching the mission. These platoons were able to break into the compound, only to be driven out by incoming fire from the 27th Mountain Battery. They quickly withdrew to and took up defensive positions in the Rubber Plantation just to the west of the mission compound. In the late afternoon Kraut launched a counterattack with his reserve, which had been held near the mission church to the south of the town. The attack came down the west side of the compound towards Methven's right flank. As the German askaris charged past 1/3rd KAR's leading platoons, they came under a withering flanking fire which broke up the attack and forced them to retreat back to the church.

As night drew in, Methven was able to extricate his company from the killing ground. They then withdrew up the road to the column's defended camp.[12] The company had lost 15 killed and 35 wounded, while 1/3rd KAR, now concentrated in the Rubber Plantation, dug-in in a position of all-round defenses.

The following morning (October 19) 1/3rd KAR sent patrols into Lukuledi, which was found to be deserted. During the night, Kraut had withdrawn his companies east towards Ndanda. "The enemy, believed to be six companies of the Gold Coast Regiment, was driven off, but in order to protect our supplies and material lying at Chigugu and Chiwata, Major Kraut retired to the first of these places. As well as Chigugu and Chiwata, Ndanda, where we had large stores of war material, was also threatened by the enemy, who had doubtless, in my opinion, been reinforced at Lukuledi. The enemy from Lukuledi might at any moment attack our lines of communication, capture our stores and supplies, and so put us out of action. We had no means of protecting our lines of communication locally, for the few thousand men we had were required for fighting. As, however, the force had to be kept alive, the danger had to be overcome in some other way."[13] The battalion occupied the fort and mission compounds and sent patrols into the surrounding bush, where a number of patrol actions took place. Colonel Orr next planned to advance on and take the enemy supply dump at Ndanda with the main body of the column, while the 25th Cavalry, supported by 1/3rd KAR, would raid the supply dump at Massasi, south of Lukuledi. In preparation for his move against Ndanda he had all the mortar sections of his subunits formed into a composite mortar company at his HQ.

The main body of No. 1 column moved off from their camp north of Lukuledi early on the 21st, leaving only the baggage and camp followers there under the cavalry's regimental transport officer. The 25th Cavalry and 1/3rd KAR began marching south along the Massasi road at 5:30 a.m. and had entered the cleared ground south of the mission church when they came under heavy and sustained machine-gun fire. They were under attack by von Lettow-Vorbeck, who had arrived to retake the mission with six companies when he learned of Kraut's withdrawal. The cavalry immediately took cover in the church and brickyards west of the track while the KAR pulled back to the mission and fort. Von Lettow-Vorbeck's companies then began to encircle the mission and church, cutting communications with the main column.

At 7:45 a.m., the Germans opened fire on the fort and compounds with two field guns, adding to the discomfort of the KAR, who were now under fire from almost all sides. With calls for ammunition coming in from all quarters, Company Quartermaster Sergeant Hamis Bin Juma, DCM, led his porters, carrying ammunition for the Rifle Companies in the fort and mission compounds, across the open, fire-swept ground, and then had them collect and carry the wounded to the Regimental Aid Post located in the center of the fort. During the action, he lost six porters killed and 27 wounded. CQMS Bin Juma was subsequently awarded a Bar to his African Distinguished Conduct Medal.

At about 9:30 a.m., one of the three messengers dispatched by Lieutenant-Colonel Fitzgerald was able to reach the main column and inform Colonel Orr of the situation. Orr immediately ordered the 129th Baluchis to move south of the Lukuledi River and take up positions from where they could prevent the complete encirclement of the mission and fort. At the same time, the 27th Mountain Battery moved into fire positions from where they could engage the *Schutztruppe* companies, and their gunnery proved so accurate that the Germans were forced away from the fort and compound.

Meanwhile, Major Kraut had crossed the Lukuledi River three-quarters of a mile east of the Ruponda Road and attacked the base camp. Here his detachment captured the baggage and killed the transport officer, Captain NJM Barry, and several of the Sowars[14] under his command, along with all the animals and a number of camp followers. Kraut then withdrew eastwards through the bush, north of the river. Fighting continued around the fort and mission until the late forenoon, but by 11:30 a.m., von Lettow-Vorbeck's companies begun to break contact and pull back to the south. The German commander regrouped during the afternoon and launched an assault against the fort at 5 p.m., but the attack was broken up, and he finally retired. "Owing to unfavourable circumstances we had not succeeded in inflicting a decisive defeat on the enemy at Lukuledi, and the operation had only in part gained its objective, but the enemy's losses must be regarded as serious."[15]

The following day (the 22nd), No. 1 column was forced to withdraw to its original positions at Ruponda. With the loss of his baggage, Orr's sub-units were running short of food and ammunition, and having overstretched his supply line, it was proving difficult to replenish them. Kilwa Force did not resume its advance until early November when Linforce was pushing Wahle's companies down the Lukuledi River. The columns of Kilwa Force and Linforce finally linked at Tschiwata on November 14.

Three weeks after the Battle of Mahiwa von Lettow-Vorbeck learned that he had been promoted to Major-General by the Kaiser. He was, at this time, pulling his main body south towards the Portuguese frontier, having decided to abandon German East Africa and invade Portuguese East Africa. With great skill, he withdrew his troops across the Makonde Plateau, reaching the Kintangari Valley on November 20, unaware that an attempt to resupply him was in preparation in Bulgaria.

The exploits of von Lettow-Vorbeck that had been regularly reported in the press had made him a popular hero in Germany. As a result of this, there arose a demand in the press and by the public that assistance should be sent to him to allow him to continue his fight in East Africa. As public pressure mounted, the German Government decided to attempt to resupply him. But the question was how this might be done. To use another blockade runner or a U–Boat would prove hazardous. Even if one was able to break the British blockade in the North Sea, traverse the Atlantic to the Southern Hemisphere and then breach the British blockade of the East African coast, it would prove almost impossible to make safe landfall. The proposal was then made, and agreed, to employ one of the German Navy's Zeppelins.

The navy had two large Zeppelins available to them that were suitable for such an operation, the L57 and L59, each measuring 741 feet (226 meters) in length. L57 was initially chosen for the mission but was destroyed during a storm as she undertook test flight trials following her modification. L59 was then quickly converted to replace her. The modifications to L59 enabled her to carry a cargo of 15 tons of supplies, including machine guns, spare parts, ammunition, medical supplies, food, and a medical team. As it would be impossible for L59 to return from her mission to East Africa, it was planned that she would be cannibalized on arrival. Her outer envelope, which was made of cotton instead of the

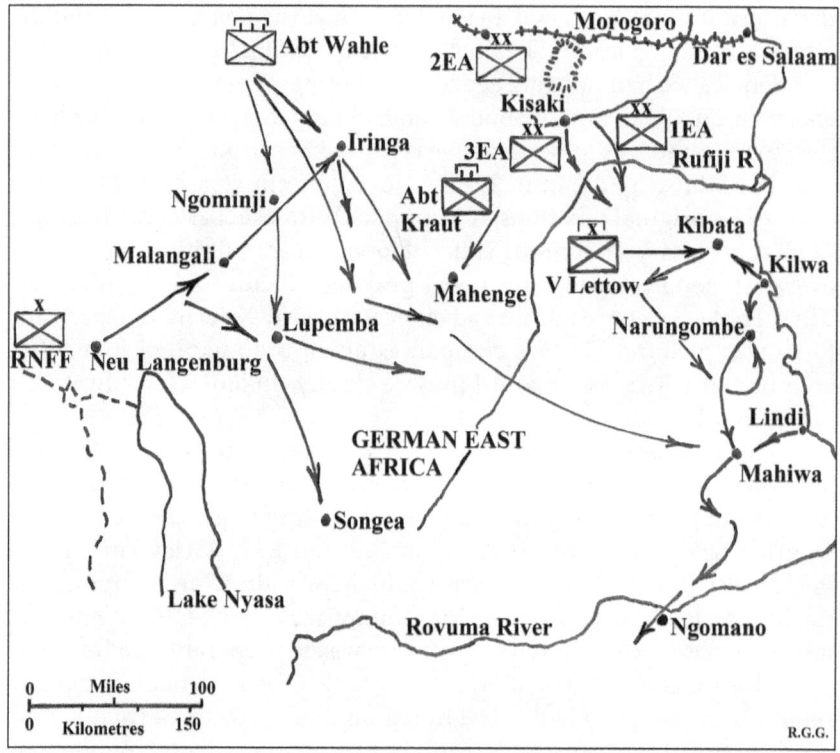

Withdrawal to the Rovuma, October–November 1917 (map by the author).

linen fabric generally used, would be used to make tents and uniforms; the muslin linings would be turned into bandages; the main frame of aluminum would be converted into wireless towers or used as building material, and her engines would become generators; nothing would be wasted.

On November 3, 1917, following her modification for the mission, L59 took off from the Zeppelin Factory at Friedrichshafen, arriving at Jamboli, Bulgaria, 29 hours later. Here she was handed over to Lieutenant-Commander Ludwig Bockholt, who would command the mission, code named "China Show." At Jamboli her new all-volunteer crew set about fitting extra hydrogen gas tanks and loading the cargo of munitions, weapons and supplies. Lieutenant-Commander Bockholt had been ordered by the Naval High Command to maintain radio silence until he was well into his mission. Only then was he to try and contact von Lettow-Vorbeck, using a cipher telegram, and inform him of the resupply mission and arrange a suitable rendezvous point.

British Intelligence, however, having cracked the German Navy's wireless codes, was fully aware of the mission and its destination from its inception. General van Deventer was warned of it, and No. 4 Squadron, RNAS and No. 26 (SA) Squadron, RFC, operating in East Africa, were put on alert, with orders to intercept L59 when the time came. At the same time, Major Richard Meinertzhagen, at this time head of intelligence in Cairo, had a fake recall message prepared for transmission, using the German naval cipher codes, while General van Deventer, as soon as he learned of "China Show" and its destination, ordered 2/2nd KAR and 1st Cape Corps from No. 3 Column to get up the 1,669-foot (600-meter) escarpment and on to the Makonde Plateau to stop Köhl's detachment at Tschiwata Mission from reaching the plateau and prevent any attempted landing by L59.

On the 13th, 2/2nd KAR marched south to Minjales and began its ascent of the escarpment, followed the next day by 1st Cape Corps. The force had concentrated on the top of the escarpment in the early hours of the 15th, and with 2/2nd KAR leading, advanced to cut the Tschiwata-Mwiti road. They reached the road at 9:30 a.m. and were in immediate contact with the withdrawing *Schutztruppe* of Wahle's command. Von Lettow-Vorbeck had ordered all his column commanders to withdraw to Nambindinga. "The march to Nambindinga was carried out under continuous fighting between the 15th and 17th November. I wanted to make the enemy complete the concentric march of his columns, advancing northwest and south, so as to effect a junction; then, when the enemy's masses were helplessly crowded on a narrow area, I could march where I liked. On November 17th I had to take a fateful decision at Nambindinga. The continual bush-fighting was threatening to consume all our ammunition. It would have been madness to go on with this fighting, which could not bring about a favourable decision. We had therefore to withdraw."[16] Von Lettow-Vorbeck marched from Nambindinga that same day, while No. 3 Column entered the settlement on the 18th, having been in constant contact with the enemy. Here they captured a field hospital and a large number of fit men that had been left behind by von Lettow-Vorbeck when he withdrew. The two battalions went firm to rest and to await the remainder of the column, who were moving up to join them. They did, however, begin aggressive patrolling. For the next three or four days the British lost all contact with von Lettow-Vorbeck until, on November 21, a patrol from 1st Cape Corps commanded by Lieutenant EP Stubbs intercepted an enemy column of 30 Germans and 78 askaris under the command of Captain Looff at Kitangari. Looff had been ordered to surrender to the British by von Lettow-Vorbeck.

Meanwhile, in Bulgaria on November 21, after two aborted departure attempts due to bad weather over the Mediterranean, L59 eventually began her mission. She flew south over Adrianople, across the Sea of Marmara and down along the coast of Turkey and then over Crete, where she ran into electrical storms which very nearly terminated the mission. She crossed the coast of Egypt near Mersa Matruh at 5:15 a.m. on the 22nd and carried on to Dakhla Oasis before heading towards the Nile River, which she then followed south. Late that afternoon Bockholt broke radio silence to advise von Lettow-Vorbeck of his mission. Shortly after the reduction gear housing in one of her engines cracked, disabling the engine, it was found that with this reduction in power, she could no longer transmit messages but could still receive them.

At 2:50 a.m. on November 23, L59 was 125 miles (200 kilometers) west of Khartoum, cruising southwards and still waiting for a reply from von Lettow-Vorbeck. The trip had not been without its hazards as heat turbulence rising from the desert, which was quickly cooled in the cold night air, affected her hydrogen gas, and she nearly went down. Her crew too were suffering from the effects of the mission, many experiencing headaches and hallucinations, and all were affected by fatigue. Shortly after passing Khartoum, Bockholt received a signal telling him to abort the mission. He was told that Newale, three days' march north of the Rovuma River, where von Lettow-Vorbeck's radio station was located, had been taken and that the *Schutztruppe* had been driven from the Makonde Plateau and were under attack from the Portuguese. It was not the message that Bockholt expected, and as he could not transmit, he could not verify the validity of the message. But it was not the fake message transmitted by British Military Intelligence.

The message was, in fact, from the German Naval High Command. The day before L59 began her epic flight von Lettow-Vorbeck's last remaining radio station, based at Newale, went off the air prior to the *Schutztruppe* marching into Portuguese East Africa. It was thought that the transmitter could only receive, but a final, weak transmission had been made before the station was closed down and dismantled. This transmission, though indistinct, was picked up by German Embassy stations in neutral and friendly countries and relayed to Germany. It eventually reached the Naval High Command, and a recall signal was transmitted from the Naval Signals station at Nauen. Jettisoning the bulk of his cargo, Bockholt ordered L59 turned around and flown back north, running into trouble over Turkey when the Zeppelin began to lose buoyancy. But overcoming this problem, L59 arrived back at Jamboli on the morning of November 25, having flown 4,200 miles (6,759 kilometers) in 95 hours.[17] On landing at Jamboli, Bockholt was informed that the Kaiser had approved him being given an immediate award of the *Order Pour le Mérite*.

Thirteen. Mahiwa, Lukuledi Mission and the Rovuma

From the Kintangari Valley von Lettow-Vorbeck had marched towards the Rovuma River and the settlement of Newale, just north of the Portuguese border. Before crossing into Portuguese East Africa, he had decided to streamline his troops into a small, tough, independent fighting column of not more than 200 Germans and 2,000 askaris, who would live on what they could capture or forage. He was of the opinion that by taking such a step, he would compel the Allies to maintain large numbers of troops and military equipment in the field trying to catch or destroy his force. "On 20th November we reached Nevale [*sic*], where we were joined by the patrols which had secured our southern flank, and the reorganization of the force was finally carried through. At Nevale the last men unfit for marching were left behind, and on 21st November we marched south to the Rovuma with 300 Europeans, 1,700 Askari, and 3,000 bearers and other natives.[18] Every man was loaded to his full capacity. In general, as the supplies were consumed, the bearers no longer required were left behind, so as to keep the number of consumers as low as possible. In many cases we had to refuse the urgent requests of our good old bearers to remain with us, a large number offering to carry on without pay, some even without either pay or rations; these were ready to provide their own rations from what we threw away and Pori fruit. The quartermaster at that time, Naval Lieutenant Besch, reorganized the supplies and transport service very efficiently. He deserves the chief credit for the force's ability to carry on."[19] Governor Schnee vehemently opposed von Lettow-Vorbeck's decision, wanting him to surrender, but he was overruled.

Leaving several hundred Germans and 600 askaris at Newale to surrender to the British, von Lettow-Vorbeck crossed the Rovuma at Ngomano into Portuguese East Africa and began marching up the Lujenda River. His column had with it two field guns and 35 machine guns. "Early in the morning of November 25th, 1917, our advance guard waded across the Rovuma, a little above the Ludjenda [*sic*] confluence; the main force of nine companies followed in the course of the forenoon, the rearguard about two days' march in the rear. Captain Goering with three companies had crossed much further downstream to surprise a Portuguese camp reported there. We had no news of Captain Tafel, and I thought it probable that he would strike the Rovuma much further west. The feeling that we were cut off from all support, as well as the absolute uncertainty as to the fate before us, had produced what is popularly known as 'allgemeine Wurcktigkeit' (absolute callousness). Undisturbed by the tactical situation, our hunting parties went on with their work, and their shots were, as afterwards transpired, distinctly heard by the enemy."[20]

The only active German forces now left in German East Africa were the companies under the command of Captain Theodor Tafel.[21] He had been forced to withdraw from Mahenge on October 9 by a Belgian column, abandoning his field hospital with 92 Germans and 242 askaris who were taken prisoner. Tafel marched to M'gangira on the Luwegu River, and from here he intended to push south and eventually join von Lettow-Vorbeck. However, General Northey dispatched two flying columns from his Rhodesia-Nyasaland Field Force under the commands of Lieutenant-Colonels Hawthorne (2/1st KAR, 1st and 2nd SA Rifles and 5th SA Infantry) and Fair (1st Rhodesia Native Regiment and a company of the Northern Rhodesia Police) to pursue and capture him. These columns kept up a constant harassment of Tafel's force as he concentrated on the Luwegu, and on November 6 he attempted to break for the Portuguese frontier, marching through Kiturika and Depate for the Rovuma.

A further two British columns were quickly dispatched in an attempt to intercept Tafel. The first, Lieutenant-Colonel Shorthose's 1/4th KAR, from Fort Johnson at the southern end of Lake Nyasa, marched rapidly via Tunduru for Liwale and bumped the German column. Following a short, sharp skirmish, Shorthose was forced to pull back to Tunduru. The second column, consisting of detachments from the 129th Baluchis, 2/4th KAR and a squadron of the 25th Indian Cavalry, commanded by Major Brian Hawkins, was waiting to link up with Shorthose's column when they were hit by Tafel's force. Hawkins's detachment suffered heavy casualties in the encounter before he was able to break contact and withdraw.

A Belgian column consisting of the *1e* and *10e Bataillons de Marche*, commanded by Commandant Herion, eventually caught up with Tafel's rearguard following a hot pursuit from Liwale. In the skirmish that followed the rearguard was driven off, leaving behind their wounded and large quantities of equipment. With Tafel's retreat from the Mahenge-Liwale area, it was decided to withdraw Herion's column before the rainy season set in, and Northey's Field Force took over the pursuit. Shorthose's column at Tunduru was reinforced while Hawthorne's was withdrawn to rest and reequip.

As van Deventer's troops followed von Lettow-Vorbeck across the Makonde Plateau to the Portuguese frontier, Tafel, in ignorance of this, marched between the British advance force and main body. As soon as he realized what he had done, he tried desperately to break south, but van Deventer's troops were all around him. His soldiers and porters were rife with fever and on the verge of starvation, so after several days without food, Tafel decided to surrender before his men just lay down and died.

Thirteen. Mahiwa, Lukuledi Mission and the Rovuma

A meeting was arranged for noon on November 28 at which Tafel surrendered his command of 18 officers, 92 German other ranks, 1,200 askaris and 2,200 porters. Unbeknown to him, only an hour's march to the south, across the Rovuma in Portuguese territory, was a large tract of farmland which had been seized by von Lettow-Vorbeck. It would have provided his column with enough food for a fortnight. With Tafel's surrender to the Gold Coast Regiment and 55th Coke's Rifles, the campaign in German East Africa ended. There only remained the task of hunting down and killing or capturing von Lettow-Vorbeck and his highly motivated, small, well-led columns, which were now on the rampage in Portuguese East Africa.

The British commander, General van Deventer, was well aware of the difficulties facing him in the hunt for von Lettow-Vorbeck now that he had crossed into Portuguese East Africa. Difficulties he outlined in his dispatch to the Secretary of State for War: "It was evident that the difficulties of operating in Portuguese East Africa would be considerable. The portion of Portuguese East Africa bounded by the Rovuma and Zambesi Rivers, Lake Nyasa and the sea, is but little smaller than France. Much of this vast area was a terra incognita to Europeans, and no accurate maps were available. In some parts, the natives were as yet unsubdued, while in others they were in more or less open rebellion."[22] He went on to note, "In fact, Portuguese East Africa appeared an ideal theatre for the operations of a commander of a compact and mobile force, tied to no base, independent of lines of communication, and adept in the art of 'living on the country,' whose aim would probably be to avoid encounters with superior forces and to remain in being as long as possible. It was therefore clear that the forthcoming operations, though on a much smaller scale than those of 1917, would be arduous and exacting, and had to be considered in the light of a new undertaking."[23]

Not only that but van Deventer had to use the coming rainy season to reorganize his troops, as he had been instructed by the War Office to send all Indian Army units and the Nigerian Brigade home or to other theaters. He was to continue operations with columns formed primarily by the King's African Rifles and the Gold Coast Regiment.

He planned to pursue, harry and wear down von Lettow-Vorbeck's troops and, above all, prevent their marching into Nyasaland or returning to German East. The Gold Coast Regiment was sent to Port Amelia (now Pemba) in Portuguese East Africa in December, where they were joined by 4/4th KAR and 22nd Mountain Battery. These units were placed under the command of Lieutenant-Colonel Richard Rose and were designated "Rosecol."[24] While a second column formed by 1/2nd and 2/2nd KAR under the command of Lieutenant-Colonel George

Giffard and designated "Kartucol"[25] arrived at Port Amelia in January 1918, at the same time, 3/2nd KAR were deployed to Mozambique as "Mobforce." Operations were planned to begin in late January, at the end of the rainy season.

Van Deventer had yet another problem, however, the Portuguese government in Lisbon had been overthrown in December and power seized by Sidónio Pais, who was thought to be pro–German. As a result, the civil and military authorities in Portuguese East Africa, thinking he would make a separate peace with Germany, were loath to cooperate with the British. However, this fear proved unfounded, and Pais informed the British that the Portuguese troops on the Western Front would remain under Allied control, while General van Deventer would command all operations against the Germans in Portuguese East Africa. In his dispatch of September 30, van Deventer wrote, "Early in February I visited the Acting Governor-General of Portuguese East Africa at Lourenco Marques in connection with the decision of our respective Governments that the Senior Officer of the Allies should command all forces operating against the Germans, and that a combined Headquarters Staff should be formed. I met with a most cordial reception, and Major Perry da Camara, of the Portuguese Cavalry, joined my Staff. After meeting General Northey at Beira, and inspecting the Port Amelia line, I visited Colonel Rosa, Commander-in-Chief of the Portuguese forces, at Mocimboa-da-Praia, and formally assumed command of the Allied forces."[26]

FOURTEEN

Portuguese East Africa

ON CROSSING THE ROVUMA on November 25, 1917, von Lettow-Vorbeck attacked a Portuguese force, 1,200 strong, under *Commandante* Teixeira Pinto at Ngomano. Pinto had arrived at Ngomano on the previous day following an arduous march from the south, with the express purpose of stopping the Germans from crossing into Portuguese territory. Pinto's troops were, however, poorly led and motivated. They were reluctant to fight, and their defensive fire towards the *Schutztruppe* as von Lettow-Vorbeck launched an enveloping attack on their camp, supported by fire from his last remaining mountain gun, was ineffectual. "While our light mountain-gun fired on the enemy's entrenchments from the west, and while at the same time several companies engaged the enemy on this side as also from the north, Captain Koehl's detachment crossed the Ludjenda half a mile above Ngomano, marched through the high wood on that bank and made a determined attack on the enemy's camp from the south. I took up my position on a little hill west of the camp, near our guns. Immediately behind me the last company of General Wahle's force to cross the river was advancing along a valley. In front I had a fairly good view of the enemy's entrenched positions. The enemy's machine guns were not shooting badly, and their fire was at times directed upon our little sand hill, from which I had to send into cover a number of Europeans and Askari, who had collected there immediately and were visible to the enemy. The clear ring of the enemy rifles, which we had heard before, and the absence of trench-mortars, made it probable that the enemy were Portuguese. We had already learned to distinguish clearly between the dull, full detonation of our '71, the sharp crack of our S-rifle, the double report of the English rifle and the clear ring of the Portuguese rifle of a little over 6 mm. calibre. Even our Askari had noticed at once that in short skirmishes the speed with which the enemy trench-mortars always got the range of our positions had been very harassing.

"Our '71 rifles threw up so much smoke that it was impossible to guard against this. To-day, however, there were no mine-throwers, and the treacherous smoke of our good old rifles was not so bad. On the other hand, when they did hit their target they made a very considerable hole. Our Askari soon realized that to-day they were able to bring their soldierly superiority to bear without being handicapped by inferior weapons. 'Today is the day of the old rifles!' they shouted to the German leaders, and from my hill I soon saw the firing line of Koehl's detachment storm the enemy's entrenchments at the double and capture them. This was the signal for attack on the other fronts also. From all sides they charged the enemy, who was badly shaken by the concentrated fire. Scarcely more than 200 of the enemy force, about 1,000 strong, can have survived. Again and again our Askari troops, in search of booty, threw themselves ruthlessly upon the enemy, who was still firing; in addition, a crowd of bearers and boys, grasping the situation, had quickly run up and were taking their choice of the pots of lard and other supplies, opening cases of jam and throwing them away again when they thought they had found something more attractive in other cases. It was a fearful melee. Even the Portuguese Askari already taken prisoner, joined in the plunder of their own stores. There was no alternative but to intervene vigorously. I became very eloquent, and, to make an example, dashed at least seven times at one bearer I knew, but each time he got away and immediately joined in the looting somewhere else. At last I succeeded in restoring discipline."[1]

The Portuguese askaris had panicked, and the German askaris, out of control, began to slaughter them using their preferred weapon, the bayonet. There followed two hours of bitter and bloody carnage, in which around 190 Portuguese askaris and their officers were massacred as their camp was overrun and looted. The *Schutztruppe* captured 250,000 rounds of small arms ammunition, large quantities of medical supplies, and enough modern rifles to replace the Model 1871 rifles still carried by the majority of the Germans' askaris. They also captured six machine guns and 30 horses.

Von Lettow-Vorbeck impressed 300 of the 450 Portuguese askaris he had taken prisoner as bearers to carry his captured stores and ammunition and then released the remaining 150. The remaining survivors had fled into the bush during the attack. Before the coming of the rains in December, he marched deep into Portuguese East Africa along the Lujenda River, overrunning a number of Portuguese posts as he did so and obtaining further stores and ammunition.

For his advance into the interior of Portuguese East Africa von Lettow-Vorbeck had divided his force into three detachments, each with its own field hospital and bearers, and as a result, his columns were able to march between 15 and 20 miles (25 and 32 kilometers) a day. Throughout the heavy rains of December 1917, von Lettow-Vorbeck's main column struggled along the banks of the Lujenda, continually searching for sources of fresh food, a commodity that was always in short supply. When his detachments reached a native village, they stole the harvested crops, looted the village and killed the animals for meat, leaving a trail of desolation in their wake. Just before Christmas von Lettow-Vorbeck received a letter from van Deventer calling on him to surrender and telling him of the surrender of Tafel's command.

Though distressed by the news of Tafel, von Lettow-Vorbeck was cheered by the unexpected news that he had been awarded Oak Leaves to his *Order Pour le Mérite*, but he had no intention of giving up. He spent Christmas and New Year at Chirumba, after driving off the garrison, and stayed here until near the end of January 1918. As his food supplies began to run out, he detached two scouting parties under the commands of Captains Köhl and Göring to search the surrounding river valleys for stocks to replenish his stores. Substantial supplies were eventually located in the Medo area, so von Lettow-Vorbeck immediately marched from Chirumba to the east to take advantage of these stocks. His columns pillaged the surrounding villages and settlements of their crops and animals and shot what wild game they could, spreading further desolation. "Behind us we leave destroyed fields, ransacked magazines and, for the immediate future, starvation. We are no longer the agents of culture; our track is marked by death, plundering and evacuated villages, just like the progress of our own and enemy armies in the Thirty Years War."[2]

In late February, Brigadier-General Edwards was given command of the two columns at Port Amelia, now designated "Pamforce,"[3] along with 58th Vaughan's Rifles and the Gold Coast Mounted Infantry as Force troops. He was to operate along the road running from the Port to Medo, 120 miles (193 kilometers) to the west. As the rains subsided, Edwards began slowly pushing into the interior, establishing an advanced camp at Meza, 64 miles (103 kilometers) west of Port Amelia.

Rosecol began advancing from Meza on March 27, encountering only light enemy activity. By April 9, they were within seven miles (11 kilometers) of Medo. Opposing them were six *Schutztruppe* companies—the 3rd, 11th, 13th, 14th, 17th Field and 6th Rifle Companies—with 12 machine guns and a field gun under the command of, now Major, Franz Köhl. Edwards decided to contain the German position, which ran along the north side of the 600-foot (183-meter), two-mile (three-kilometer)-long Chirimba Hill feature, lying just south of the road, with Rosecol, while Kartucol undertook a flank attack to the south.

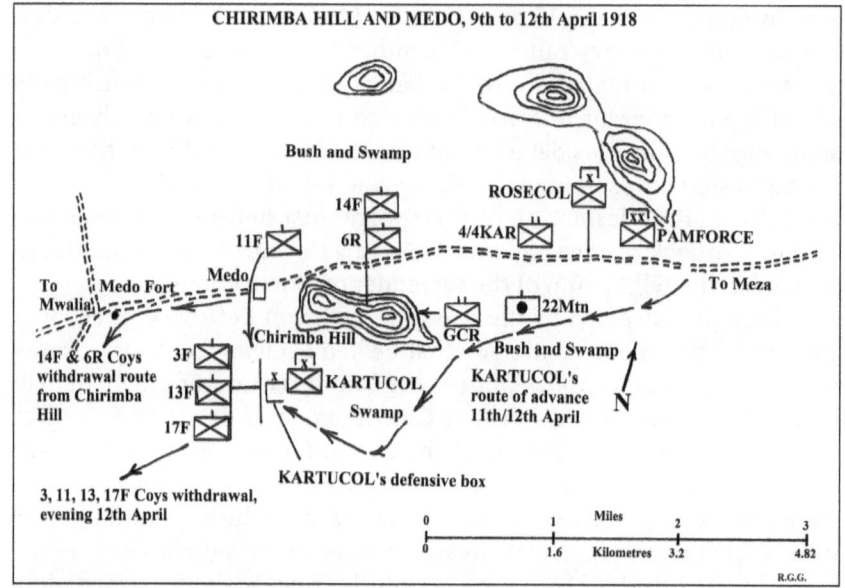

Operations against Medo (based on a sketch map from Hugh Clifford's *The Gold Coast Regiment in the East African Campaign*).

Rosecol began advancing to contact at 1:30 p.m., with a 50-man reconnaissance from the Gold Coast Regiment probing the eastern side of the hill, but it was met by heavy fire from the 14th Field and 6th Rifle Companies holding the position and forced to retire. Next morning the Gold Coast Regiment supported by 4/4th KAR attacked the position again, only to be again repulsed. In the afternoon, Kartucol began its flanking march to the south that would last through the night preparatory to a dawn attack on Köhl's right flank, held by the 3rd, 13th and 17th Field Companies. At 6 a.m. on the 12th, Rosecol mounted another attack against the hill with the Gold Coast Regiment, which advanced with "B" Company forward and supported by two mortars and the 22nd Mountain Battery. The mortars were deployed 50 yards (46 meters) behind the Gold Coast Regiment's firing line, lobbing bombs into the Germans ahead of the advancing infantry, who began driving the enemy gradually back along the hill. But unbeknown to Rose, Kartucol, with 2/2nd KAR leading, had been ambushed at 2:15 p.m. while advancing across a stretch of swamp. They were swept by heavy and accurate machine-gun fire which was followed up by a savage counterattack; the KAR could only fix bayonets and prepare to meet the advancing *Schutztruppe*, now reinforced by Köhl's reserve, 11th Field Company, which had been ordered from its positions northwest of the hill at 2:30 p.m.

Fourteen. Portuguese East Africa

Fortunately, the opposition to Rosecol had eased during the late afternoon. The 14th Field and 6th Rifle Companies facing them had begun to withdraw westwards to the old Medo fort, and at 5 p.m., "B" Company with half of "A" and half of "I" Companies of the Gold Coast Regiment were able to move around the hill's western slope and link up with 2/2nd KAR who, along with the rest of Kartucol, were embroiled in a bloody hand-to-hand fight with the Germans. Kartucol had been able to form an open square and scrape shallow rifle pits in the mud, and here they held until the Gold Coast companies came to their support. The Germans facing Kartucol were now, in their turn, forced to retire. Köhl broke contact at around 5:45 p.m., withdrawing towards Nanunga and Korewa. On the 13th, Pamforce entered Medo and two days later, with 4/4th KAR leading, marched for Mwalia, 25 miles (40 kilometers) away, in hot pursuit of the withdrawing Germans.

From the south of Lake Nyasa Brigadier-General Hawthorne, commanding Norforce[4] (formerly the Rhodesia-Nyasaland Field Force), having relieved Northey who had returned to Britain prior to taking up his appointment as Governor of British East Africa, was pushing east towards Mahua. General van Deventer began to hope that his troops might encircle the *Schutztruppe* columns, but von Lettow-Vorbeck once again evaded him, calling in all his detachments and marching to the southwest.

Pamforce caught up with them at Korewa. General Edwards tried to encircle Köhl's detachment, employing Lieutenant-Colonel AH Griffiths's 3/1st KAR column (which included half the 2/1st KAR) from Norforce, which was approaching from the west, in conjunction with Pamforce. His plan called for Griffiths to take the main road behind Köhl's position, while Kartucol mounted a frontal attack and Rosecol turned the enemy's left flank.

The operation began early on May 22. However, von Lettow-Vorbeck saw the British deploying from a lookout post on Koroma peak and sent a runner to warn the unsuspecting Khöl, whose men were at breakfast, ordering him to escape. But Governor Schnee, who was with Köhl's detachment, refused to move, and it was with great difficulty that he was finally persuaded to leave. Kartucol advanced rapidly on Köhl's front, while the 3/1st KAR column captured his camp and baggage; it was only von Lettow-Vorbeck's timely intervention with his main force that saved Köhl's detachment from complete destruction.

Having extricated Köhl's troops and inflicting heavy casualties on the enemy, von Lettow-Vorbeck broke off action and withdrew before Giffard or Rose could outflank him. Because of Schnee's stubborn refusal to move when he was asked, the *Schutztruppe* lost 70,000 rounds of irreplaceable small arms ammunition and 30,000 Rupees of useless scrip belonging to the Colonial Treasury.

Now that his forces from Nyasaland and the coast had linked up, General van Deventer ordered the establishment of a line of fortified towns running from Fort Johnson in Nyasaland through Mahua and Medo to Port Amelia on the coast. It was hoped that this line would prevent von Lettow-Vorbeck from returning north. The Gold Coast Regiment from Rosecol was ordered to provide the detachments for the various garrisons, while the 2nd KAR battalions of Kartucol continued the pursuit. Towards the end of May, however, Rosecol was disbanded, and the much-decorated Gold Coast Regiment was withdrawn to Port Amelia in preparation for its return to West Africa once its detachments in garrison rejoined the regiment, leaving only the Gold Coast Mounted Infantry in East Africa, where they served until early October.

The British pursuit had resumed in earnest by May 24. The Germans fought several rearguard actions in which they set fire to the elephant grass on the plains to forestall the advancing KAR and to assist their own escape and springing highly successful ambushes when in hill country. These continuing skirmishes were, however, eating into von Lettow-Vorbeck's precious supplies of ammunition, and it became imperative for him to replenish these fast-diminishing stocks.

From a map captured in an action along the Malema River it appeared to von Lettow-Vorbeck that the town of Alto Moloque, which he knew from gained intelligence housed a garrison of only company strength, may contain the ammunition he so desperately needed. "We marched by native tracks or straight through the bush. Several considerable streams had to be negotiated on the way. This district, too, was fertile, and we soon came across unmistakable human tracks leading towards Alto-Moloque, not to mention kraals, the first I had ever seen. They were grass huts, very thick and carefully built. Ashes were smouldering in places and the heads of hens which were lying about were still fresh. We exchanged shots with some Portuguese patrols and a few rifles with ammunition were captured."[5] Marching through the arduous Iangu Mountains to avoid the KAR he entered Alto Moloque, which he found was deserted. The garrison had fled when it learned of the German approach. Here he captured large stocks of food, maps and documents, which gave him much valuable intelligence but no ammunition. "We could see that there was a telegraph wire from Alto-Moloque to Quelimane via Ili. A large company, the Lugella Company, had its headquarters at the confluence of the Lugella with the Likungo. There were great plantations and factories and large supplies of food. Above all, it looked as if preparations were in progress to make this station a main supply

Fourteen. Portuguese East Africa

depot for food and ammunition for considerable bodies of troops. If we wished to exploit the opportunity that this situation presented, our subordinate commanders would have to act very promptly and must not be hampered by too rigid instructions."[6] From Alto Moloque he pushed south, taking Ili and Lugella but still no ammunition, a situation that was fast becoming critical.

From the constant interrogation of natives caught in their path of advance von Lettow-Vorbeck learned of a large concentration of Portuguese troops and equipment at a place called Kokosani, which lay on the railway running from Nhamacurra to Quelimane on the coast. With Captain Erich Müller's company leading, the Germans marched on Nhamacurra.

Earlier, van Deventer, suspecting that the Germans might make for the Quelimane-Nhamacurra railway, dispatched Major Eric Gore-Browne with two companies of the 2/3rd KAR to Quelimane by sea. As soon as they landed, these companies were moved up to the Nhamacurra railway terminus to reinforce Colonel Rosa's Portuguese garrison of three battalions. Von Lettow-Vorbeck's columns, meanwhile, marched rapidly south, fording the Likungo and pressing on past Nhamacurra to Kokosani. He detached Müller's company to march around the flank of the Portuguese garrison, which it successfully did, taking them by surprise and, after several hours fighting, drove them off. Müller captured two field guns with 200 rounds of ammunition abandoned by the garrison when it fled.

Though Kokosani was quite a large settlement containing a number of factories and surrounded by plantations, there were no ammunition supplies. Not long after the town was taken, a steamer came up the Nhamacurra River from the coast and unsuspectingly docked at the wharf, and a British Army doctor came ashore. He was arrested and, during his interrogation by von Lettow-Vorbeck, revealed that he was bringing medical supplies to the British forces operating in the area. This was the first news the Germans had of the presence of British troops so far south. Until now von Lettow-Vorbeck had assumed the presence of only Portuguese troops. The interrogation of the doctor went on for several hours, and it was eventually established that the railhead at Nhamacurra was where the desperately needed small arms ammunition was being dumped.

Von Lettow-Vorbeck ordered his columns to march immediately up the railway to the Nhamacurra railhead. The next day, July 2, the leading company of the German column approached the railhead and came under a storm of heavy fire, killing several of their number and pinning the others down. Von Lettow-Vorbeck, unable to achieve anything except heavy casualties if he attempted a frontal assault, ordered his men to fall back but maintain contact with the enemy, using the oncoming night to plan and prepare his attack for the next day.

Müller had the two captured field guns brought forward to give artillery support to the attack, which began with a heavy concentration of fire from the field guns and the *Schutztruppe's* 35 machine guns. The Portuguese troops holding the forward trenches panicked and fell back in disorder. The Germans, seeing the disordered route, charged forward and into them with fixed bayonets. As the panic-stricken Portuguese askaris fled through 2/3rd KAR's positions, they caused fear and anxiety among the British troops. Despite being highly agitated, the KAR companies held firm, and Major Gore-Browne ordered them to pull back to the railway station, which they did in good order, and here he was able to rally the Portuguese 21st Indigenous Company and some artillerymen.

But at 3 p.m., the attacking Germans broke through his line in a ferocious assault, forcing his men back towards the river. They were trapped. But rather than surrender, Gore-Browne attempted to lead his companies across the river. None reached the opposite bank; they were exhausted. Several sank in the river and drowned, while others were taken by the crocodiles that were prolific in these waters. At the captured railhead von Lettow-Vorbeck secured 350 new rifles, seven heavy and three light machine guns, and enormous stockpiles of small arms ammunition, more than his soldiers and porters could possibly carry, as well as an abundance of food, sugar and medical supplies.

The next day (the 4th) the Germans recovered the bodies of Gore-Browne, three of his officers and 100 soldiers of 2/3rd KAR and 21st Company. They had captured five British officers, 117 Portuguese officers and men and 421 Portuguese and British askari soldiers for the loss of three Germans, 11 askaris wounded and nine killed.

When he learned of the attack and defeat of the Anglo/Portuguese garrison at Nhamacurra, van Deventer ordered 2nd KAR to converge on the railhead, hoping to trap von Lettow-Vorbeck between them and the coast. But the Germans had marched eastward for a short time before turning northeast and crossing the Molocue River at Tibe. On July 18 they ran headfirst into a column of 3/3rd KAR, commanded by Lieutenant-Colonel HC Dickinson (Somerset Light Infantry), and in the following encounter battle that lasted for 15 hours, Dickinson, his adjutant and medical officer were captured by Lieutenant Böll's company. Dickinson remained a prisoner of the Germans until their surrender, becoming a close friend of von Lettow-Vorbeck and dying of Spanish flu at Dar es Salaam at the end of the war.

Following this encounter, von Lettow-Vorbeck pushed north for Pekera, attacking a 200-strong column of the Gold Coast Mounted Infantry on July 29, which developed into a running skirmish fought over the following two days and at the same time halting a relief attempt from Alto Ligonha before action was broken off. He took Pekera on August 1, after driving off its garrison, a troop of the Gold Coast Mounted Infantry, and from here marched to Chalau, capturing that place on the 5th.

General van Deventer and his HQ, meanwhile, had reached Port Amelia on July 29 and immediately moved inland to Nampula. Here he was met by and briefed on the tactical situation by General Edwards, commander of land operations in Portuguese East Africa. When he was told that the Germans held Chalau, he ordered all British columns to close on that place at once.

As the British approached the settlement, von Lettow-Vorbeck marched out, crossing the Likungo River on August 24. The next day he was ambushed by a company of the 2/4th KAR, commanded by Major P Garrard (24th Bn, London Regt), who shortly after making contact began a fighting withdrawal towards his positions at Numarroe, two hours march away. The *Schutztruppe* followed up, and a detachment under Captain Göring cut their way through the bush, outflanking the KAR positions and attacking their rear, which they stormed and took, forcing Garrard to surrender. Garrard's losses were three officers and 41 men killed, one officer and six men wounded. Von Lettow-Vorbeck captured two Lewis light machine guns, 40,000 rounds of small arms ammunition and large quantities of food and medical supplies.

From Numarroe he marched north, bivouacking near Regone on the 26th. Giving the town, which he knew from captured intelligence was strongly garrisoned, a wide berth, he pushed on towards Lioma. His lead elements reached Lioma on the 29th, where it found units of 1/1st KAR digging entrenchments in the bush. The 1/1st KAR had been rushed to Lioma by lorry on August 27 to take up a blocking position near the Portuguese post and halt von Lettow-Vorbeck's march north. Kartucol, following in close pursuit, was to attempt to trap him in the Luala River Valley and there force him to surrender or destroy him. The battalion dug-in in a position of all-round defense on the high ground west of the Luala River and the road running alongside it. Major Alexander Masters, MC, commanding the battalion, also placed three of his platoons, each with a machine gun, outside the defensive perimeter to the east, south and west. The platoon to the east was on the high ground on the opposite side of the valley.

Although there was an exchange of fire between the *Schutztruppe*'s advance party and the KAR outpost to the south on the 29th, nothing further occurred. The next day at noon 3/2nd KAR from Kartucol reached Lioma and took up defensive positions behind and three miles (five kilometers) north of 1/1st KAR. At 1 p.m., the platoon on the east side of the river exchanged fire with a *Schutztruppe* patrol which withdrew southwards. Then at 3 p.m., von Lettow-Vorbeck launched an assault against the position, which overwhelmed the post, killing the commander, Lieutenant AC Goldrick (Special List) and a number of his platoon. The survivors pulled back towards the battalion's main position, abandoning their machine gun, while Captain GV Sibary (Royal Scots Fusiliers) commanding "D" Company led a platoon out of the perimeter and down to the river from where he covered the withdrawal of the survivors.

Next von Lettow-Vorbeck's companies launched simultaneous attacks on the main British position from all quarters, the companies commanded by Göring and Müller having made their way around to the north of the British defenses. The Germans' determined attacks spooked the battalion's porters who fled into the bush. At one stage a large number of the enemy broke through the perimeter only to be killed by a British SNCO attached to the battalion, Sergeant Price, while two others,

Sergeants AH Thomson and W Cartnell, moved around the perimeter with their Lewis guns to support and encourage the defenders.[7] At 4:45 p.m., Masters was badly wounded, shot through the chest, and Captain SC John, MC, commanding "C" Company, took over command of the battalion.

Three miles to the north, Lieutenant-Colonel CG Phillips, MC (West Yorkshire Regt), hearing the heavy firing coming from 1/1st KAR's position, moved his 3/2nd KAR to their support, skirmishing with elements of the *Schutztruppe* that had bypassed the British position as he advanced. The battalion then launched a counterattack against Müller's and Göring's companies. The counterattack inflicted heavy casualties on these detachments, including Göring, who was badly wounded, and forced them to pull back. Von Lettow-Vorbeck recalled the survivors of the two companies and then broke off the action and withdrew, abandoning a large proportion of his baggage as he did so. German losses were high, their field hospital captured, and over 48,000 rounds of ammunition left with the abandoned baggage. British losses were 49 killed and 61 wounded.

At Lioma von Lettow-Vorbeck knew that he had been lucky to avoid being trapped; of the action, he wrote, "On the 30th and 31st of August, we had lost 6 Europeans, 23 Askari killed; 11 Europeans, 16 Askari wounded; 5 Europeans, 29 Askari missing; 5 Askari taken prisoner; 48,000 rounds of ammunition, important medical and surgical stores, a considerable number of rifle parts and the whole transport of Müller's detachment had been lost. The enemy losses were also severe, as appeared from a casualty list of the 1st battalion 1st King's African Rifles which was captured later. In addition to this battalion part of the 3rd battalion of this regiment and the 2nd King's African Rifles had taken part in the fighting against us."[8] [This is incorrect; von Lettow-Vorbeck appeared confused by the title of 3/2nd KAR, assuming the 3 stood for 3/1st KAR, none of whose members were present at Lioma.]

With the coming of darkness and with the last German attack beaten off, Captain John reorganized his perimeter and distributed his reserves of ammunition in the expectation of the enemy renewing the attack at dawn. But with the arrival of Colonel Giffard's Kartucol the next morning, 1/1st KAR, having borrowed some of their porters, pulled back to the supply depot at Muletere.

As the Germans continued their march northwards, they were pursued by Kartucol from Lioma, who hit their rearguard hard, forcing them to increase the pace of their march. The 2/2nd KAR then undertook a forced march in an attempt to overtake the *Schutztruppe* main body, which it did, catching them at midday on September 6, north of

Anguros at Pere Hills. The battalion was immediately attacked by the Germans, and in the ensuing action they were badly mauled, losing nearly all their officers and NCOs. Von Lettow-Vorbeck, not wanting to be caught up in a general action, and with Giffard within four miles (six and a half kilometers) and approaching rapidly in an attempt to outflank him with 1/2nd and 3/2nd KAR, did not follow up his attack but broke off action and withdrew into the thick bush under cover of the encroaching darkness.

Following this action Kartucol was in no condition to continue in pursuit, and Shortcol,[9] comprising 1/4th KAR and the 1st Rhodesia Native Regiment, was brought forward, while 1/2nd KAR, having sustained very heavy losses, was withdrawn and put into reserve. At the end of the month Kartucol was broken up and its units sent into garrison in German East.

Finding Portuguese East Africa becoming too hot for him to effectively operate in, and with his whole force depressed by successive defeats, hunger and growing illness, von Lettow-Vorbeck decided to return to German East. Half his men where suffering from inflammation of the lungs or bronchial catarrh, which gave them a painful, hacking cough. This inflammation of the lungs, he was now informed by his chief medical officer, Surgeon-Major Max Taute, was likely to spread throughout all his command. He split his force into four columns, whose leaders were instructed to try and maintain contact with each other then began marching north for the frontier, leaving the pursuing British far behind; those with influenza took it in turns to ride the few pack animals they had, while 80 of the worst cases were carried in litters. "No satisfactory solution of the problem of transport of the sick was to be found, short of abandoning the campaign.... We simply could not leave the sick to die in the bush."[10]

Van Deventer wrote, "It may appear extraordinary that the enemy should so often have succeeded in evading our converging columns: But the German force, well guided, generally avoided the regular tracks, and moved by native paths through the heart of the bush, which is often so thick and difficult that troops may march and counter march within a few miles of one another without gaining touch. And there were over 100,000 square miles of such bush between the Rovuma and the Zambesi. [sic]"[11] As they trekked north, a large number of the weaker askaris, porters and camp followers dropped behind the columns; many were able to rejoin their respective columns when they were allowed a day's rest, but a large number, finding camping site after camping site empty, simply gave up. Reaching Nagwamira on September 28, they waded across the Rovuma River back into German territory. Once

Fourteen. Portuguese East Africa 187

across the river von Lettow-Vorbeck rested his columns for a few days before resuming his march. While here, it was noticed that the number of bronchial catarrh cases among his troops and carriers began to drop.

Van Deventer was yet again forced to redeploy his troops, the brunt of the operations falling on Kartufor[12] (2/4th KAR and the Northern Rhodesia Regiment).[13] The 2/4th KAR marched from Fort Johnson on the southern tip of Lake Nyasa, embarked on steamers and were shipped to Sphinxhaven, then marched to Songea where they were joined by the Northern Rhodesia Regiment.

From here Kartufor prepared to intercept the *Schutztruppe*, who were closing on Songea, taking up positions astride the Songea-Wiedhafen road. But von Lettow-Vorbeck, as he pushed north from the Rovuma, learned from his patrols of this heavy concentration of troops and bypassed the settlement, pressing on towards Ubena (now Njombe), which he occupied on October 17. Here he left Major-General Wahle, who had marched and fought gallantly since the beginning of the war and had been awarded the Iron Crosses 1st and 2nd Class and the *Order Pour le Mérite*. He was wounded and extremely ill and unable to march any further. He was eventually picked up by the pursuing Kartufor and sent to a British military hospital.

The British command expected the Germans to march on Tabora and the Central Railway; instead, von Lettow-Vorbeck wheeled his force to the west, heading for Northern Rhodesia, the last place he was expected to go.

Van Deventer rushed 1/2nd KAR to Bismarckburg and 1/4th KAR to Neu Langenburg, while two companies of the Northern Rhodesia Regiment were sent to Fife, close to the German frontier. Reaching Fife on November 1, these companies immediately began preparing defensive positions and sighting their machine guns. The *Schutztruppe* approached the town the next day and were greeted by heavy fire. They responded with mortar fire, using a trench mortar captured from the Portuguese, which eventually blew up with a round in its barrel. Von Lettow-Vorbeck did not want to become embroiled in a general action and ordered his troops to break contact; bypassing Fife, he pushed on to Kasama, which he had learned was well stocked with supplies. "Various reports and statements of prisoners showed that enemy transport was moving from the Broken Hill district to Kasama, and from there onwards to Fife, with motor-cars and ox-wagons. Kasama itself seemed to be a large place and an important road centre. In any case, we could expect enemy depots on the way from Fife to Kasama, and Kasama itself would be a valuable objective."[14]

Kasama fell on November 9. But all the supplies and ammunition had been removed by the District Officer, Hector Croad, who had formed a local defense group from invalids and prisoners he had released from the town jail. On learning of the approach of the Germans, he had carried these stores to the rubber factory at Chambezi, 40 miles (64 kilometers) to the south, which he prepared to defend. He was pursued south by a detachment commanded by Captain Walter Spangenburg, who captured the Chambezi bridge on the 12th, and began making preparations to assault the rubber factory. "I had now formed the opinion that the attempt on the Chambezi depot was the more promising and important undertaking, especially as the whole position made it probable that the pursuing enemy would continue to follow and thus again afford us an opportunity to give battle."[15]

The *Schutztruppe* main body remained at Kasama until the 13th, then began marching south to link up with Spangenburg at Chambezi. Earlier, on the 12th, as he was riding his bicycle forward from the main column to get in touch with one of his advanced detachments, von Lettow-Vorbeck saw Captain Müller cycling furiously towards him. Müller's troops had captured a British dispatch rider, and he carried an extremely important telegram from General van Deventer to all British units in East Africa.

"12.11.18. To be fwded via M.B.cable and dispatch rider. Send following to General Von Lettow-Vorbeck under white flag. The Prime Minister of England has announced that an armistice was signed at 5 hours on Nov. 11th, and hostilities cease on all fronts at 11 hours on Nov. 11th. I am ordering my troops to cease hostilities forthwith unless attacked, and of course I conclude that you will do the same. Conditions of armistice will be forwarded to you immediately I receive them. Meanwhile I suggest that you remain in your present vicinity in order to facilitate communications.

"General Van Deventer.

"As message is also being sent to Livingstone, it is important Karwunfor receive this same time as enemy. Every effort must be made to get this message through to him today."

Von Lettow-Vorbeck wrote, "Our feelings were very mixed. Personally, as I had no knowledge of the real state of affairs in Germany, I felt convinced that the conclusion of hostilities must have been favourable, or at least not unfavourable to Germany. Spangenberg's detachment, which was on ahead, had to be told as soon as possible, and I immediately set out on my bicycle after it, taking with me Haouter, a *Landsturm* soldier, as my sole companion. About half-way, Reissmann's cyclist patrol of Spangenberg's detachment met me and reported that Captain Spangenberg had arrived at the Chambezi. Although I had no doubts about the correctness of the English news, our position was very uncomfortable."[16] Von Lettow-Vorbeck and Major Kraut immediately cycled to the rubber factory at Chambezi to stop Spangenburg's attack and there met DO Croad. Here von Lettow-Vorbeck received a telegram from van Deventer at midnight on the 14th which confirmed the text of the captured message.

"13.11.18. To Norforce. Karwunfor[17] via Fife. Send following to General von Lettow-Vorbeck under white flag: War Office London telegraphs that Clause 17 of armistice signed by the German Government provides for unconditional surrender of all German forces operating in East Africa within one month from November 11th. My conditions are; First: hand over all allied prisoners in your hands, Europeans and natives to nearest British troops forthwith. Second: bring your forces to Abercorn without delay, as Abercorn is the nearest place at which I can supply you with food.

"Third: hand over all your arms and ammunition to my representative at Abercorn. I will, however, allow you and your officers and European ranks to retain their personal weapons for the present in consideration of the gallant fight which you have made, provided that you bring your force to Abercorn without delay. Arrangements will be made to send all Germans to Morogoro and to repatriate German askaris. Kindly send an early answer giving probable date of arrival at Abercorn and numbers of German officers and men, askari and followers."

"Without being in a position to examine the ground in detail," von Lettow-Vorbeck wrote, "I had to tell myself that the conditions imposed upon us were inevitable, and must be loyally carried out. I met the British Commissioner, who had come from Kasama to the Chambezi rubber factory, at the river at eight o'clock on the morning of the 14th. There I handed to him a telegram to His Majesty, in which I reported what had happened and added that I would act accordingly. The Commissioner told me that the German fleet had revolted, and that a revolution had also broken out in Germany; further, if he was to accept a report which was official but had not yet been confirmed, the Kaiser had abdicated on November 10th."[18] Von Lettow-Vorbeck immediately returned to his main force and marched them back to Kasama, arriving on the 16th. On reaching the settlement he handed his written unconditional surrender to Major EBB Hawkins, DSO (West Yorks Regt), commanding 1/4th KAR, who had by this time retaken the town. Then at noon he and his command began their march to Abercorn, 1/4th KAR following at dawn the next day.

Fifteen

The Last German General

NINE DAYS LATER, on November 25, 1918, the *Kaiserlichen Schutztruppe für Ostafrika*, with Major-General Paul von Lettow-Vorbeck at their head, marched into Abercorn. Brigadier-General Edwards had come from Tabora to receive the official surrender, while 1/4th KAR and the Northern Rhodesia Regiment provided a guard of honor. At midday the *Schutztruppe* paraded in front of the government offices; von Lettow-Vorbeck was introduced to the British officers present, and he in turn introduced his own officers. He then ordered his men to lay down their arms. The German askaris discarded their equipment; once they had laid down their weapons, they were then marched off by companies to the internment camp set up a mile (one and a half kilometers) from the settlement. Their officers and German other ranks were allowed to retain their personal weapons in accordance with van Deventer's telegram of the 13th.

Von Lettow-Vorbeck, the last German General to surrender to the Allies, surrendered 155 Germans, 1,168 askaris and 1,516 native porters. He also handed over 777 Portuguese askaris and followers and more than 800 women. Besides their rifles, the *Schutztruppe* surrendered a field gun, 24 medium machine guns and 14 British Lewis light machine guns.

Following the signing of the formal surrender documents, von Lettow-Vorbeck and his officers were invited to dinner by the British, but he refused, going instead to inspect the camp where his askaris were interned. His men complained bitterly about the conditions of the camp and asked him to lead them against their captors and continue the campaign. Von Lettow-Vorbeck quieted his men, then went to see General Edwards.

The next day the *Schutztruppe* were marched to Bismarckburg, escorted by Hawkins's 1/4th KAR, and from here they were ferried across Lake Tanganyika to Kigoma, where they boarded trains and were carried to Tabora and into internment camps preparatory to their

Fifteen. The Last German General

repatriation. Von Lettow-Vorbeck and the other Germans were then taken to Dar es Salaam, arriving on December 8. Here they found that the influenza pandemic that was spreading rapidly across East Africa was rife among the occupying forces and townspeople: "Escort officers told me that frequently five or seven English officers had died [daily] of this disease at Dar-es-Salaam. We soon came across its traces among ourselves. Infection had probably taken place while we were on the ship on Lake Tanganyika, and subsequently on the train. It spread from man to man in the concentration camps in Dar-es-Salaam. Captain Spangenberg was going about with me in the town shortly after his arrival at Dar-es-Salaam. Then he felt ill, and though his iron constitution had successfully overcome all the hardships of the campaign, he died in hospital on December 18 of influenza and inflammation of the lungs.

"Almost all the Europeans in our camp were attacked by it, and it was very sad that in addition to Captain Spangenberg, nine other Europeans, in all, therefore, ten per cent, of our strength, succumbed. Numbers of our Askari interned at Tabora also died."[1] Von Lettow-Vorbeck himself was laid low by the pandemic and was desperately ill for ten days, but he gradually recovered. He and 114 of his surviving officers and men remained in Dar es Salaam until January 17, 1919, and then embarked for Germany, sailing via Cape Town to Rotterdam in Holland, thence by train to Berlin.

On March 2, 1919, von Lettow-Vorbeck, mounted on a horse and escorted by his surviving officers, marched through Berlin and the Brandenburg Gate cheered by a jubilant crowd. During his four-year campaign, he had forced the Allies to maintain upward of 160,000 combat troops in the field. Of the British Imperial forces alone, 3,443 were killed in action, 6,558 died from disease or accident, 7,777 were wounded and 1,310 were missing or captured. The British forces also lost 140,000 horses, mules, donkeys and oxen. As for the *Schutztruppe*, they recruited 3,007 Germans as officers and NCOs, 12,100 askaris and impressed several thousand native porters; their losses were 439 Germans and 1,290 askaris killed in action, 23 Germans killed accidentally, 277 Germans died of disease, 874 Germans and 3,669 askaris wounded and 4,510 missing, 2,718 Germans and 4,275 askaris were taken prisoner and two Germans and 2,847 askaris deserted.

When he crossed into Portuguese East Africa, von Lettow-Vorbeck and his command became, to all intents and purposes, a marauding bandit gang. They left a trail of destruction and devastation as they progressed through the country which was to affect the region for years to come. In the grand scheme of things his continuation of hostilities in Portuguese East Africa did not achieve what he had hoped it would,

Major-General Lettow-Vorbeck parading through Berlin (Bundesarchiv, B.145 Bild-P008268/Foto:o.Ang, 1 March 1919).

as the British had begun drawing down their military commitment in East Africa towards the end of 1917 and had no intention of committing any further troops to hunt for him. The entire campaign, however, took place within a few miles of the equator and covered thousands of square miles of country, at times in the blazing sun, at others in torrential rainfall.

All the troops of the belligerent nations performed amazing feats of physical endurance in this and the other African campaigns, marching and fighting in desert, tropical and subtropical conditions, in jungle and rainforest and across vast open plains, facing not only their respective enemies but wild animals, insects, disease, hunger and thirst. Had it not been for the momentous events taking place on the battlefields of Europe, the campaigns that took place in Africa would be as well known as those that took place on the Western Front, Gallipoli and on the Eastern Front.

On June 28, 1919, at Versailles, the final act of the Great War took place. The proceedings of the Peace Conference, that officially ended hostilities, began. They lasted for just under an hour, concluding with the German plenipotentiaries, Herr H Müller, Minister for Foreign Affairs, and Dr. Bell, Minister for Railways, signing the treaty on behalf of Germany. In the treaty Germany renounced her colonial possessions. German East Africa came under British control as "The Protectorate of

Fifteen. The Last German General

Tanganyika Territory." (In 1964, following independence and unification with Zanzibar, Tanganyika became the Republic of Tanzania.)

After his return to Germany in 1919, von Lettow-Vorbeck married his fiancée, Margarethe Wallrath, whom he had not seen since taking up his command in East Africa in 1914. They had two sons and two daughters. He remained in the army despite attempts to involve him in the politics of the Weimar Republic. Fourteen months after his return to Germany, von Lettow-Vorbeck—with Majors Georg Kraut and Franz Köhl and Captain Max Wintgens as his staff officers—commanded the *Freikorps* troops that ended the Spartacist uprising in Hamburg. In March 1920 Von Lettow-Vorbeck, with the covert support of Field Marshal von Hindenburg, became a leading figure in the Kapp Putsch. During March 13–17, Dr. Wolfgang Kapp, a right-wing radical, attempted to seize power in Berlin using units of the *Freikorps*. The Social Democrat government, which wanted to impose a military rule to put down the anarchy prevailing in Germany, fled to Stuttgart after the commander of the army, General Hans von Seeckt, refused to allow the army to be used to restore order. Von Lettow-Vorbeck's involvement in the Kapp Putsch, however, saw him arrested, court-martialed, cashiered from the army and imprisoned.

After his release, von Lettow-Vorbeck took a job as an import-export manager in Bremen, and in 1926 he met Colonel Richard Meinertzhagen, who was visiting the city. He then went into politics, and between May 1928 and July 1930 he served as a Reichstag Deputy for the monarchist German National People's Party, which he left in 1930 to join the Conservative People's Party. In 1929, while serving as a Reichstag Deputy, he was invited to London to be a guest of honor at the British East Africa Expeditionary Force anniversary dinner, where he met Field Marshal Jan Smuts—his old adversary. Both he and Smuts stayed with Richard Meinertzhagen at his home in Kensington Gardens during their visit to London, and the three men became close friends. In the national election of 1930, he gained the best result of the Conservative People's Party in his electoral district of Upper Bavaria but failed to be reelected.

He intensely disliked and distrusted Hitler and his National Socialist German Workers' Party (the Nazis) and, approaching his relative Hans-Jürgen von Blumenthal, suggested forming a coalition with the Stahlhelm against the National Socialists, which came to nothing. In 1935, Hitler, by now Chancellor and Führer of Germany, offered von Lettow-Vorbeck the ambassadorship to the United Kingdom, which he coldly refused as he was not prepared to join the Nazi Party, a requirement of the job. This refusal led to him being kept under close surveillance by the Gestapo. Von Lettow-Vorbeck had been restored to rank in the army shortly after his release from prison, and in 1938, at the age of 68, he was promoted to General of Infantry on the retired list.

His two sons, Rüdiger and Arndt, and his stepson Peter, were killed in action during the Second World War while serving in the Wehrmacht, and his house in Bremen had been destroyed during the bombing by the Allies. After the German surrender, he and his surviving family depended for a time on food packages sent to him by his friends Richard Meinertzhagen and Field Marshal Smuts. He visited East Africa in 1953, where he was welcomed by the British colonial officials with military honors.

On March 9, 1964, 11 days before his 94th birthday, Paul von Lettow-Vorbeck died at his home in Hamburg-Altona, where he lived with one of his daughters, and was buried in the Vicelin Church, Pronstorf, Schleswig Holstein.

Governor Schnee, on his return to Germany, accompanied Major-General von Lettow-Vorbeck when he and the other returning officers and men marched through the Brandenburg Gate to the acclaim of the Berlin crowds. He entered politics, joining the German People's Party, and was elected to the Reichstag where he served as a representative until 1932, when he resigned from the party. In 1926 Schnee was appointed President of the Federation of Germans Abroad and became the leading proponent of German colonial interests. He held this post until 1933. He was appointed to the Lytton Commission—the League of Nations Manchuria Commission—following the Manchuria Incident, where he was involved in the negotiations taking place between China and Japan.

In 1933, Schnee, by now an ardent Nazi, joined the National Socialist German Workers' Party and was elected to the Reichstag as a Nazi Deputy, a post he held until the defeat of Germany in 1945. Because of his affiliations and beliefs, he was barred from public office following the collapse of Nazi Germany. He was killed in a car accident in Berlin on June 23, 1949.

Major-General Kurt Wahle, who had been left at Ubena in October 1917 where, wounded and ill, he had been picked up by 2/4th KAR and sent for treatment at a British military hospital, rejoined von Lettow-Vorbeck when he arrived in Dar es Salaam as a prisoner of war on December 8, 1918. Despite his age—he was the oldest combatant of any nation who fought during the war—he had fully recovered from his wounds and illness. He returned to Germany with von Lettow-Vorbeck, Governor Schnee and the other Germans of the *Schutztruppe* when they were repatriated in January 1919. He was one of those who marched with von Lettow-Vorbeck through the Brandenburg Gate. He died aged 72 on June 19, 1928.

Captain Max Looff, following his surrender to the 1st Cape Corps on November 21, 1917, was taken first to Lindi then to Dar es Salaam. Not long afterwards Looff and the surviving members of the *Königsburg*, along with the German members of the *Schutztruppe*, then held by the British, were moved to Egypt. The officers were sent to a prisoner of war camp located at Sidi Bishr near Alexandria, while the NCOs and other ranks were interned at Toura near Cairo. In 1918 he and the other prisoners were sent to England, where they were interned near Hull on the east coast of Yorkshire. They remained here until 1919 when they were carried to Rotterdam, where they were reunited with von Lettow-Vorbeck and his party who were en route to Germany. From Rotterdam the entire group was carried by train to Berlin.

On his return to Germany, Captain Looff was placed on the retired list. He was recalled to the Navy on May 24, 1939, with the rank of Vice-Admiral, but despite the outbreak of war in September, he was given no active command. When the war in Europe ended in 1945, he was in the Soviet occupation zone, which became East Germany. He died in East Berlin on September 20, 1954.

Lieutenant-General Dirk van Deventer returned to Pretoria after the war. He had been made a Knight Commander of the Order of the Bath and promoted to full general. He died in Pretoria on August 17, 1922.

Colonel Richard Meinertzhagen, after leaving East Africa in November 1916, served as Chief of Intelligence in the Middle East. In late 1918 he was attached to HQBEF in France, and after the armistice, he became Sir Edmund Allenby's Chief Political Officer and was at the Paris Peace Conference in 1919. Meinertzhagen was involved in the creation of the Palestine Mandate which eventually led to the creation of Israel; he retired from the army in 1925. With the outbreak of World War II in 1939, he returned to military service as a Lieutenant-Colonel in Military Intelligence. Four days after the United Nations voted in favor of the partitioning of Palestine, which led to the foundation of the State of Israel—December 3, 1947—Chaim Weizmann, its first President, wrote to Meinertzhagen to tell him how much Israel owed him for his contribution in the formation of the Jewish State. In 1948, Meinertzhagen, a respected ornithologist, along with Dr. Philip Clancey, went on an ornithological expedition which covered Arabia, the Yemen and Aden, then across to Africa where they traveled through Somalia, Kenya, Ethiopia and South Africa. Meinertzhagen died on June 17, 1967.

Following World War I, Jan Smuts, along with Botha, was a key negotiator at the Treaty of Paris. He strongly believed and advocated in favor of reconciliation with Germany and the imposition of limited reparations. He returned to South Africa following the Paris Conference, and when Botha died, he was elected Prime Minister, a post he held until his party was defeated in the 1924 general election. He became Deputy Prime Minister in the coalition government of JBM Hertzog in 1933 after nine years in the political wilderness. When Hertzog advocated neutrality with the outbreak of war in 1939, his motion was defeated in the South African Parliament and the coalition split. The Governor-General, Sir Patrick Duncan, refused Hertzog's request to dissolve Parliament and hold a general election; instead he asked Smuts to form a government. On May 24, 1941, Smuts was made a Field Marshal in the British Army.

Following the end of the war in 1945, Smuts was the South African representative in San Francisco at the drafting of the Charter of the United Nations. He was elected as Chancellor of the University of Cambridge in 1948; that same year he lost power when his party was defeated in the general election which brought the pro–Apartheid Daniel Malan's Reunited National Party to power. Field Marshal Smuts died on September 11, 1950, at his farm of Doornkloof, Irene, near Pretoria.

Appendix I

British Order of Battle, January 1916

1st EA Division

2nd EA Brigade: 25th Royal Fusiliers, 29th Punjabis, 129th Baluchis, 3rd Kashmir Rifles, Cape Corps Battalion.
1st SA Mounted Brigade: 1st, 2nd and 3rd SA Horse, SA Scouts.
Two unbrigaded companies 1st KAR.
Mounted Troops: EA Mounted Rifles, East Africa Squadron, 17th Indian Cavalry, KAR Mounted Infantry Company (formed by a half company 3rd KAR).
Div Artillery: 17th Mountain Battery, 7th Battery, RA (formed by cadres from 2nd and 6th Batteries, RA, from Mauritius), 1st and 2nd SA Batteries.

2nd EA Division

1st EA Brigade: 2nd Loyal North Lancs, 2nd Rhodesia Regt., 130th Baluchis, 3rd KAR.
2nd SA Brigade: 5th, 6th, 7th and 8th SA Infantry.
3rd SA Brigade: 9th, 10th, 11th and 12th SA Infantry.
Mounted Troops: 10th Armoured Car Battery (originally a section of 1st Squadron, RNAC Division from South West Africa).
Div Artillery:
4th Indian Mountain Brigade: 28th Mountain Battery, 5th Battery (Calcutta Volunteer Bty), 1st Light Battery, RA, 4th (H) Battery, RA.
SA Field Brigade: 2nd, 4th and 5th SA Batteries.

Lake Victoria Detachment

98th Hyderabad Infantry, 4th King's African Rifles, Baganda Scouts, Nandi Scouts, Machine Gun Section.

Appendix II

British Order of Battle, March 1916

1st EA Division

1st EA Brigade: 2nd Loyal Nth Lancs, 40th Pathans, 129th Baluchis, 3rd KAR.
2nd EA Brigade: 25th R. Fusiliers, 2nd Rhodesia Regt, 29th Punjabis, 130th Baluchis.
Mounted Troops: 4th SA Horse, East Africa Squadron, 17th Indian Cavalry, East African Mounted Rifles, KAR Mounted Infantry Company, Belfield's Scouts, 1st and 10th Armoured Car Batteries.
Divisional Artillery: 27th & 28th Mountain Batteries, 7th, 8th & 9th Batteries.

2nd EA Division

3rd SA Infantry Brigade: 9th, 10th, 11th & 12th SA Infantry Battalions.
1st SA Mounted Brigade: 1st, 2nd & 3rd SA Horse, SA Scouts, half Company SA Motor Cycle Corps, 4th Armoured Car Battery.
Divisional Artillery: 2nd, 4th & 5th SA Batteries.

3rd EA Division

2nd SA Infantry Brigade: 5th, 6th, 7th & 8th SA Infantry Battalions.
2nd SA Mounted Brigade: 5th, 6th & 7th SA Horse, half Coy SA Motor Cycle Corps, 5th Light AC Battery.
Unbrigaded: 1st Battalion, Cape Corps.
Divisional Artillery: 1st & 3rd SA Batteries.

Army Troops

Mounted: 4th South African Horse and Belfield's Scouts attached to 1st

EA Division, No. 10 Light Armoured Car Battery, and South African Motor Cyclist Corps.

Infantry: 2nd KAR (newly raised and still in training, not yet operational)

Pioneers: 61st Pioneers, less one company; South African Pioneers less four sections.

Artillery: No.9 Battery, No.10 (Heavy) Battery, No.11 (Heavy) Battery, 134th Howitzer Battery, 38th Howitzer Brigade, Trench Mortar Brigade.

Aviation: No.4 Squadron, Royal Naval Air Service, No.26 SA Squadron, Royal Flying Corps, Kite Balloon Section.

Miscellaneous: North-West Railway Volunteer Maxim Machine Gun Section, East African Intelligence Corps.

Lines of Communication Troops: 5th Indian Light Infantry, 17th Indian Cavalry, 63rd Palamcottah Light Infantry, 101st Grenadiers, Bharatpur Infantry, Jind Infantry, Kapurthala Infantry, 3rd Gwalior Rifles, Rampur Infantry, 2nd Kashmir Rifles, Cape Corps, Arab Rifles, Company 61st Pioneers, East African Pioneer Company.

Lake Victoria Detachment

17th Indian Infantry, 98th Hyderabad Infantry, 4th King's African Rifles, Baganda Scouts, Nandi Scouts, Machine Gun Section.

APPENDIX III

Versailles Treaty— Articles Regarding German Overseas Territories

Conditions agreed to by the German representatives at Versailles concerning the German overseas territories. These being Part IV of the Treaty of Versailles; articles 118 to 127.

PART IV. GERMAN RIGHTS AND INTERESTS OUTSIDE GERMANY

Article 118

In territory outside her European frontiers as fixed by the present Treaty, Germany renounces all rights, titles and privileges whatever in or over territory which belonged to her or to her allies, and all rights, titles and privileges whatever their origin which she held as against the Allied and Associated Powers.

Germany hereby undertakes to recognize and to conform to the measures which may be taken now or in the future by the Principle Allied and Associated Powers, in agreement where necessary with third Powers, in order to carry the above stipulation into effect.

SECTION I.—GERMAN COLONIES

Article 119

Germany renounces in favor of the Principle Allied and Associated Powers all her rights and titles over her overseas possessions.

Article 120

All movable and immovable property in such territories belonging to the German Empire or to any German State shall pass to the

Government exercising authority over such territories, on the terms laid down in Article 257 of Part IX (Financial Clauses) of the present Treaty. The division of the local courts in any dispute as to the nature of such property shall be final.

Article 121

The provisions of Sections I and IV of Part X (Economic Clauses) of the present Treaty shall apply in the case of these territories whatever be the form of Government adopted for them.

Article 122

The Government exercising authority over such territories may make such provisions as it thinks fit with reference to the repatriation from them of German nationals and to the conditions upon which German subjects of European origin shall, or shall not, be allowed to reside, hold property, trade or exercise a profession in them.

Article 123

The provisions of Article 260 of Part IX (Financial Clauses) of the present Treaty shall apply in the case of all agreements concluded with German nationals for the construction or exploitation of public works in German overseas possessions, as well as any sub-concessions or contracts resulting there from which may have been made to or with such nationals.

Article 124

Germany hereby undertakes to pay, in accordance with the estimate to be presented by the French Government and approved by the Reparation Commission, reparation for damage suffered by French nationals in the Cameroons or the frontier zone by reason of the acts of the German civil and military authorities and of German private individuals during the period from January 1, 1900, to August 1, 1914.

Article 125

Germany renounces all rights under the Convention and Agreements with France of November 4, 1911, and September 28, 1912, relating to Equatorial Africa. She undertakes to pay to the French Government, in accordance with the estimate to be presented by that Government and approved by the Reparation Commission, all the deposits, credits, advances, etc., effected by virtue of these instruments in favor of Germany.

Article 126

Germany undertakes to accept and observe the agreements made or to be made by the Allied and Associated Powers or some of them with any other Power with regard to the trade in arms and spirits, and to the matters dealt with in the General Act of Berlin of February 26, 1885, and the General Act of Brussels of July 2, 1890, and the Conventions completing or modifying the same.

Article 127

The native inhabitants of the former German overseas possessions shall be entitled to the diplomatic protection of the Governments exercising authority over those territories.

* * *

PART IX. FINANCIAL CLAUSES

Article 257

In the case of the former German territories, including colonies, protectorates or dependencies, administered by a Mandatory under Article 22 of Part I (League of Nations) of the present Treaty, neither the territory nor the Mandatory Power shall be charged with any portion of the debt of the German Empire or States.

All property and possessions belonging to the German Empire or to the German States situated in such territories shall be transferred with the territories to the Mandatory Power in its capacity as such and no payment shall be made nor any credit given to those Governments in consideration of this transfer.

For the purposes of this Article the property and possessions of the German Empire and of the German States shall be deemed to include all the property of the crown, the Empire or the States, and the private property of the former German Emperor and other Royal personages.

* * *

Article 260

Without prejudice to the renunciation of any rights by Germany on behalf of herself or of her nationals in the other provisions of the present Treaty, the Reparation Commission may within one year from the coming into force of the present Treaty demand that the German Government become possessed of any rights and interests of German nationals in any public utility undertaking or in any concession operating in Russia, China, Turkey, Austria, Hungary and Bulgaria, or in the possessions or dependencies of these states or in any territory formerly belonging to Germany or her Allies, to be ceded by Germany or her Allies to any Power or to be administered by a Mandatory under the present Treaty, and may require that the German Government transfer, within six months of the date of demand, all such rights and interests and any similar rights and interests the German Government may itself possess to the Reparation Commission.

Germany shall be responsible for indemnifying her nationals so dispossessed, and the Reparation Commission shall credit Germany, on account of sums due for reparation, with such sums in respect of the value of the transferred rights and interests as may be assessed by the Reparation Commission, and the German Government shall, within six months from the coming into force of the present Treaty, communicate to the Reparation Commission all such rights and interests, whether already granted, contingent or not yet exercised, and shall renounce on behalf of itself and its nationals in favor of the Allied and Associated Powers all such rights and interests which have not been so communicated.

Chapter Notes

Chapter One
1. The German colony's topography was hugely variable with mountains and fertile areas in the northwest, grasslands in the northeast, a dry, sandy and rock-strewn center and vast forest areas in the southwest.
2. Von Lettow-Vorbeck: *My Reminiscences of East Africa*.
3. *Ibid.*
4. The 2nd KAR had been reduced to a single company in 1906, and this company was subsequently disbanded in 1913. The unit was reconstituted on the 1st April 1916 as the 2nd Regiment KAR.
5. The *City of Winchester* was the first British ship to be taken in the war.
6. Von Lettow-Vorbeck.
7. *Ibid.*
8. Imperial Service Battalions were Indian State Forces offered by their Rulers to the Raj for war service.
9. The Belgian *Force Publique* was comprised of 21 independent Field Companies and a combined artillery and engineer company in 1914. The *Troupes de Katanga* at this time were a semiautonomous force comprising a Battalion HQ, four *Compagnies de Marche*, a cyclist company and four garrison companies numbering 2,875 officers and men. Following the instructions from the Vice-Governor of Katanga to assist British operations and to defend Belgian territory, the *Troupes de Katanga* were reorganised into battalions numbered *Ie, IIe and IIIme Bataillons de Marche* for service along the eastern frontier and in support of the British in Northern Rhodesia. Later a fourth battalion, the *11e Bataillon de Marche*, was also formed. The *Compagnie d'Artillerie et de Génie* was stationed in Boma at the mouth of the Congo River throughout the war.
10. Major-General Baron Charles Henri Marie Ernest Tombeur, 1867–1947.

Chapter Two
1. Col Richard Meinertzhagen: *Army Diary 1899–1926*.
2. *Ibid.*
3. *Ibid.*
4. Lieutenant-Colonel Charles W Horden, *Official History, Military Operations, East Africa, 1914–1918*.
5. Horden.
6. Meinertzhagen.
7. *Ibid.*
8. Von Lettow-Vorbeck.
9. Meinertzhagen.
10. Horden.
11. Sir Charles Lucas: *The Empire at War*.

Chapter Three
1. Von Lettow-Vorbeck.
2. Henry Peel Ritchie, VC, RN, survived his wounds, retiring in 1917; he was promoted Captain on the retired list on the 29th January 1924 and died on the 9th December 1958 at the age of 83.

Chapter Four
1. Von Lettow-Vorbeck.
2. A Subadar was a Viceroy Commissioned Officer (VCO) in the infantry of the Indian Army. Indian officers could not receive a Sovereign's Commission until after World War I. Indian officers were promoted from NCO ranks to Jemadar

(wearing rank badges of a Lieutenant) and commanding an infantry platoon or cavalry troop; Subadar (Infantry) Risaldar (Cavalry), wearing rank badges of a captain and second in command of an infantry company or a cavalry squadron; and Subadar Major or Risaldar Major, wearing rank badges of a major and, after the commanding officer of an infantry or cavalry regiment, its most important member, advising on administrative matters and Indian customs. The Subadar Major or Risaldar Major could also be called on to take command of a company or squadron. The officers of the Indian State forces, however, received their commissions from their own rulers, not the British.
3. Von Lettow-Vorbeck.
4. *Ibid.*
5. *Ibid.*

Chapter Five

1. The exploits of Pieter Pretorius were the inspiration for Wilbur Smith's novel *Shout at the Devil.*
2. Von Lettow-Vorbeck.
3. Reichskolonialamt Records.
4. *Ibid.*
5. *Ibid.*

Chapter Six

1. Capt Angus Buchanan, MC. *Three Years of War in East Africa.*
2. *Ibid.*
3. *Ibid.*
4. *Ibid.*
5. Horden.
6. *Ibid.*

Chapter Eight

1. Meinertzhagen.
2. *Ibid.*
3. *Ibid.*
4. Wilbur Taylor Dartnell was born William Thomas Dartnell; he changed his name while living in South Africa before the War.
5. Von Lettow-Vorbeck.
6. Horden.
7. Von Lettow-Vorbeck.
8. *Ibid.*
9. *Ibid.*
10. See Appendix One.

11. The 7th SA Infantry Battalion had been raised from Australian and New Zealand expats residing in South Africa.
12. On 6th October 1915 the 2nd Loyals commander, Lieutenant-Colonel Jourdain, had received orders to withdraw the machine-gun sections from each of his Rifle Companies and form them into a machine-gun company. When the 2nd Loyals were redeployed to Egypt in December 1916, the 2nd LNL MG Company remained in East Africa, having been transferred to the Machine Gun Corps as No. 259 Machine Gun Company.
13. AE Capell, *The 2nd Rhodesia Regiment in East Africa.*

Chapter Nine

1. Buchanan.
2. Meinertzhagen.
3. Horden.
4. Von Lettow-Vorbeck.
5. *Ibid.*
6. Meinertzhagen.
7. See Appendix Two.

Chapter Ten

1. Aniceto Afonso and Carlos de Matos Gomes. *Portugal e a Grande Guerra.*
2. Von Lettow-Vorbeck.
3. Meinertzhagen.
4. *Ibid.*
5. Von Lettow-Vorbeck.
6. Horden.
7. The Kashmir Rifles Battalion was a composite battalion formed by the half battalions of the 2nd and 3rd Kashmir Rifles.
8. Schnee had met his wife while on local leave in New Zealand while serving as District Administrator and Deputy Governor of German Samoa at the turn of the century.
9. The 1st and 2nd South African Rifles, though infantry, were formed into squadrons and troops with each battalion having four squadrons each of 110 officers and men and a HQ squadron.
10. Prior to the reorganization of the King's African Rifles the letter "R" in a 1st KAR Company's title showed that it was comprised of reservists recalled to the colours.

Chapter Notes

Chapter Eleven

1. Von Lettow-Vorbeck.
2. Sir Hugh Clifford, KCMG: *The Gold Coast Regiment in the East African Campaign*.
3. Von Lettow-Vorbeck.
4. Besides the detachments of Tafel and Lieberman, there were also the detachments of Captain Ernst Otto (23rd, 24th Field, 6th Rifle and 14th Reserve Companies), Captain Paul Stemmermann (3rd, 14th, 18th, 22nd Field and 4th Rifle Companies), and Captain Hans Schulz (4th, 9th, 13th and 21st Field Companies) engaged in the Uluguru and Kisaki operations.
5. Von Lettow-Vorbeck.
6. Lieutenants Harold Swifte and Hugh Barrett were subsequently awarded Military Crosses, while Pvts AS Peters and RG Hill were awarded Distinguished Conduct Medals for their actions during the siege.
7. On the 30th September General Smuts had sent a letter through the lines to Governor Schnee, with a copy to von Lettow-Vorbeck, calling on them to surrender. Von Lettow-Vorbeck correctly deduced from this letter that the British had outrun their resources and refused the offer.
8. The 1st Battalion, 2nd Regiment, The King's African Rifles.
9. General Smuts's dispatch to the Secretary of State for War, 28th February 1917.
10. Von Lettow-Vorbeck.
11. Von Lettow-Vorbeck's artillery consisted of one of the last remaining 105-mm *Königsberg* guns, a 4.1-inch howitzer and two mountain guns,
12. Clifford.
13. *Ibid.*
14. Von Lettow-Vorbeck.
15. Clifford.

Chapter Twelve

1. General Hoskins dispatch to the Secretary of State for War, 30th May 1917.
2. The 1st Battalion, Cape Corps Coloureds, was raised in South Africa from South Africans of mixed race in December 1915 and arrived in East Africa in February 1916. It returned to South Africa in December 1917 and then went to Egypt where it joined the 160th Bde, 53rd British Division, serving in that division from July 1918 to May 1919. In March 1917 the newly raised 2nd Battalion was sent to East Africa to reinforce General Northey's command.
3. Von Lettow-Vorbeck.
4. Buchanan.
5. *Ibid.*
6. Von Lettow-Vorbeck.
7. *Ibid.*
8. *Ibid.*
9. *Ibid.*
10. H Moyse-Bartlett, *The King's African Rifles.*
11. Clifford.
12. Gen van Deventer's dispatch to the Secretary of State for War, 21st January 1918.
13. Von Lettow-Vorbeck.
14. *Ibid.*
15. Sergeant Mafinde was subsequently awarded a Military Medal for his conduct on this occasion and during the later fighting at Bweho Chini.
16. Capt WD Downes, MC: *With the Nigerians in German East Africa.*
17. O'Grady's Linforce column consisted at this time of, besides the 25th Fusiliers and 1/2nd KAR, the 3/2nd and 3/4th KAR, Bharatpur Infantry and No. 259 Machine-Gun Company.
18. Buchanan.
19. *Ibid.*
20. Major-General Wahle's command consisted of Captain Rothe's detachment—the 19th and 20th Field and Tanga *Landsturm* Companies—Captain Lieberman's detachment—3rd and 9th Field, 4th Rifle, 14th Reserve and 'S' and 'O' Companies.

Chapter Thirteen

1. Von Lettow-Vorbeck.
2. *Ibid.*
3. Downes.
4. *Ibid.*
5. The fighting at Nyangao was the last action involving the 25th Royal Fusiliers. They had only been able to field 120 officers and men at the beginning of the action, the strength of a half company, and by the end of the fighting, there were less than 50 all ranks fit for service.
6. Von Lettow-Vorbeck.

Chapter Notes

7. Captain ID Difford: *The Story of the 1st Battalion Cape Corps.*
8. Clifford.
9. Colour-Sergeant Michael Cuneen was a British Senior NCO attached to the Gold Coast Regiment.
10. Clifford.
11. No. 1 column had a two-gun section of 27th Mountain Battery attached to it at this time.
12. Captain Methven subsequently received a bar to his Military Cross for his gallantry during this action, while Sergeant Mamprusi, MM, was awarded the African Distinguished Conduct Medal.
13. Von Lettow-Vorbeck.
14. In the Indian Army a cavalry trooper was known as a Sowar, while an infantry private was a Sepoy.
15. Von Lettow-Vorbeck.
16. *Ibid.*
17. L59 was subsequently employed on a number of bombing and reconnaissance missions from her base at Jamboli over the following months. Then in early April 1918 she took off to bomb the British Naval Base at Valetta in Malta. Having crossed the Balkans and the Strait of Otranto, she was spotted on the 7th by the commander of the German coastal submarine *UB53*, Lieutenant JLE Sprenger, flying at about 700 feet (214 meters). Shortly after, Sprenger heard two short detonations followed by an enormous flame, which engulfed the Zeppelin, and it crashed into the sea with the loss of all hands. She was not lost to enemy action, as neither the British nor the Italians reported destroying a Zeppelin. Her loss, apparently, was due to an accident on board.
18. The 2nd, 3rd, 4th, 9th, 10th, 11th, 13th, 14th, 17th, 18th, 19th, 20th, 21st and 25th Field Companies, 14th Reserve Company, 'S' and 'I' Companies and the 3rd, 4th, 5th, 6th and 8th Rifle Companies.
19. Von Lettow-Vorbeck.
20. *Ibid.*
21. Tafel had under command 1,639 officers and men of the 1st, 5th, 6th, 7th 15th, 22nd, 23rd and 29th Field Companies, 1st and 2nd Rifle Companies, "L" Company and the Pangani detachment, plus 3,732 porters and camp followers.
22. Gen van Deventer's dispatch to the Secretary of State for War, 30th September 1918.
23. *Ibid.*
24. Rose Column.
25. 2nd King's African Rifles Column.
26. Van Deventer.

Chapter Fourteen

1. Von Lettow-Vorbeck.
2. Ludwig Deppe: *Mit Lettow-Vorbeck durch Afrika.*
3. Port Amelia Force.
4. Northey Force.
5. Von Lettow-Vorbeck.
6. *Ibid.*
7. Captain Sibary was subsequently awarded the Military Cross, while Sergeants Thomson and Cartnell each received the Distinguished Conduct Medal.
8. Von Lettow-Vorbeck.
9. Shorthose Column.
10. Von Lettow-Vorbeck.
11. Van Deventer.
12. 2/4th King's African Rifles Column.
13. The recently redesignated Northern Rhodesia Police (Military Branch).
14. Von Lettow-Vorbeck.
15. *Ibid.*
16. *Ibid.*
17. 1/4th King's African Rifles Column.
18. Von Lettow-Vorbeck.

Chapter Fifteen

1. Von Lettow-Vorbeck.

Bibliography

Adler, FB, AE Lorch, and HH Curson. *The South African Artillery: German East Africa and Palestine 1915–1919.* (1958)
Amery, LS. *German Colonial Claims.* (1929)
Aniceto, Afonso, and Carlos de Matos Gomes. *Portugal e a Grande Guerra.*
Armstrong, FC. *Grey Steel: J.C. Smuts, A Study in Arrogance.* (1937)
Arnold, John. *The African Distinguished Conduct Medal.* (1998)
Blumberg, HE. *Britain's Sea Soldiers: A Record of the Royal Marines During the War 1914–1919.* (1927)
Boyd, W. *An Ice Cream War.* (1982)
Brelsford, WV (ed.). *The Story of The Northern Rhodesia Regiment.* (1990)
Buchanan, MC. *Capt Angus: Three Years of War in East Africa.* (1920)
Capell, AE. *The 2nd Rhodesia Regiment in East Africa.* (1923)
Clark, Peter. *West Africans at War.* (1986)
Clifford, Hugh. *The Gold Coast Regiment in the East African Campaign.* (1920)
Collyer, JJ. *The South Africans with General Smuts in German East Africa 1916.* (1939)
Corbett, JS, and Sir H Newbolt. *Official History (Naval Operations).*
Crafford, RR. *Jan Smuts.* (1945)
Crowe, JHV. *General Smut's Campaign in East Africa.* (1918); *War Memoirs.* (1942)
Cundall, Frank. *Jamaica's Part in the Great War.* (1925)
Dane, Edmund. *British Campaigns in Africa and the Pacific, 1914–1918.* (1919)
Dennis, LG. *The Lake Steamers of East Africa.* (1996)
Deppe, Ludwig. *Mit Lettow-Vorbeck durch Afrika.* (1919)

Difford, Ivor. *The Story of the First Battalion Cape Corps, 1915–1919.* (1920)
Downes, WD. *With the Nigerians in German East Africa.* (1919)
Dyde, Brian. *The Empty Sleeve: The Story of the West India Regiments of the British Army.* (1997)
Farwell, Byron. *The Great War in Africa.* (1986)
Fendall, Brig-Gen CP. *The East African Force 1915–1919.* (1921)
Feyver, WH. *The Distinguished Service Medal 1914–1920.* (1982)
Frankland, A. *The 101st Grenadiers.* (1927)
Gardener, Brian. *German East.* (1963)
Gardner, B. *German East. The Story of the First World War in East Africa.* (1963)
Gardner, B. *On to Kilimanjaro.* (1963)
Gladding, RG. *At the Going Down of the Sun: The African Campaigns of World War One.* (2016)
Graham, CAL. *The History of the Indian Mountain Artillery.* (1957)
Hancock, WK. *Smuts.* (1962)
Harding, Colin. *Frontier Patrols: A History of the British South Africa Police and other Rhodesian Forces.* (1937)
Haywood, A, and F Clarke. *History of the Royal West African Frontier Force.* (1964)
HMSO (War Office). *Field Service Regulations, 1914, General Staff, War Office.*
HMSO (War Office). *The Monthly Army List, 1914–1818.*
Hodges, G. *The Carrier Corps 1914–1918.* (1986)
Horden, Lt-Col Charles. W. *Official History, Military Operations, East Africa, 1914–1918.* (1941)
Hoyt, Edwin P. *The Germans who Never Lost: The Story of the Königsberg.* (1968)

Bibliography

Hoyt, Edwin P. *Guerrilla: Colonel von Lettow-Vorbeck and Germany's East African Empire.* (1981)

Iliffe, John. *Africans; The History of a Continent.* (1995)

Ingham, K. *A History of East Africa.* (1962)

Jose, Arthur W. *The Official History of Australia in the War of 1914–1918, Vol IX, The Royal Australian Navy.* (1941)

Katzenellenbogen, SE. *South Africa and the War of 1914–18.* (1973)

Keble Chatterton, Cmdr E. *The Koenigsberg Adventure.*

Lawford, JP, and WE Catto. *Solah Punjab: The History of the 16th Punjab Regiment.* (1967)

Lewin, Evans. *The Germans and Africa.* (1915)

Liddle-Hart, Capt Sir B. *War in Outline: History of the First World War.*

Lucas, Charles. *The Empire at War.* (1925)

Maxwell, RM. *Jimmie Stewart—Frontiersman.* (1992)

Meinertzhagen, Richard. *Army Diary 1899–1926.* (1960)

Miller, C. *The Battle of the Bundu: The First World War in East Africa.* (1974)

Millin, SG. *General Smuts.* (1936)

Moore, Capt John, RN. *Jane's Fighting Ships of World War I.* (1919)

Moseley, L. *Duel for Kilimanjaro.* (1963)

Moyse-Bartlett, H. *The King's African Rifles.* (1956)

Nutting, A. *Scramble for Africa.* (1970)

Page, Malcolm. *KAR, A History of the King's African Rifles.* (1997)

Shankland, P. *The Phantom Flotilla.* (1969)

Smyth, Brig Sir J, VC, MC. *The Story of the Victoria Cross.* (1963)

Stewart, Lt-Col R, MVO. *The Victoria Cross.* (1928)

Strachan, Hew. *The First World War.* (2003)

Strachan, Hew. *The First World War in Africa.* (2004)

Thatcher, WS. *The 4th Battalion DCO Tenth Baluch Regiment in the Great War (129th Baluchis).* (1932)

Union of South Africa, General Staff, Defence Headquarters. *The Union of South Africa and The Great War, 1914–18: Official History.* (1922)

Von Lettow-Vorbeck, Gen P. *My Reminiscences of East Africa.* (1920)

Waters, RS. *History of the 5th Battalion (Pathans) 14th Punjab Regiment.* (1936)

Wigmore, L, and B Harding. *They Dared Mightily.* (1986)

Wilde, AT. *Regimental History of the 4th Battalion, 13th Frontier Force Rifles (Wilde's).* (1932)

Wilson, CJ. *The Story of the East African Mounted Rifles.* (1938)

Wylly, HC. *The History of Coke's Rifles.* (1930)

Young, Francis Brett. *Marching on Tanga: (with General Smuts in East Africa).* (1938)

War Diaries

National Archives, Kew, London. (WO 95/ WO 123/WO 161)
2nd Loyal North Lancashire Regiment.
Mounted Infantry Company.
1st King's African Rifles.
2nd King's African Rifles.
3rd King's African Rifles.
4th King's African Rifles.
29th Punjab Regiment.
129th (Duke of Connaught's Own) Baluchis.
130th Baluchis.
South African Mounted Brigades.

Index

Abercorn (Mbala) 13–15, 109, 189–190
Adamstor (Portuguese cruiser) 97
Aden 11, 195
Adler, Capt. Otto 39
Adrianople 170
Adye, Lt.-Col. D.R. 108
Aitken, Maj.-Gen. Arthur Edward 20–21, 23, 26–27; demoted to colonel and ordered home 31; orders evacuation of Tanga 29; refuses stores and machine gun evacuation 30
Akure, Company Sgt.-Maj. Belo, DCM, MM 149
Albertville 66
Alexandre del Commune (Belgian Government steamer) 14, 66
Alexandria 195
Ali, Subadar Mardan 40, 205*ch*4*n*2
Allenby, Field-Marshall Sir Edmund 195
Alto Ligonha 183
Alto Moloque 180–181
Amorim, Lt.-Col. Massano de 96
Anguros 186
Apartheid 196
Apel, Lt.-Cmdr. Hans 133
Arabia 195
Arusha 12, 76, 87, 95, 99, 148, 150
Aslin, Lt. Robert, RNR 79
Astraea (British cruiser) 10–11
Augar, Capt. 93
Auracher, District Commissioner 23–24
Austro-Hungarian Empire 7
Azevedo, Capt. Benedito de 123

Bagamoyo 121
Baringo 10
Baron Dhanis (Belgian steamer) 66
Barrett, Lt. E.H. 76
Barrett, Lt. Hugh Treherne, MC 128, 207*ch*11*n*6
Barry, Capt. N.J.M. 166

Bauer, 1st Lt. 75–76
Bauman 93
Baumstark, Capt. Paul 17, 24
Baxter, Capt. G.L. 111, 128
Beaumont, Capt. G.N. 129
Behobeho-kwa-Mahinda 137
Beira 174
Belfield, Sir Henry Conway 7, 23
Belgium 7
Belgian Congo 1, 4, 65–67, 108
Belgian Army 172
Belgian Army formations and units: *Force Publique* 14, 205*ch*1*n*9; *Group Mobile nord* 108–109; *Group Mobile sud* 108–109 (*1e Bataillon de Marche* 172; *1er Régiment de Marche* 108; *2e Régiment de Marche* 108; *3e Régiment de Marche* 108; *4e Bataillon de Marche* 142–143; *4e Régiment de Marche* 108; *6e Bataillon de Marche* 108–109, 142, 148; *9e Bataillon de Marche* 142; *10e Bataillon de Marche* 172; *13e Bataillon de Marche* 142–143, 148); *Troupes de Katanga* 14–15 (*Ier Bataillon de Marche, Troupes de Katanga* 15, 60; *IIème Bataillon de Marche, Troupes de Katanga* 205*ch*1*n*9; *IIIème Bataillon de Marche, Troupes de Katanga* 15)
Bell, Dr, Minister for Railways 192
Berkeley, Maj. R.E. 46
Berlin 191, 194–195
Berrange, Brig.-Gen. C.A.L. 99
Besch, Naval Lt. 171
Beves, Brig.-Gen. Percival Scott 81–82, 101, 137–138, 143, 150–152, 159, 161
Bharata (British ship) 30
Biharamuli 108
Bismarckburg (Kasanga) 56, 70, 109–110, 187, 190
Blaxendale, Maj. Walter 125–126
Bloomfield, Capt. William Anderson, VC 118

Blumenthal, Hans-Jürgen von 193
Bock, Col. (Rtd.) Heinrich *Freiherr* von 12, 100
Bockholt, Lt.-Cmdr. Ludwig 168; awarded *Pour le Mérite* 170
Boemcken, Maj. Julius von 115, 131
Boer War 63
Boggis, Air-Mechanic, RNAS 48
Böll, Lt. 183
Bombaja-Ngombe 86–87
Bombay (Mumbai) 20, 37, 50
Bombo 10
Booth, Sgt. (later Capt.) Frederick Charles, VC, DCM 141–142
Botha, Gen. Louis (Prime Minister of South Africa) 138, 196
Botha, Brig.-Gen. Manie 98–99; resigns 108
Bowker, Corporal D.M.P. 118
Brandenburg Gate 191, 194–195
Brandis, Capt. Ernst von 78–79
Braunschweig, Capt. Friedrich 41, 111–112
Bray, Lt. P.V.R. 115
Bremen 193
Bridges, Maj. T. McG. 43
Bristow Pvt. Harry, DCM 73
Britain 3–4, 7–8, 14, 16, 96
British Admiralty 18–19, 32; orders increase of warships to East Africa 50, 64
British Army 1, 196
British Army formations and units: 1st East African Brigade 80–83, 85, 87, 100–101, 105, 113, 115, 137, 143, 150–153, 156, 163, 166–167, 197–198; 1st East African Division 80–81, 84–87, 89, 92–95, 98, 100–101, 103, 105–107, 109, 113–115, 118, 132, 143, 197–198; 1st KAR 9, 13, 16–17, 36–40, 47, 109–112, 124–125, 127–129, 141–142, 172, 179, 184–185, 197, 206*ch*10*n*10; 1st Rhodesia Native Regiment 129, 141–142, 172, 186; 2nd Battalion, Loyal North Lancashire Regiment 20, 26–30, 42–46, 57–59, 81–84, 130–131, 197–198; 2nd East African Brigade 80, 92–93, 101, 113, 115, 117–118, 132, 136, 143, 150–152, 156, 163, 197–198; 2nd KAR 71, 131–136, 143–144, 146–147, 151–154, 156, 161, 163, 169, 173–174, 178–179, 183–187, 199, 205*ch*1*n*4; 2nd LNL Machine Gun Company 83, 105, 134, 136, 206*ch*8*n*12; 2nd Rhodesia Regiment 56, 81–83, 88–89, 101, 115, 197–198; 2nd West India Regiment 95, 121, 143–144; 3rd East African Brigade 131; 3rd East African Division 95, 98, 100–101, 113, 115, 118, 120, 130, 198; 3rd KAR 9, 12–13, 16, 23, 38–39, 43, 45–46, 57–59, 74–76, 88–89, 101, 103–104, 115–117, 132, 135–136, 143, 150, 152, 163, 165–166, 181–183, 197–198; 4th KAR 10, 34, 36–37, 41–45, 108, 140, 142–143, 149, 161, 172–173, 178–179, 183, 186–187, 189–190, 194, 197, 199; 6th Field Battery, RA 87; 6th KAR 71, 142; 7th KAR 71; 8th Field Battery, RA 88, 198; 9th Field Battery, RA 89, 198; 10th Heavy Battery, RA 100, 199; 11th (Hull) Heavy Battery, RA 143, 199; 14th Howitzer Battery, RA 136; 25th (Service) Battalion, Royal Regiment of Fusiliers 56–57, 59, 86, 105, 144, 146–147, 156–157, 161, 197–198, 207*ch*13*n*5; 134th (Howitzer) Battery, RGA 88, 199; Arab Rifles 16, 199; Baganda Rifles 108; British South Africa Police 15, 109, 129, 141; East African Mounted Rifles 16, 21–22, 41–42, 44, 74–76, 197–198; East African Regiment 16, 57; "EDFORCE" (Edwards Force) 142 ; KAR Mountain Battery 110 112, 125, 128; KAR Mounted Infantry Company 44–45, 74–76, 103, 142, 149–150, 197–198; "Kartucol" (2nd KAR column) 174, 177–179, 184–186; "Kartufor" (2/4th KAR column) 187; "Karwunfor" (1/4th KAR column) 188–189; "Kilwa Force" 143, 150, 153–154, 163, 167; King's African Rifles 8–9, 40, 43, 56, 71, 115, 126, 128–130, 132, 134, 136, 143, 152–153, 157, 166, 173, 178, 180, 182, 184; "Lake Force" 108–109, 197; "Linforce" (Lindi Force) 148, 153, 156–158, 161–162, 167; Machine Gun Corps (1st Armoured Car Battery 105, 198; 5th Light Armoured Car Battery 198; 4th Armoured Car Battery 198; 7th Light Armoured Car Battery 163; 10th Armoured Car Battery 83, 197–199; No.259 Machine Gun Company [formerly 2nd LNL Machine Gun Company] 143–144, 161); Masai Scouts 16; "Mobforce" (Mozambique Force) 174; Mounted Infantry Company 73–74, 88; Nandi Scouts 108 148, 197, 199; Northern Rhodesia Police (Military Branch) 13, 15, 60, 109, 125, 128, 141–142, 172, 208*ch*14*n*13; Northern Rhodesia Regiment (formerly the Northern Rhodesia Police) 187, 190; No. 3 column 151–152, 161–162, 169; No. 4 column 161–162; No.26 (SA) Squadron, Royal Flying Corps 81–82, 104–105, 135, 169, 199; "Pamforce" (Port Amelia Force) 177, 179; Rhodesia-Nyasaland Field Force 62, 98, 109, 115, 124, 172, 179; "Rosecol" (Rose column) 173, 177–180; Royal Marines Light

Index

Infantry 121; "Shortcol" (Shorthose column) 186; West African Frontier Force (WAFF) (Gold Coast Mountain Battery 95, 117; Gold Coast Mounted Infantry 177, 180, 183; Gold Coast Regiment 95, 106, 115–117, 132, 134–136, 143, 151–154, 163–165, 173, 178–180; Nigerian Brigade 130, 137–138, 153–154, 156–160, 162, 173 [1st Battalion, Nigeria Regiment 130, 149, 154, 156, 158–160; 2nd Battalion, Nigeria Regiment 130, 137, 154–155, 160; 3rd Battalion, Nigeria Regiment 130, 153, 160–162; 4th Battalion, Nigeria Regiment 130, 142–143, 148, 154–155, 160; 300th Field Ambulance 130; Gambia Company 130, 159–160; Sierra Leone Carrier Corps 130; West African Field Ambulance 130; West African Frontier Force Artillery 130, 159; Zanzibar Rifles 121])
British Cape Squadron 10–11, 13, 50
British Colonial Office 12, 31
British Committee of Imperial Defence 13
British East Africa (Kenya) 9–10, 13, 16, 31, 41–42, 61, 71, 80, 94, 143, 179, 195
British East Africa Command 108, 193
British War Office 41, 57, 62, 86; orders reinforcements sent to East Africa 56; takes over control in East Africa 31
British West Africa 95
Brits, Maj.-Gen. Coen 95, 118–120, 130
Browning, Capt. C.S. 134
Buchanan, Capt. Angus, MC 86
Buiko 101, 103
Bukakata 108
Bukama 65
Bukari, Acting Sergeant, DCM and Bar 116
Bukerebe Island 77
Bukhora 110
Bukoba 41, 57–59, 61, 66, 76–78
Bulgaria 167, 169
Bura Hills 80
Burgess, Lt.-Col. C.R. 108
Butler, Capt. John Fitzhardinge Paul, VC, DSO 115, 117
Bweho Carti 155
Bweho Chini 154–156
Bweho Ju 155
Byron, Lt.-Col. J.J. 89

Cairo 195
Camara, Maj. Perry da 174
Cambridge University 196
Cameroon 95
Cape Delgado 97
Cape Town 3, 62, 64–65, 191
Capell, Lt.-Col. A.E. 56

Cartnell, Sergeant W., DCM 185, 208*ch*14*n*7
Castro, Gen. Joaquim Pimenta de 96
Caulfield, Capt. Francis Wade., RN 23–24, 29, 31
Central Railway 101, 106–107, 109, 113, 120, 122, 124, 130, 141, 143, 187
Chaimite (Portuguese gunboat) 97–98
Chala heights 85
Chalau 183
Challenger (British cruiser) 50, 121
Chambezi 188–189
Chapman, Capt. 16
Chappuis, 1st Lt. Udo von 16, 35
Charlton, Rear-Adm. E.F.B. CB, RN 121
Chatham (British cruiser) 18–19, 32, 37, 50
Chemara 132–134
Chigugu 165
China 3
Chirimba Hill 177
Chirumba 177
Chiwata 163, 165
Chole Bay 37, 50
Christiansen, Reserve Lt. Carl 49
Chumo 135
City of Winchester (British ship) 11, 13
Clancy, Dr Philip 195
Clark, Capt. C.H.B. 125–126
Clarke, Petty Officer T.J., CGM, RN 36
Collins, Capt. H.G., RA 47
Colville, Capt. A.M. 44
Congo Act, 1885 7, 12, 14
Copenhagen 49
Cornwall (British cruiser) 50
Corson, Lt., DSC, RN 35–36
Costa, Afonso da 96–97
Crete 170
Crewe, Brigadier-Gen. Sir Charles 108–109
Croad, District Officer Hector 188–189
Cull, Flight-Cmdr. John Tulloch, RNAS 48, 52
Cuneen, Colour-Sgt. Michael 163, 208*ch*13*n*9
Cunha, Maj. A da 123
Cunliffe, Brigadier-Gen. Frederick Hugh Gordon., CB, CMG 130, 137–138, 155, 159, 162
Curado, Capt. Francisco 122
Cutler, Sub-Lt. H.D., RNVR 32–34

Dakawa 113, 115
Dakhla Oasis 170
Dar es Salaam 3, 8, 10–11, 13–14, 19, 34–35, 43, 50, 53–54, 56, 80, 121, 130, 183, 191, 194–195
Dardanelles 50

Index

Dartmouth (British cruiser) 18
Dartnell, VC, Lt. Wilbur Taylor (born William Thomas) 59; commanding 3 (25RF) Troop 73; posthumous Victoria Cross 74
Davis, Capt. H.H. 44
Defu River 93
Dennistoun, Lt.-Cmdr. G.H., RN 47
Depate 172
Dessel, Volunteer Dr 26
Deventer, Lt.-Gen. Sir Louis Jakobus (Dirk) van 62, 85, 87, 91, 93–94, 98, 100–101, 106–109, 113–115, 124, 130, 139, 148–149, 153, 157, 169, 172–174, 177, 179, 181, 183, 186–190; command in East Africa 143; command of 2nd EA Division 95; knighted and death 195
Dickinson, Lt.-Col. H.C. 183
Diobahila 108
Dobson, Maj. J.W. 122
Dodoma 106–107, 139–140, 148
Doornkloof, Irene 196
Döring, Capt. Robert 104–105
Downer, Lt. 136
DPM Intelligence Unit 71, 72
Driscoll, DSO, Lt.-Col. D.P. 56
Drought, Capt. J.J. 44
Drury-Lowe, Capt. Sidney, RN 18–19, 32–33
Dudley, Lt. Arthur, RN 68
Duncan, Sir Patrick (Gov.-Gen. of South Africa) 196
Duplex (British armed steamer) 32
Durban 32
Dutumi 118
Dutumi River 117
Dyke, Lt.-Col. P.H. 105, 148–149, 162

Edwards, Brigadier-Gen. William Frederick Savery, CB, CMG, DSO 121, 142, 177, 179, 183, 190
Egypt 131, 170, 195
Engare Nanjuka River 86–87
Enslin, Brig.-Gen. Barend 101, 113, 118–119, 130
Erdmann, 2nd Lt. 40
Ethiopia 195
Euphorbein Hill 93
Europe 96

Fair, Maj. Charles Henry, DSO 60, 128–129, 172
Fairweather, Lt.-Col. J.M. DSO 124, 126
Federation of Germans Abroad 194
Feldmarshall (German ship) 35
Fife (Mwenzo) 15, 60, 187
Fifi see *Kingani*

Filsell, Lt.-Col. Harold Stuart. R. DSO 133, 151
Fischer, Maj. Erich 87
Fitzgerald, Lt.-Col. T.O. 101,103, 165–166
Fitzmaurice, Cmdr. Raymond, RN 32
Flindt, Maj. R.L. 109, 111, 126
Fort Johnson 140, 172, 180, 187
Fort Kyaka 34
Fox (British light cruiser) 20, 23, 25, 30, 32, 34–36, 65; bombards Tanga 29
France 3, 7, 95, 173
Franken, 1st Lt. Gotthold 109
Franz Ferdinand, Archduke 7
Freeth, Lt.-Col. J.C. 89, 91, 126
Freikorps 193
Fremantle, Western Australia 50
Friedrichshafen 168
Fullerton, Capt. E.J.A., RN 50
Fungurume 65

Galbraith, Capt. James Edward Evans, DSO 128–129
Gallehawk, RNR. Midshipman Arthur Noel 32, 34
Gamble, Admiral Sir David, RN 64
Garrard, Maj. P. 183–184
Gazi 17, 73
Geiro 149
Gengini Island 51
Geraragua 86
Gerlich, Lt. 40
German Army formations and units: 1st Field Company 12, 26, 39, 104–105, 119; 1st Rifle Company 121; 2nd Field Company 112, 124; 2nd Rifle Company 121; 3rd Field Company 104–105, 117, 150, 177–178; 3rd Rifle Company 121, 150; 4th Field Company 27, 29, 39, 117, 159; 4th Rifle Company 38, 117, 122–123, 150, 159; 5th Field Company 13, 34, 104, 110, 124; 5th Rifle Company 124, 128; 6th Field Company 26–28, 39, 83; 6th Rifle Company 26–27, 156, 177–179; 7th Field Company 34, 41; 7th Rifle Company 27, 39, 42; 8th Field Company 74, 87, 124, 126; 8th Rifle Company 27, 87, 124, 159; 9th Field Company 39, 73, 83, 93, 100, 117, 150; 9th Rifle Company 21–22, 27, 87; 10th Field Company 16, 21, 34–35, 110, 124, 127–129, 150, 156; 10th Rifle Company 56, 60, 150; 11th Field Company 21–22, 39, 119, 150, 177–178; 13th Field Company 12, 27, 29, 39, 117, 159–160, 177–178; 14th Field Company 41, 43–45, 81, 100, 117. 156, 159, 177–179; 14th Reserve Company 150; 15th Field Company 16, 38–39, 81,

Index 215

83, 100, 124; 16th Field Company 16, 25–27, 29, 104–105, 124, 145–147; 17th Field Company 16, 24–27, 39, 119, 150, 156, 159, 177–178; 18th Field Company 56, 81, 87, 100, 117, 132; 19th Field Company 100, 124, 128, 144, 147; 20th Field Company 122–123, 144; 21st Field Company 21, 117, 150, 156, 160; 22nd Field Company 56, 100, 117, 121; 23rd Field Company 56; 24th Field Company 56, 59–60, 83, 93, 100, 124, 126; 25th Field Company 124, 127–129; 26th Field Company 43, 124–126; 27th Field Company 81, 100, 119, 150; 28th Field Company 87, 99; 29th Field Company 56, 59–60, 109; 30th Field Company 81, 87, 119, 132; Angoni Levies 150; Arab Company, Irregulars 27, 38–39; "C" Company 125; Dar es Salaam *Landsturm* Company 121; Detachment Bahnschutz 115; Detachment Batzner 156; Detachment Haberkorn 156; Detachment Wilhemstal 115; *Königsberg* Company 52, 110–111, 121; "L" Company 110, 124, 127; No. III Field Hospital 140; *Ostafrikaschutztruppe* 3, 16, 21–23, 34, 39, 41, 52–53, 56, 60, 70, 72–73, 85, 87, 89, 91–94, 97, 99, 101, 103–106, 110–111, 113–115, 117–121, 123, 126–127, 129–131, 136–138, 142–144, 147–148, 150–154, 156–162, 166, 169–170, 175–180, 182–185, 187–188, 190, 194–195 (accompanied by women on operations 38; distribution of guns and stores captured at Tanga 21; strength of 7–8); Ruanda "A" Company 124–125; Ruanda "B" Company 125; "S" Company 147; *II Seebataillon* 3; Tanga *Landsturm* Company 115, 122–123, 144, 147; "W" Company 81, 87, 119
German East Africa 1, 7–8, 10, 31, 36, 41, 61, 71–72, 76, 80, 94, 96, 108–109, 122, 124, 167, 172–173, 186
German People's Party 194
German South West Africa 3–4
Germany 3, 96, 150, 191–193, 196
Giffard, Lt.-Col. George J. 37, 39, 136, 161, 173–174, 179, 185–186
Gil, Maj.-Gen. Jose Cesar Ferreira 96–98, 122; recalled to Portugal 124
Goldenfels (German ship) 11
Goldrick, Lt. A.C. 184
Goliath (British battleship) 20, 23, 34–36; sunk in the Dardanelles 50
Gordon, Squadron-Cmdr. Robert, RNAS 50, 71
Gore-Browne, Maj. Eric Antony Rollo 75, 181–183

Göring, Capt. Karl 159–160, 171, 177, 184–185
Gouta 44
Graf von Götson (German armed lake steamer) 14, 68–70
Graham, Lt.-Col. B.R. 23; killed 89
Grant, Col. H. 143
Griffiths, Lt.-Col. Alexander Harcourt, DSO 128, 179
Griffiths, Capt. Howard Thomas 152
Grote, Freiherr 93
Gulf of Aden 10–11
Gurribe Hill action 43
Gwendolen (British armed lake steamer) 46

Hadhramaut (South Arabia) 11
Hall, Capt. W.D. 150
Hamburg 49, 193–194
Hammerstein, Capt. von 26; died of wounds 40
Handeni 101, 103–105
Hannyngton, Brigadier-Gen. John Arthur 101, 103, 113, 115, 131–133, 140, 143, 153
Hanson, Capt. G.J. 40
Haouter, Landsturm 188
Hatia 163
Hawkins, Maj. Bryan, DSO 172, 189–190
Hawthorne, Brig-Gen George M.P. 17, 109–112, 127–128, 172, 179
Haxthausen, 1st Lt. Wilhelm von 42–45
Hedwig von Wissmann (German armed lake steamer) 14, 66–70
Helmuth (British armed tug) 34–36, 121
Herero 3
Herion, Commandant 172
Hertzog, J.B.M. (Prime Minister of South Africa) 196
Hickson, Lt.-Col. L.H. 43–45
Hill, Pvt. R.G., DCM 128, 207*ch*11*n*6
Himo 80
Hindenburg, Field-Marshall Paul von 193
Hinrichs, Lt.-Cmdr. Herbert 123
Hitler, Adolf 193
Hobson, 2nd Lt. F. 155
Hodson, Col. F.A 15, 60
Holland 191
Holtham, Surgeon-Lt., RN 36
Hope, Sub-Lt. Douglas, RN 64–65
Hoskins, Maj.-Gen. Arthur Reginald, CMG, DSO 95, 105, 132, 134, 142; ordered to Mesopotamia 143; takes command in East Africa 139
Howard, Lt. the Hon. Bernard, RFC 135
Hoy, Maj. C.N. 149
Hughes, Col. 62
Hull, Yorkshire 195

216   Index

Hulseberg, Lt.-Col. H. 132–133
Hyacinth (British cruiser) 10–11, 37, 49, 145–146

Iangu Mountains 180
Ibrahim, DCM, Corporal Ismail 45
Igali Pass 141
Igamba 109
Ikoma 148–149
Ikoma Hill 43
Ilembule Mission Station 129
Ili 180–181
India 4, 91
Indian Army 13, 20, 30, 173
Indian Army formations and units: 1st Battery, Calcutta Volunteer Artillery 13; 3rd Lahore Division 143; 5th Indian Light Infantry 95, 144, 150, 199; 13th Rajputs (The Shekhawati Regiment) 20, 25–27, 28; 17th Indian Cavalry 74–76, 197–198, 199; 17th Indian Infantry 108, 199; 22nd Mountain Battery 143, 151, 173, 178; 25th Indian Cavalry, (Frontier Force) 130, 163, 165–166, 172; 25th (Railway) Company, Sappers and Miners 20, 101; 26th (Railway) Company, Sappers and Miners 20, 101; 27th Bangalore Brigade 20; 27th Mountain Battery 13, 21–22, 94, 101, 104, 116, 133–134, 136, 143–144, 153, 164–166, 198; 28th Mountain Battery 20, 30, 40, 42, 43–44, 57–58, 100, 124, 126, 197–198; 29th Punjab Infantry 13, 22, 57–58, 89, 92, 104–105, 117, 197–198; 30th Punjab Infantry 138, 142, 161; 33rd Punjab Infantry 143, 151–153; 40th Pathans 71, 131, 134, 150, 152, 198; 55th Coke's Rifles 130, 173; 57th Wilde's Rifles (Frontier Force) 71, 115, 117, 132, 143; 58th Vaughan's Rifles 177; 61st King George's Own Pioneers 20, 25–26, 28; 31, 101, 104, 144, 147, 199; 63rd Palamcottah Light Infantry 20, 27, 28, 37, 199; 98th Hyderabad Infantry 20, 27, 77–79, 108, 199; 101st Grenadiers, Bombay Infantry 20, 27, 29–30, 36, 38, 40, 199; 127th Baluchis 130; 129th (Duke of Connaught's Own) Baluchis 71, 92, 121, 131–136, 143, 163, 166, 172, 197–198; 130th (King George's Own) Baluchis (Jacob's Rifles) 71, 73–74, 81–83, 88, 93, 101, 104–105, 115, 138, 142, 197–198; Indian Expeditionary Force "B" 20, 22–23, 31, 205ch1n8; Indian Expeditionary Force "C" 13, 16–17, 20–21, 23, 31; Indian Volunteer Maxim Battery 17, 22
Indian State Forces: 2nd Kashmir Rifles 20, 26–30, 38, 40, 105, 137, 199; 3rd Kashmir Rifles 20, 26–30, 117, 197; 3rd Gwalior Rifles 20, 26–27, 30, 199; 28th (Faridkot) Company, Sappers and Miners 20, 59, 101, 138; Bhurtpore Infantry 13, 161, 199; Jind Infantry 13, 199; Kapurthala Infantry 13, 21, 199; Kashmir Rifles composite battalion 105 Rampur Infantry 13, 199
Ipiana Fort 109
Iringa 124, 140
Irugwa Island, Lake Victoria 46
Israel 195
Itaka 142
Italian Somaliland 10

Jackson, Adm. Sir Henry, RN (First Sea Lord) 64
Jahore, Sultan of 95
Jamboli, Bulgaria 168, 170
Japanese forces 95
Jasin 38–41, 72
Jericho Farm 15
Johannesbruck (Mabogoro) 141
John, Capt. Stanley Conway, MC 185
Jollie, Lt.-Col. F. 74–76
Jourdain, Lt.-Col. C.E.A. 58
Jubaland 9, 16–17
Juma, Company Quartermaster Sergeant Hamis Bin, DCM and Bar 166
Juma, Company Sergeant-Maj. Mama 163

Kabalo 65
Kagera River 34, 77
Kahe 80, 85, 87, 91–95, 101
Kahe Hills 93
Kaiser Willhelm II (German ship) 35–36
Kajiado 81
Kalambo River 110
Kang Mountains 113
Kapp, Dr Wolfgang 193
Kapp Putsch 193
Karmala (British ship) 25
Karema 109
Karonga 13
Karungu 42, 46
Karwazi Hill 57
Kasama 14, 187–189
Kasigau 72, 81
Katanga 15, 62–63
Kaufmann, 2nd Lt. 40
Kavirondo (British armed lake steamer) 43–44, 77–79
Kemondo Bay 77
Kempner, Lt. Franz 103
Kenya *see* British East Africa
Kepler, Maj. Arthur 39, 40
Khartoum 170

Index

Kiaya Bay 57
Kibata 131–136
Kibati 108
Kidatu 115
Kidodi 115
Kigali 108
Kigoma 66, 70, 108–109, 190
Kihende 156
Kikarunga Hill 115, 117
Kikumbuliro 122
Kilimanjaro 8, 12, 21, 23, 72, 80–81, 85–86, 94, 98
Kilimatinde 107
Kilindoni 37
Kilosa 113, 115, 122, 140
Kilwa 121–122, 131–132, 135, 140, 143–144, 150, 153, 157
Kimbambabwe 138
Kinfauns Castle (British armed merchant cruiser) 32, 36
King-Hall, Vice-Adm. Herbert 10–11, 32, 36–37, 48–50, 52
King Manuel of Portugal 96
Kingani (German armed lake steamer) 14, 66–69
Kintangari Valley 167, 169, 171
Kionga 97
Kionga Triangle 97
Kipembawe 142
Kipenio 138
Kisaki 115, 117–120–121 207*ch*11*n*4
Kisii 41–42
Kisinga 128–129
Kisumu 10, 41–42, 57, 77
Kitambi 132
Kitanda 141
Kitchener, Field-Marshal Lord 86
Kitoho Hill 117
Kitovo Hills 85
Kituio Hill 146
Kiturika Hills 150, 153, 172
Kivambo 123
Kivu 63, 76
Kiyombo 136
Knox, Capt. R.F.B. 43
Kock, Lt.-Cmdr. Georg 52
Köhl, Capt. Franz 156, 169, 175–179, 193
Kokosani 181–182
Koller, Reserve Lt. 77–79
Komo Island 18
König (German ship) 35
Kondoa *see* Kondoa-Irangi
Kondoa-Irangi 98–101, 106, 148
Konick, Maj. de 60–61
König (German ship) 11
Königsberg (German light cruiser), 10–11, 13, 16–20, 32–34, 36–37, 53–54, 97, 123, 195; scuttled and guns removed 48–52
Königsberg guns 91, 93–94, 100, 106, 110–111, 114, 118, 121, 136
Korewa 179
Kornatzki, Capt. Friedrich von 35; killed by Meinertzhagen 100
Korogwe 103–104
Koroma Peak 179
Kraut, Maj. Georg 21–22, 81–83, 87, 89, 91, 101, 104–106, 124, 127, 129–130, 140, 163, 165–166, 193
Kronberg (German blockade-runner) 49
Kuhn, Lt. 127
Kungulio 120
Kuria Muria Islands 13

Lake Chala 87, 91
Lake Eyassi 148, 150
Lake Jipe 85
Lake Kivu 76, 108
Lake Natron 148
Lake Nyasa (Lake Malawi) 13, 46, 110, 140–141, 172–173, 179, 187
Lake Rukwa 141
Lake Tanganyika 14, 41, 64–65, 70, 76, 108, 110, 190–191
Lake Victoria Nyanza (Lake Victoria) 10, 14, 41–42, 46, 57, 77, 108, 148
Langenn-Steinkeller, Maj. Erich von 34, 56
Larsen, Maj. 148–149
Latema-Reata Nek 87, 89, 91
Latema spur 88–89
Laurentic (British auxiliary cruiser) 50
Law, Lt.-Col. 144, 146, 148
League of Nations 194
Lee, Lt.-Cmdr. John R, RNVR 64
Lembeni 94
Leopoldville 70
Lettow-Vorbeck, Arndt 194
Lettow-Vorbeck, Gen. Paul Emil von 2–5, 7–8, 10, 12, 14–16, 24, 26, 28–31, 34, 38–41, 43, 52, 54–56, 70, 72, 77, 80–81, 87, 91–92, 99–101, 106, 108, 113, 117, 120–122, 124, 130, 132–133, 135–137, 140, 143–144, 148, 150, 153, 156–158, 161–162, 166, 169–173, 175–176, 179–189, 195, 208*ch*13*n*18; awarded Iron Crosses 1st and 2nd Class 94; awarded Oak Leaves to *Pour le Mérite* 177; awarded *Pour le Mérite* 138; laid low by Spanish flu 191; marries, arrested and cashiered 193; promoted to major general 167; surrenders 190; under Gestapo surveillance and death 194; writes to Kaiser regarding command situation 53

Index

Lettow-Vorbeck, Rüdiger 194
Lewis, Capt. H.V. MC 135
Lieberman, Capt. Eberhard von 119, 145, 150–154, 207*ch*12*n*20
Likungo River 180, 182–183
Lilley, Lt.-Col. Harry Arthur, DSO 42, 149
Lindi 18, 34, 122, 124, 140, 143–144, 146, 150, 153–154, 156–157
Lindini 122
Linkangara Mountains 158, 162
Lioma 184–185
Lisbon 174
Little Nhigu 119
Livingstone 14
Liwale 122, 131, 143, 172
Liwinda Ravine 154
Llanstephen Castle (British ship) 65
Llewellyn, Col. E.H. (Commandant King's African Rifles) 130
Lol Kissale Hill 99
London 56, 138, 193
Longido 16, 21–23, 74–76, 81, 85–86, 91
Looff, Capt. Max 10–11, 13, 18–19, 33, 36, 54, 121–124, 147; orders scuttling of *Königsberg* 52; promoted and awarded Iron Cross 1st and 2nd Class 53; surrenders 169; vice-admiral in Kriegsmarine and death 195
Lourenco Marques 174
Lower Saxony 3
Luala River 184
Lualaba River 65
Luale Chini 154
Lubembe Peninsula 77
Lugella Company 180
Lugella River 180–181
Luita 148–149
Lujenda River 171, 175–176
Lukalanka 142
Lukigura River 105–106
Lukuga 65, 67–70
Lukuga River 66
Lukuledi Mission Station 158, 163, 165–167
Lukuledi River 18, 144–145, 148, 157, 163, 166–167
Lumi River 14, 85
Lupemba 126, 129–130
Lupembe 112, 127
Lutende 150
Luwegu River 172
Luwiwa 109
Lyle, Lt.-Col. R.A. 137
Lytton Commission 194

Mafia Island 11, 18–19, 32–33, 36–37, 50–51

Magadi 16, 81, 148
Magomera, Colour-Sergeant, DCM 128
Mahansi 126
Mahenge 124, 127, 130, 140, 144, 172
Mahenge Plateau 109, 122
Mahiwa 158; battle of 159–160, 162, 167
Mahiwa River 159
Mahua 179–180
Mahuta 122–123
Mainprise, Maj. B.W., RE 89
Majita Peninsula, Lake Victoria 46
Makallah Bay 11, 13
Makatumbe Lighthouse 10
Makinda 105–106
Makonde Plateau 94, 122–124, 167, 169–170, 172
Maktau 73, 81
Malan, Daniel 196
Malangali 125, 129
Malangali Ridge 111–112
Malema River 180
Malleson, Brig.-Gen. Wilfrid 80–82, 87; abandons command 88; competence questioned 84; returns to India 91; takes command of 1st EA Brigade 85
Malongwe 143, 148
Mambala River 15
Mamprusi, Sergeant Yessufu, DCM, MM 164–165
Manganza 140
Maning, Lt.-Col. F. 34
Mann, Maj. G.D. 159
Manza Bay 49
Mara Bay 45
Mara River 45
Margerini 16
Marie (German blockade-runner) 94
Marriot, Capt. T. MC 129
Masai Kraal 92–93
Masai Steppes 99, 149
Massasi 122, 143, 165–166
Masters, Maj. Alexander Charles, DSO, MC 111–112, 184–185
Matakia, Sgt., 3rd KAR 45
Matamondo 113
Matandu Valley 140, 144, 150
Matombo Mission Station 115
Mauri 103–104
Mawerenye 155–156
Mayani 144, 146
Mbemkuru River 144
Mbirikia Hill 136
Mbuyuni 72, 85
McCarthy, Lt. J.J. 14
Mdogo 73
Medo 177, 179–180

Index

Meinertzhagen, Lt.-Col. Richard, CBE, DSO 20–21, 23–26, 29–30, 58, 72, 94, 100, 169, 193–194; appointed chief of intelligence, East Africa 71; feels Gen. Mallison should be shot 88; latter career and contribution to foundation of Israel 195
Mendes, Maj. Moura 96
Mersa Matruh 170
Mersey (British monitor) 50–52, 121, 145–146
Mesopatamia 47.
Methner, Lt. 159
Methven, Capt. E.B. MC 154, 163–165, 208*ch*13*n*12
Meza 177
M'gangira 172
Mgeta Mission Station 118
Mgeta River 118–119, 121, 137, 139, 140
Mhonda 113
Mhulu 158
Migeregere 143
Mihambia 153–154
Mikikama 151
Mikindani 122
Mikocheni 101
Mimi (British naval motor-boat) 65–67, 69
Minerva (British cruiser) 145–146
Mingoyo 146, 148
Minjales 169
Mitchell, Lt. Philip Edmund, MC 128
Mitole 132
Mitonono 156
Mivambo 97
Mkalama 148
Mkalamo 104–105
Mkalamo Bridge 104
Mkalinzo 137–138
Mkapira 127–129
Mkwaya Creek 144, 146
Mkwaya Village 146–147
Mkwere 162
Mlali 118
Mnero Mission Station 156
Mnindi 150–151
Mnitshi 154
Mocimboa-da-Praia 174
Mohambika Valley 144, 146
Mohambika Village 148
Molitor, Col. Philippe 108–109
Molocue River 183
Mombasa 16–17, 22–23, 30, 32, 38, 73, 106
Mombo 103
Montford, Lt. D.R. 77–78
Montgomerie, Maj. H.G. MC 142
Morogoro 11, 101, 103, 105–106, 113, 115, 120, 153, 189

Moshi 12, 80
Mount Kenya 10
Mount Kilimanjaro *see* Kilimanjaro
Mount Meru 95
Mount Oldeani 148
Mount Saisi 15, 60–61
Möwe (German survey ship) 14, 18
Mozambique Channel 49
Mpapau 113–114
Mpotora 144
Mrweka 148
Msiha River 106, 113
Mssongossi River 118
Mtama 158, 160
Mtua 157–158
Mtumbei Hills 131, 134, 136
Mtumbi Juu 134–135
Mtupiti River 146
Muansa (German armed lake steamer) 42–44
Muavenet-i Milliye (Turkish Torpedo Boat) 50
Müller, Capt. Erich 181–182, 184–185, 188
Müller, Herr H. (Minister for Foreign Affairs) 192
Mumbai *see* Bombay
Murray, Lt.-Col. Ronald Ernest "Kaffir," DSO, DCM 109–110, 127–129, 141–142
Murray, Lt. L.G. 37
Musoma 45–46
Mwaika Hill action 44
Mwalia 179
Mwanza 41–43, 46, 108
Mwembe 140
Mwengei 136
Mwete 73
M'zima 21

Nafouba Island, Lake Victoria 44
Nagwamira 186
Nahauga 158
Nahungo 156
Nahungu 144
Nairobi 9, 16, 41–42, 85
Naitiwa 144, 146, 150
Nakadi River 159
Namaqua 3
Namanga 74, 76
Namanga River 22
Nambindinga 169
Nambunjo Hill 154
Namema 109–110
Nampula 183
Namupa Mission Station 158, 160
Nangoo 163
Nanunga 179

Narumbego 158
Narungombe 151, 153–154
Narunya 144
Nauen Naval Signals Station 170
Naumann, Ist Lt. Heinrich 142–143, 148–149, 162; war crimes 150
Naval Africa Expedition 64, 70
Nazi Party 193–194
Ndanda 163, 165–166
Nderema 105
Ndessa 153–154
Nengidi River 157
Neu Gottorp 109
Neu Iringa 109–112, 124–126, 130, 139, 141
Neu Langenburg (Tukuvu) 56, 109–110, 124–125, 129, 141
Neu Moshi 12, 23–24, 26, 29, 38, 85, 87, 91, 93, 95, 98, 101
Neu Utengule 141
Newala 122–123, 170–171
Newbridge (British ship) 32
Ngapa 144
Ngerengere 115
Ngomano 171, 175
Ngombeni Village 37
Ngominji Depot 124–126
Ngongo River 146
Nguru Mountains 113
Nhamacurra 181–183
Nhamacurra River 182
Nhica 97
Niger (British warship) 64
Nile River 170
Niororo Island 33, 48
Njangalo 113
Njombe 112
Njoro 81
Njoro Drift 81
Njoro River 81–82
Nkessa 117
Northern Rhodesia (Zambia) 5, 13, 34, 56, 59, 62, 76, 141, 187
Northern Rhodesia Medical Service 125
Northey, Brigadier-Gen. Edward 62–63, 98, 109–110, 112, 115, 124–125, 129, 140–142, 172, 174; appointed Governor British East Africa 179
Npingo 154
Nrunya 156
Numarroe 183–184
No.4 Squadron, Royal Naval Air Service 48, 50, 71, 81–82, 146–147, 169, 199
Nussey, Brigadier-Gen. A.H.M., DSO 108, 118–120
Nyangao 157–161
Nyanza (British armed lake steamer) 77–79

Nyasaland (Malawi) 9, 34, 125, 173, 180
Nyengedi River 157–158

Odebrecht, Sub-Lt. 66, 69
O'Grady, Brigadier-Gen. Henry de Courcy 132, 134, 140, 143–144, 146–148, 156–157, 160–162, 207*ch*12*n*17
Okousa Island 33
Old Utengule 141
Olsen, Col. Frederick V. 15, 62, 76, 108
Onyett, Lt. Harry Thomas, MC 129
Operation "China Show" 168–169
Orr, Lt.-Col. G.M. 143, 151, 163, 165–167
O'Sullevan, DSO, Maj. John Joseph 60–61
Otto, Capt. Ernst 39, 93, 100
Oukenoueoue Island, Lake Victoria 44

Palestine 195
Pangani River 91, 93, 100–101, 103–104
Pangutini 136
Pare Mountains 80, 85, 100–101
Paris Peace Conférence, Versailles 192, 193, 195–196
Parker, Second-Lt. W. 73
Patterson, Lt., RN 35–36
Pegasus (British cruiser) 10–11, 17, 18, 44, 125
Pekera 183
Peking (Beijing) 3
Pere Hills 186
Peters, Pvt. A.S., DCM 128, 207*ch*11*n*6
Phillips, Lt.-Col. Charles George, DSO, MC 147, 185
Pinto, *Commandante* Teixeira 175
Pioneer (Australian cruiser) 50
Pires, Maj. J. 122
Port Amelia (Pemba) 173–174, 177, 180, 183
Portugal 96
Portuguese Army formations and units: 1st Mountain Battery 98; 2nd Battery, Artillery Group 7 96; 2nd Mountain Battery 98; 3rd Battalion, Infantry Regt 15 (Tomar) 96; 3rd Battalion, Infantry Regt 21 (Penmacor) 96; 4th Mountain Battery 98; 4th Squadron, 3rd Cavalry 96; 4th Squadron, 10th Cavalry 96; 21st Indigenous Company 182–183; Artillery Groups 4, 5, 8 98; Infantry Regiment 23 (Coimbra) 98; Infantry Regiment 24 (Aveiro) 98; Infantry Regiment 28 (Figueira de Foz) 98
Portuguese East Africa (Mozambique) 4, 96–98, 122, 138, 140, 143, 167, 170–171, 173–174, 176, 183, 186, 191
Präsident (German ship) 18–19
Pretoria 196

Index

Pretorius, Maj. Pieter J, DSO 37, 48
Price, Lt.-Col. Cyril. P., CMG 73, 121
Price, Sergeant 184
Prince, Capt. Tom von 12; killed at Battle of Tanga 29.
Pronstorf, Schleswig Holstein 194
Pugu 8, 11, 41
Pugu River 115
Pyramus (British light cruiser) 50

Quelimane 180–181

Ramsgate 64
Ras Kasone Peninsula 24, 26–27
Ras Kisimani 36
Reata heights and nek 89, 161
Red House 25–26
Red Sea 18
Regone 184
Reichstag 193–194
Reunited National Party 196
Ritchie, Capt. Henry Peel, VC, RN 35–36, 205*ch*3*n*2
Roberts, Maj. C.E. 159–160
Rodger, Lt.-Col. T.A. 109–112, 124, 126
Rondo Plateau 158
Rosa, Col. 174, 181
Rose, Lt.-Col. Richard Aubrey de Burgh, DSO and Bar 154, 173, 178–179
Rosenthal, Lt. 66
Rothe, Capt. Wilhelm 122–124, 144, 207*ch*12*n*20
Rothert, Capt. Paul 99
Rotterdam 191
Rougesi Passage, Lake Victoria 44
Rovuma River and Delta 94, 97–98, 122–124, 136, 140, 158, 170–173, 175, 186–187
Ruaha River 139–140
Ruanda 108
Rubens (British ship) *see Kronberg*
Ruckteschell, 1st Lt. Walter von 160
Rufiji River and Delta 18–19, 32–34, 36–37, 49–51, 113, 120–122, 130, 133, 137–140
Ruga Ruga 13, 15, 34, 41, 59–60, 77–78
Ruhuje River 127, 130
Ruponda 156–157, 163, 166–167
Rusisi River 76
Russia 3, 7, 95
Ruwa River 85, 91, 93–94, 98
Rwonga Hill 57

Sabath, Sergeant-Maj. 158
Sadani 121
St. Boniface Mission Station 142
St. George, (British steamer) 70
St. Leger-Hansard, Lt. A.J. 77–78

St. Michael 108–109
St. Moritz Mission Station (Galula) 141–142
Saisi River 15, 142
Salaita 72, 81–83, 85, 87, 131
Salaita Hill 81–83
Salale 18–19
Salisbury Bridge 16
San Francisco 196
Sango Bay 77
Sanja River 87
Sankisia 65
S'Antenecai, Reserve Lt. von 80
Sarbiland, Subadar, IOM 2nd Class 134
Sargeant, Lt.-Col. J. 143, 148
Saunderson, Lt. Robert de Bedick 164–165
Schaedel's Farm 144, 146–147
Schaeffer's Farm 144, 146
Schiller, Reserve Lt. 36–37
Schnee, Frau Ada von 109
Schnee, Dr Heinrich Albert 7–8, 11, 34, 53, 109, 171, 179; admonished for attempting to undermine von Lettow 54–55; Nazi Deputy and death 194
Schönfeld, Lt. 67
Schönfeld, Reserve Cmdr. 52
Schulz, Capt. Hans 83, 113, 117, 132–133
Sea of Marmara 170
Serengeti Plain 72, 81–83, 85, 87
Severn (British monitor) 50–52, 121, 145–146
Shaw, Capt. Gerald S. 115–116, 134, 153
Sheppard, Brigadier-Gen. S.H., DSO 91–94, 101, 105, 113, 137–138
Shewa, Sgt. Mafinde, MM 155, 207*ch*12*n*15
Shirati 42–43
Shorthose, Lt.-Col. W.J.T. 140, 172
Sibary, Capt. George Vincent, MC, Royal Scots Fusiliers 184, 208*ch*14*n*7
Sidi Bishr 195
Sidónio Pais 174
Silva, Maj. Leopoldo da 123
Silveira, Maj. de 97–98
Singapore (and mutiny) 95
Singh, Lt.-Col. Raghbir 38, 40
Smith, Lt. S.B. 154
Smith-Dorrien, Lt.-Gen. Sir Horace 62; forced to resign command in East Africa 63, 79
Smuts, Lt.-Gen. (later Field-Marshal) Jan Christian:[en}87, 91–95, 98–99, 101, 103–108, 113, 115, 120–121, 124, 130, 132, 137, 139, 194; accepts command in East Africa following Smith-Dorrien's resignation 63; arrives in East Africa 85; condemns Gen. Mallison a coward 88; offered command

221

in East Africa, but refuses 62; ordered to London 138; Prime Minister of South Africa and death 196
Soames, Maj. L.M. 37
Soko Nassai River 93
Solf, Minister Dr 7
Somali (German ship) 11, 13, 18–19
Somalia 195
Songea 141, 187
Songwe 13
Songwe River 141–142
Ssongo Ssongo Island 132
South Africa 1, 3–4, 62–64, 108, 144, 195–196
South African Army 62; special Medical Boards established,
South African Army formations and units: 1st Battalion, Cape Corps 1, 142, 149, 162, 169, 197–199, 207*ch*12*n*1; 1st SA Mounted Brigade 71, 85, 93, 99, 106, 108, 118–120, 130, 197–198; 1st SA Rifles 109, 111, 127, 172, 206*ch*10*n*9; 2nd Battalion, Cape Corps 207*ch*12*n*1 ; 2nd SA Infantry Brigade 71, 81, 83–84, 93, 101, 118–119, 138, 197–198 2nd SA Mounted Brigade 101, 113, 118–119, 130, 198; 2nd SA Rifles 109–111, 124, 126, 172; 3rd SA Field Battery 144, 198; 3rd SA Infantry Brigade 71, 85, 93, 99, 106, 197–198; 4th SA Horse 91, 93–94, 198; 5th SA Field Battery 87, 117, 197; 5th SA Infantry Battalion 81–83, 89, 105, 172, 197–198; 5th SAMR Battery 110–111, 125, 127, 129; 6th SA Infantry Battalion 81–83, 89, 105, 197–198; 7th SA (ANZ) Infantry Battalion 82–83, 89, 100, 124, 126, 150–151, 197–198, 206*ch*8*n*11; 8th SA Infantry Battalion 82, 89, 91, 100, 150–152, 197–198; 10th SA Horse 149; 10th SA Infantry Battalion 99, 197–198; 11th SA Infantry Battalion 100, 197–198; 12th SA Infantry Battalion 91, 100, 197–198; Belfield's Scouts 82–83, 88, 198; South African Engineers 125; South African Motor Cycle Corps 100, 107, 124, 198–199; South African Pioneers 122, 199
Spalding, Lt. 40
Spangenburg, Capt. Walter 188–189; dies of Spanish flu 191
Spanish flu pandemic 183; spreads across East Africa 191
Spartacists 193
Speke Gulf, Lake Victoria 44
Sphinxhaven 47, 187
Spicer-Simson, Cmdr. Geoffrey, DSO, RN 64–65, 67–70, 110
Sprockhoff, Sub-Lt. Leonhard 97, 122–123

Stahlhelm 193
Stanlyville 70
Stemmermann, Capt. Paul 117
Stennett, Maj. H.M. 14
Steumer, Capt. Willibald von 41, 59, 77, 140
Stewart, Lt.-Col. J.A. 25
Stewart, Maj.-Gen. James M. 13, 17, 21, 23, 42, 57–58, 80, 85–87; command of Nairobi Area 31; resigns after row with Smuts 91
Stonor, Capt. W.G. 17
Store 92
Storrs, Surgeon Capt. E.G. 125
Stosch, Lt. von 93
Stubbs, Lt. Edgar Perceval, MC, 1st Cape Corps 169
Stuttgart 193
Suba River 39–40
Sudi Bay 94
Sullivan, DCM, Pvt. Michael 45
Sumani, DCM, Colour-Sergeant 17
Susuni Hill 43
Sutherland, Lt. 149
Swifte, Lt. Harold, MC 127, 207*ch*11*n*6
Sybil (British armed lake steamer) 45–46

Tabora 108–109, 122, 124, 130, 141–143, 148, 187, 190–191
Tabora (German ship) 34, 36
Tafel, Capt. Theodor 15–16, 119, 140, 144, 171–173, 177, 208*ch*13*n*21
Tamboua Bay 67
Tandamuti Hill 146
Tanga 8, 34, 38, 49, 54, 71, 101, 147; battle of 22–32
Tanga Bay 25
Tanga-Neu Moshi Railway 103
Taute, Surgeon-Maj. Max 186
Taveta 12, 72, 80–83, 85, 87, 91–92
Taylor, Lt.-Col. A.J. 150
Thistle (British gunboat) 145–146
Thomas, Col. 142
Thompson, Sgt. A.H., DCM 185, 208*ch*14*n*7
Thompson, Maj. 89, 91
Thorneycroft, Capt. E.G.M. 41; killed 42
Thornley, Cmdr. G.S., RN 42–46, 57, 77–78, 108
Tighe, Maj.-Gen. Michael J. 20, 32, 38–39, 56, 58, 61, 80–82, 87, 89; command of Mombasa Area 31; promoted and given command in East Africa 47; recalled to India 91; takes command of 2nd EA Division 85
Tilbury 64–65
Tirimo 148
Tombeur, Maj.-Gen. Baron Charles Henri Marie Ernest (Vice-Governor of Katanga)

14, 76–77, 98, 108–109; appointed commander of all Belgian forces in Eastern Congo 62;
Tomlinson, Lt.-Col. A.J. 141–142
Toura 195
Toutou (British naval motor-boat) 65–69
Towse, Lt.-Col. Harold B. 108
Trotha, Lt.-Gen. Lothar von 3
Tryon, Capt. Spencer 146
Tsavo River 13, 21
Tschipwada River 158
Tschiwata 167, 169
Tshunjo Pass 113
Tsimbe 137
Tunduru 172
Turkey 170
Tyndall, Maj. 121
Tytler, Lt.-Col. H.C. 161

Ubena (Njombe) 187, 194
Ufiome 99, 148
Uganda 10, 34, 77
Uganda Railway 7, 41, 43, 73
Ujiji 109
Ukerwe 108
Ulanga River 130
Uleia 115
Uluguru Mountains 115, 117, 120
Umba River 38–40
Umba Valley 38, 72
Umbulu 99
United Nations 195–196
Upton, Able Seaman George, DSM, RN 36
Usambara 101
Usambara Mountains 80, 100
Usambara Railway 23, 98, 100
Utete 122, 131, 136

Vanga 16, 38, 73
Vaughan, Lt. J.H. 129
Vengeance (British battleship) 121
Victoria Cross 1
Voi 73
Volkwein, Reserve Lt. 119

Wahle, Maj.-Gen. (Rtd.) Kurt 34, 56–57, 108–109, 124, 129–130, 140, 144, 146–148, 154, 156–159, 161–162, 167, 169, 175, 207*ch*12*n*20; death 195; invades Northern Rhodesia 59–60; learns of awards of Iron Crosses 1st and 2nd Class and *Pour le Mérite* 187; oldest combatant of any nation 194
Wainwright, Lt. A.E., RN 69

Wallrath, Margarethe 193
Wallrath, Peter (Lettow-Vorbeck's stepson) 194
Walmsley, Lt. Leo, RFC 135
Wami River 113
Wamwibi, Pvt. Mulandi, DCM 75
Wapshare, Maj.-Gen. Richard 20; given command in East Africa 31; ordered to Persian Gulf 47
Ward, Lt.-Col. L.E.S. 12, 36–37
Wavell, Capt. A.J.B. 16–17
Wehrmacht 194
Weimar Republic 193
Weizmann, Chaim 195
West Africa 1
Westhoven, Medical Lt. Dr. 13–14
Weymouth (British cruiser) 18, 50
Wheeler, Capt. Edmund George 116
Whittall, Lt.-Cmdr., RN 83
Wiedhafen 141, 187
Wildman, Lt. Arthur Henry 73–74
Wilford, Lt.-Col. A.L., DSO 150
Wilhelm II, German Kaiser 5, 94, 138, 167, 170; abdication of 189
Wilhelmshaven 3, 49
Wilhelmstal (Lushoto) 103
Wilkinson, Lt.-Col. C.W. 122
Wilson, Cmdr. Robert Amcotts, RN 50
Wilson, Temporary Lt. Thomas 76
Winifred (British armed lake steamer) 42–44, 46, 77–79
Wintgens, Capt. Max 108, 124–126, 129–130, 140–141, 143, 193; awarded *Pour le Mérite* 142
Woodruffe, Capt. John S. 73
Woods, Lt. Richard Cheetham 154, 163–164
World War I 196
World War II 195
Wülfingen, Capt. Bock von 41–42, 121

Yemen 195

Zambezi River 173, 186
Zanzibar 10–11, 17, 193
Zeiten (German ship) 11, 13
Zeppelin L57 167
Zeppelin L59 167–170, 208*ch*13*n*17
Zimmer, Lt.-Cmdr. Gustav 14, 18, 65–66, 68–70
Zingel, Lt. Joseph 125
Ziwani Ridge 146–147
Zuganatto 103
Zuganatto Bridge 103–104

www.ingramcontent.com/pod-product-compliance
Lightning Source LLC
Chambersburg PA
CBHW032041300426
44117CB00009B/1141